Human Rights and Constituent Power

With the emergence of modern human rights in the Universal Declaration, what remained of a radical political potential of the discourse withdrew: statism and individualism became its authorised foundations and the possibilities of other human rights traditions were denied. The strife that once lay at the heart of human rights was forgotten in an increasing juridification. This book seeks to recover the radical political pole of human rights. It looks to the debates surrounding constituent power – the 'power of the people' – in order to understand different possibilities for the discourse. Using continental political philosophy and critical legal theory, *Human Rights and Constituent Power* presents a very different conception of human rights, more at home on the riotous streets than in courtrooms and parliaments.

Illan rua Wall is a Senior Lecturer in Law at Oxford Brookes University. He graduated with distinction from University College Cork (BcL) and NUI, Galway (LLM in International Human Rights Law). He holds a PhD in Legal Theory and Human Rights from Birkbeck College.

Human Rights and Constituent Power

Without Model or Warranty

Illan rua Wall

Routledge
Taylor & Francis Group

LONDON AND NEW YORK

First published 2012
by Routledge
2 Park Square, Milton Park, Abingdon, Oxon OX14 4RN

Simultaneously published in the USA and Canada
by Routledge
711 Third Avenue, New York, NY 10017

Routledge is an imprint of the Taylor & Francis Group, an informa business

British Library Cataloguing in Publication Data
A catalogue record for this book is available
from the British Library

Library of Congress Cataloging in Publication Data

Wall, Illan Rua.
   Human rights and constituent power : without model or warranty /
Illan Rua Wall.
     p. cm.
   Includes bibliographical references and index.
   ISBN 978-0-415-58497-5 (hbk)—ISBN 978-0-203-80487-2 (ebk)
   1. Human rights.   I. Title.
   K3240.W3485 2011
   341.4'8—dc22

                                           2011008525

ISBN: 978-0-415-58497-5 (hbk)
ISBN: 978-0-415-82403-3 (pbk)
ISBN: 978-0-203-804872 (ebk)

Typeset in Times New Roman
by RefineCatch Limited, Bungay, Suffolk

Invention is always without model and without warranty. But indeed that implies facing up to turmoil, anxiety, even disarray. Where certainties come apart, there too gathers the strength that no certainty can match.

Nancy and Lacoue-Labarthe

Contents

Acknowledgements

I would like to thank Costas Douzinas, perhaps more than anyone; he supervised the beginnings of this work during my PhD at Birkbeck College and has continued to encourage and challenge me. His friendship, generosity and insight have affected every fibre of this work. To my co-conspirators at Birkbeck, Brookes and beyond, Matt Stone, Carolina Olarte Olarte, Suhraiya Jivraj, Ben Golder and Máiréad Enright, I owe not just my gratitude but my sanity. I would like to express my thanks to those who have read elements of this work with a critical eye and for their insightful comments which I have (perhaps unwisely) not always followed: Julia Chryssostalis, Gilbert Leung, Jess Whyte, José Manuel Barreto, Nathan Moore, Richard Bailey, Oren Ben-Dor, Sarah Keenan, Chris Lloyd, Honor Brabazon, Philip Kaisary, Rory Rowan, Chris Butler and Deirdre Duffy. Many thanks also to my PhD examiners, Igor Stramignoni and Emilios Christodoulidis, whose comments were invaluable. Oscar Guardiola-Rivera, Elena Loizidou, Patrick Hanafin, Victoria Ridler, Joanne Ahern, Marcus Rediker, Elizabetta Bertollino, Aoife O'Donoghue, Vincent Keter, Emily Mierisch, Ricardo Sanín, Sarah Ramshaw, Sara Knuckey and all the singularities who have at various stages made up the wonderfully inoperative community at Birkbeck and beyond have challenged me and urged me on. The Critical Legal Conference has always provided a wonderful opportunity to present to and test my work on, but the friendships that have grown from that transitory event are invaluable.

Oxford Brookes University has been particularly supportive. The law department has helped with time, funding and readers. Without this assistance, the book could not have been completed. I would like to thank the School of Law at Birkbeck College, University of London, for its generous provision of the Ronnie Warrington Scholarship. The Gilbert and Tobin Center for Public Law at the University of New South Wales and the School of Law at the University of Melbourne kindly provided visiting fellowships during the completion of this book. Queens University Belfast, Birkbeck College, the University of Glasgow, the University of Utrecht, the University of New South Wales, the University of Essex and London Metropolitan University all provided me with opportunities to present this work in embryonic forms at conferences, workshops and seminars.

I would also like to thank the blogs Critical Legal Thinking, Human Rights in Ireland and Irish Left Review, which remain interesting spaces of engagement.

I would like to thank my parents, William Wall and Elizabeth Kirwan, and my brother, Oisín Wall, for all the years of support, love and patience (although they suggest that there was very little patience).

Finally, to Bríd, *a stór, mo chroí* – this is yours before and after all else. It bears your singular mark on every page.

Chapter 1

Democracy, radical politics and a differential human rights

Human rights is a law that both allows for the resolution of political dispute *and* supports resistance to state power. The traditional subject of human rights demands her internationally guaranteed rights against an overbearing state. She forces the state to respect her rights, resisting its aberrant activity, by pleading before a judicial body. Thus, human rights posits a law of resistance, seeking to restrain and police the state in the worst excesses of its force and power. It does this by becoming the language *of* the state. Resistance is translated into a common language, thereby allowing a judge to decide its legitimacy.[1] I want to begin by marking a difference: human rights transcend and resolve political conflict, but they also properly belong to political conflict.[2] The discourse thus takes its place at the junction of politics and law, both a political demand and the juridical decision. Human rights have a difference at their heart (demand *and* decision). However, the former pole of this difference is denied by the traditional discourse. The everyday presentations of human rights see these two aspects (conflict and resolution, authoritative demand and deliberation or decision) as two sides of one coin, thereby inexorably tying demand to decision. The point of this book is to recover the radical pole of human rights and challenge the closing down of the political implicit in juridification.

The conception of human rights as 'authoritative demands' demonstrates this point. As *authoritative* demands they are structured by a prior authorization, attuning resistance to the language of the state. This facilitates resistance to state power, but also (re)inscribes state power itself. Crucially, the translation places the moments of demand and decision together in a necessary relation. The resistant demand, expressed in the language of rights, is dependent on the juridical for its completion. If these two moments necessarily belong together in human rights, if they form one phenomenon, then essentially they can be united in one moment: decision is rendered as the *essential* moment because it synthesizes the various demands. Thus, we find a human rights indisassociably linked to the juridical. A political conflict placed in the language of human rights is *completed* by the decision of an authority. Human rights discovers an identity in the juridical, a closed sense of itself.[3] What initially appears as a differential structure becomes unified in the (re)giving of law. The tension between demand and decision is thus 'resolved' by privileging the latter.

This book will argue that both the enunciation of a demand and the decision are equally important, but that the only way to understand this is to recover their *different* senses. The enunciation of a demand must be distinguished from a decision on that conflict. They are not two aspects of the same phenomenon merely distinguished by time, but, rather, they differ in their very nature. By thinking about what is radically democratic in rights it is possible to recover this difference. It is only due to the withdrawal of the radical democratic sentiment that human rights can be reduced to a legal framework – in the very projection of this framework as the totality of human rights the withdrawal is re-produced and re-inscribed. Human rights are no longer understood in terms of political creation, but rather as the pre-existing solution to individual conflicts, filtered through the judicial wing of the state or its international avatars. In fact, modern human rights themselves are constituted by this withdrawal of the creative potential, that is by their pre-constitution in the Universal Declaration of Human Rights (hereinafter, the UDHR) and the Covenants. Prior to that, human rights spoke through a variety of voices – from the radically democratic to the reactionary.[4] However, after the UDHR it becomes difficult to see the differential sense of human rights because an authoritative document exists. This blocks the multiplicity of rights-positions by implicitly claiming to write the totality of the human through her rights. But let me be clear: I am not suggesting that modern human rights could or should be swept aside. Rather, I argue it is both necessary and possible to think about a *differential discourse of human rights*.

To recover the radical in human rights it is necessary to understand them through the collective and alegal nature. I am sure this will strike many as strange because human rights are usually thought of as both legal and individual. But my purpose is not to reiterate human rights as they have been represented for the last 60 years, but rather to recover and recreate a space for the radical within the discourse. It is useful to understand this in the context of radical democratic theory. Mouffe suggests that there are actually two traditions in what is now called 'democracy' or modern democracy:

> The novelty of modern democracy, what makes it properly 'modern', is that, with the advent of the 'democratic revolution', the old democratic principle that 'power should be exercised by the people' emerges again, but this time within the symbolic framework informed by the liberal discourse, with its strong emphasis on the value of individual liberty and human rights. Those values are central to the liberal tradition and they are constitutive of the modern view of the world. Nevertheless, one should not make them part and parcel of the democratic tradition whose core values, equality and popular sovereignty, are different.[5]

Mouffe's central argument is that the conjunction of 'liberal democracy results from the articulation of two logics which are incompatible' and, in the final instance, paradoxical: democracy with its 'power to the people' and liberalism with its limitation by the rule of law.[6] She insists that this difference of democracy and liberalism should not be thought of as two separate, distinct and pure traditions, but as two poles, each constantly infecting the other with its logic. Nevertheless, she maintains that there remain two logics or poles of thought.[7]

For Mouffe, human rights remain a separate tradition to democracy, thoroughly liberal in their pedigree. I want to challenge the *necessity* of this categorization. I will ultimately argue that it is possible to conceive of human rights in a non-metaphysical sense, that is, from within the radical democratic tradition. But, for now, I will say that to simply cede human rights to the liberal tradition is to fail to understand the significance of the democratic tradition in human rights. What is more, the overemphasis of the human rights–liberal nexus misunderstands the everyday practice of human rights. Evans ably critiques this in the context of international law: '[F]ocusing so singularly on international law elevates the *legal* approach beyond its potential, offers a distorted view of progress in providing protection for human rights, obfuscates the structural roots of human rights violations and overlooks the inconvenient fact that international law is politically motivated.'[8] In fact, human rights is often used as a means of generating democratic movements more focused on the power of the people (the constituent power) than on the limitation of that power. The problem is that because human rights are only understood through the UDHR and its like, the political creation of constituent power is elided from such a usage. To recover the radical pole or logic of human rights (and thereby re-establish its differential structure) requires an alternative approach.

A 'differential structure' means, on the most basic level, that the essence of human rights cannot be simply rendered as some sense of limitation of the people or 'authoritative demand' of an individual. In fact, it would mean that there could be *no essence of human rights* or, at least, no essence separable from their performance in each instance. To understand the radical democratic pole of human rights, it is necessary to start from constituent power. If I were to do this by half-measures, I would say that some rights are radical and some are not. Thus, maybe the rights to association, speech or strike all put the 'common man' against the 'power of the state'. At the pinnacle of this might be something like self-determination or even the right to revolution, which cannot be secured legally. I will not follow this course, however. Such a crude portrayal of the difference of human rights would focus too much on the normative content of rights and not enough on the manner in which they are performed. This rendering of the difference of human rights (as between different rights) is perpetually repeated in concerned tones in classrooms, courts and academic conferences with the question: 'But what happens when one human right conflicts with another?' The answer is, of course, the conflict is resolved with one or other norm. Such a structuring runs exactly counter to my project. The difference of human rights is not normative and cannot be resolved. It is precisely the tension *between* the poles that makes human rights a politically productive discourse. To rejuvenate this tension, the forgotten constituent power of human rights must be recovered.

Although modern human rights are constituted by the withdrawal of the radical, a trace of radical politics remains within them. This trace of the radical means that there is an effervescent democratic *potential* (in the sense of constituent power) within the discourse that conventional renderings mystify. It is not that I want to revive the right to revolution and deny traditional rights talk. The point is that even in traditional rights talk a radical trace remains.[9] Similar to the democratic and liberal poles that Mouffe highlighted earlier, a differential human rights would not have two separate camps that remain pure and uncontaminated. It is the difference and the constant tension between the poles of human rights that make them such a crucial part of modern politics and law. There is a constant contamination between them. Thus, there can be no proper, given and static essence of human rights.[10] Rather, there is constant *oscillation or vibration* between the poles of limitation and creation, a certain *trembling* between decision and demand. It is neither pole that defines human rights but the oscillation, trembling or vibration itself.[11]

The vision of human rights as limitation or empowerment-before-the-law is ideologically hegemonic. The point of this book, therefore, is to recover the second pole of radical political creation. The premising of decision and the importance of authoritative demands leads human rights to be understood merely as limitation on the *cracy* (force) of the *demos*. The effect of such a framework is that human rights increasingly pacifies politics. With this trembling of the difference within human rights I have introduced the most important theme that runs through this work. The withdrawal of the radical in human rights is the manner in which human rights loses touch with the fundamental difference at its heart. The differential core of human rights is destroyed by reducing it to international legal questions of standard setting, reporting and enforcement. To understand this differential character in its essence it is necessary to retrace the radical in human rights. In this, I will mirror Nancy and Lacoue-Labarthe's idea of re-treating or retracing the political. In their analysis, the political has withdrawn from politics, it has 'retreated'. This means that 'the question of the political, that is the question as to its exact nature or essence, retires or withdraws into a kind of evidence or self-givenness, in which that which is political in politics is taken for granted or accorded a kind of obviousness which is universally accepted.'[12] Our time is no longer concerned with the nature of the political, rather it is 'given' or 'obvious'. Politics is presupposed as that which happens after and in the wake of the economy, and is ultimately determined by the economy. In this, politics itself is erased under the sign of the market.[13] It is not difficult to see there that the 'nature' of politics remains entirely 'given' or unquestioned except insofar as the economy demands. The political has retreated from politics.

This reduction of the political into the givenness of everyday politics leads Nancy and Lacoue-Labarthe to give 're-treat' a second sense – the re-treating of the political – a sense that 'implies a necessary and urgent retreating, retracing or rethinking of the political'.[14] In the context of this urgency to re-treat the retreat, philosophy should withdraw from politics in order to allow it to rethink the political. This is crucial, as the traditional move is to advance philosophy in order to provide the ground of politics. The political, however, is not a ground that would lend metaphysical weight to specific political determinations. Rather, what occurs is the withdrawal *from* politics, re-treating the retreat of politics with its philosophical pre-givens.[15] This necessitates a withdrawal from everyday politics, in order to trace the possibility of the political. This can then be reinserted into politics, but the questions of politics themselves have changed. Nancy and Lacoue-Labarthe's analysis of the political will be loosely mirrored in this work. There is, of course, a variety of differences between the analyses. The political is very different from human rights, however, the method of seeking to recover the possibilities of that site, tool, or discourse, remains.

By way of a guide to this work; the first substantive step after this introduction is to challenge the hegemonic idea of human rights. Thus, in Chapter 2, I trace three strategies of pacification in the human rights historiography. Rarely, if ever, is a radical sense of human rights understood. Rather, the current practice is rendered natural by showing an inexorable progress towards international human rights law. To do this, it carefully selects historical subjects. Through a progression of patricians, nobles and bourgeois subjects, human rights is shown to accord to the 'best' moments of bourgeois western politico-legal history. A very clear teleological causality is constructed here, with progress rendered as the secular version of the divine hand of providence. Other heterogeneous movements are reduced so that they mirror the present (or at least an idealized version of current practice). They are pacified by being rendered *just* as human rights movements. Having sketched the pacification of human rights history, I go on to ask what we can learn from the manner in which the Haitian Revolution and the abolition of the slave trade are written for human rights law. The point of this is to ask why one moment is privileged (abolition) and the other (Haiti) is silenced. In this, I demonstrate a certain structuring of the human rights imaginary around the quasi-colonial triplet of victim, rescuer and oppressor.

In Chapter 3, in order to explain the withdrawal of the radical, I look to Locke's right to revolution. On first reading, it would seem that this would be the apogee of the radical in human rights. However, on closer inspection we find in Locke precisely the withdrawal that I want to demonstrate. Property is the axis through which his right to revolution operates. It binds the social together and allows a revolution to overthrow the political constitution, while maintaining the social constitution of inequality. Property is written into human nature, thereby allowing only limited political reform. At this moment, where the radical appears most evident, we actually find one of the clearest efforts to withdraw that which is most political in rights. This early instance is placed alongside an analysis of human rights as they are enacted today. There we find only the slightest trace of the radical. This is because modern human rights are only truly constituted when the radical withdraws, leaving only ghostly traces of their prior potentiality. The second half of the chapter suggests that it is the deep structures of individualism and statism that maintain and keep out radical voices. I seek to deepen the traditional critiques of Burke, Bentham and Marx, through the addition of Heidegger's critique of humanism. With this, individualism and statism become symptoms of a more fundamental problem in human rights: their metaphysical core. Through an all too brief introduction to Heidegger, I challenge the renderings of the subject, temporality and being in humanism. This marks the closing of the first section of the book (Chapters 1 to 3). The focus on humanism and human rights is concluded and I hope that my critique of the current state of human rights is clear.

In the second section of the book (Chapters 4, 5 and 6) I propose to withdraw from the liberal rendering of rights and instead to question the sense of democracy – of the *cracy* (force) of the *demos*. At its most basic, democracy suggests that power belongs to the people to make and remake the polity – this is the constituent power of the book title. The purpose of these chapters is primarily to explore the sense of constituent power as distinct from the explanations provided by the constituted order that it founds. In other words, I want to explore constituent power as such, rather than as and for the constituted order. In Chapter 4, I examine the work of the Abbé Sieyès and Immanuel Kant. These works demonstrate a number of variations, but, ultimately, show a view of the constituent that is deeply tied to the constituted order. In a totalizing and crude dialectic, the constituent is understood not in its essence, but rather in relation to what it will institute. In other words, the constituent is defined by the constituted order that it creates. Authority is the linchpin here. As Loughlin says, constituent power gives authority to modern democracy. However, to think a different non-metaphysical and radical human rights, it will be necessary to challenge the necessity of authority in the configuration of right. Kant provides an interesting counterpoint. Unlike Sieyès, he understands the unauthorizability of constituent power – the *salto mortale*. There is a tension within his oeuvre between the rejection of the morality of revolt and the complex argument that the sympathy for (or even will to) revolution is evidence of moral progress. Nevertheless, constituent power essentially remains unthinkable in his project.

To break this prefiguring of the constituent, I move to consider a number of very different conceptions of constituent power. Georges Sorel, Walter Benjamin and Georges Bataille provide three themes that I follow throughout what remains of the book. From Sorel, the sense of a radical being together emerges; from Benjamin, I show an alegal (although mysticized) moment of change; and finally, from Bataille, there appears a radical challenge to the economic form of utility, calculation and commensurability. Each in his own way demonstrates a thinking of constituent power that is not tied to a determinate end (constituted order). Rather, they suggest a means without end(s). However, each attempt fails and this is crucial. I do not propose any of their schemas, but rather suggest that they open the possibility of a different constituent power. In Chapter 6, I ask who the subject of this different constituent power is. In particular, I am interested in recovering 'the people' from substantialism (see Schmitt for instance) and from the tendency to fold it into the constituted order (like Kelsen). Through Derrida and Rancière, I offer two different deconstructions of the people. The first looks to

Derrida's attack on the notion of pure presence. In this, the challenge is to understand the people temporally, as deferred but not pacified in an infinite suspension of constituent power. The second, through Rancière, differs the people from itself. It challenges the sense of the people as a unitary actor. This marks the end of the second section of the book. At this stage, I hope that a different sense of constituent power (that is, without model or warranty) is beginning to emerge. However, it is still, in many senses, oceans away from a radical sense of human rights.

In section three I begin to bring constituent power and human rights together in a radically different manner, by looking to Jean-Luc Nancy and his ontology of being singular plural. This turns the previous questioning of the people inside out. I begin by setting out Heidegger's sense of being-together, focusing on the problematic idea of the *Volk* (the people) in *Being and Time*. Challenging this, I argue that the totalization involved in an *ontological* idea of gathering renders Heidegger deeply problematic. This introduces Nancy's critique of those who set the idea of a community to work in creating and defending community. I briefly sketch his notion of an *inoperative* community. From this, the beginning of a different sense of human rights emerges, one that does not unavoidably start with the individual and then move to the state. Rather, the ontological status of the inoperative community allows us to think differently about questions of law and the political. Being-together is now the starting point for a radical ontology.

Chapter 8 seeks to take seriously the assertion in human rights that the nexus between human *being* and the political gives rise to a different and new political impetus. The problem with this nexus is, of course, biopolitics. Foucault demonstrated that the development of human rights is concurrent with and intimately connected to disciplinary structures of biopower and capitalism. This questioning allows me to pose the problem of the subject of human rights from a critical perspective. With Agamben, the political is cleared of actors, but, with Rancière, it becomes merely a matter of resubjectivization. Meshing these ideas, I look to Nancy's sense of singularity to think an anti-juridical (alegal) non-subject. This opens onto Nancy's critique of biopower. He argues that what is so problematic in our recent political configuration is not so much the matter of 'power through life' but rather a question of 'technology of emplacement' – *ecotechnics*. This reframing of the problem allows me to close the chapter with the question of world creation as distinct from the manner in which global capitalism is world destroying.

The final step then is to fold these political and ontological insights back into human rights. However, with this folding, the questions change. No longer is it a matter of the radical in human rights, as though there were some sort of substance that could be rediscovered. There is not simply a different set of rights whose object would be properly and exclusively radical. Rather, it is a matter of the constituent potential *in* rights. To demonstrate this, I look at two attempts to put forward different rights. Raoul Vaneigem's version is a failure as it attempts completely to inscribe human being – *graphephilia* is the danger of biopolitics *par excellence*. By the same token, Henri Lefebvre's idea of the right to the city gets to the heart of the matter. It posits a right of world creation where the right itself does not go untouched by the object it seeks to facilitate. It is a matter of seeing the possible manners in which 'human rights' can be thought that reveal their essential political function of unveiling the possibility of the political. This is found, I suggest, in the awkward neologism 'right-ing'. The subtitle of this book ('without model or warranty'), which is taken from Jean-Luc Nancy, suggests that to rework human rights in a non-metaphysical fashion, it is necessary to begin to question the reliance on 'legitimacy', which suggests a transcendent authority that might give warranty for certain action. Right-ing has no authority, no sovereign power over others. Instead, it starts from the in-between of relation, from the possibility of world creation.

***

As I finish this introduction, the snow is falling on a dark and wintry London. The student protests have begun to quieten down after a cacophonous month on the streets and in occupation. Ireland lies in an abject despair after the rapacious incompetence of its political elite and the IMF intervention. Once again, Greece is in flames, with a general strike manifesting the power of labour and the police, with truncheons and gas, manifesting the power of law. It seems to me that now is the moment to rethink the political givens of our time. Perhaps for the first time since the fall of communism in western Europe, we have entered a crisis of worlds. The pacifying and neutering thinking of human rights must give way to a more militant and collective sense. Human rights mean nothing if they do not provide the tools to resist the everyday network power of what Nancy called 'soft totalitarianism'. This book is written in an attempt to clear some ground, to write a space in which human rights may be reimagined. However, it also hazards a number of positions. To be merely analytic about human rights is to miss the great antagonistic spirit that they so often name. This book is an attempt not to found or ground some new orthodoxy, but rather to write of the task of thinking politically about the possibilities of human rights – possibilities that have everywhere withdrawn. I think today, more than ever, the challenge is to think a human rights more at home on riotous streets than between the hallowed walls of supreme courts or in the leather-bound chairs of power.

Chapter 2

Challenging human rights histories

> The role of the one who speaks is therefore not the role of the legislator or the philosopher, between camps, the figure of peace and of armistice, in that position of which already Solon had dreamt and also Kant. To establish oneself between adversaries, at the centre and above them, to impose a general law on each and to found an order that reconciles: this is not at all what is at issue. At issue, rather, is the positing of a right marked by dissymmetry, the founding of a truth linked to a relation of force, a weapon-truth and a singular right. The subject that speaks is a warring – I won't even say a polemical – subject.
>
> Foucault, *Society Must Be Defended*

In 1932 the surrealist group penned a declaration entitled 'Murderous Humanitarianism'. In it, they argued with perspicacity that humanitarianism and the embryonic human rights discourse is bound to a western colonial capitalist military machine.[1] When this strain of thought is placed alongside the human rights of the UDHR we find the basic division of the politics of humanism: anti-humanism attacks the mystification of humanism and its *mission civisatrice* and humanism roundly denies the anti-colonial anti-humanism of the radicals with cries of nihilism. These battle lines have long been drawn. What the surrealists demonstrated, along with subsequent postcolonial critiques, is the manner in which human rights becomes a morality of (imperial) power while simultaneously mystifying this function. I want to retrace this division through a critique of the 'church history'[2] usually told about human rights: a narrative that sacrifices any perceived negative aspects of the lineage and tells a purified story. This forms the basis of the surrealist critique of their contemporary humanitarian discourses that shrouded colonial violence in a cloak of morality. I argue that, to begin to see the possibilities of human rights, it is necessary to understand the manner in which these possibilities are withdrawn. Thus, in this chapter and the next, I will look at the manner in which human rights is constructed so as to exclude radical politics. This purification is crucial; however, unlike the surrealists, I want to suggest other possibilities for human rights: neither mystifying moral warranties nor the drowning out of imperial violence, but, rather, the possibility of radical political demands.

To begin, let me schematically sketch the traditional historical narrative of human rights. There are various different emphases within this discourse, but they all tend towards the same self-glorifying end. They usually begin with Mesopotamia, Greece or Rome. Ancient histories or theological texts provide 'roots' across various cultures. Then skipping a millennium or so, the next episode is provided by the theological thought of Europe as it begins its rapacious expansion around the globe (although generally the violence of the colonial is elided). With Hobbes, Locke and the liberal constitutionalists, rights begin 'properly' to take shape. Various episodes can be taken from the 'long 19th-century' (1789 –1914)[3] depending on which of the various 'branches of the human rights tree' the author wishes to highlight: the French Declaration for civil and political rights; the Hague conventions for humanitarianism; the anti-slavery movement for 'civil society'; various socialist labour struggles for economic and social rights; or even nationalism and self-determination for third generation rights. Finally after the inter-war experiments with minority rights and the horror of the Second World War our international age arrives. At this point many of the histories tend to stop, and instead shift to the 'political' and 'legal' description of the post-war 'present'.[4]

I want to suggest that these histories, despite their various emphases, ultimately utilize three strategies that determine what is thinkable in human rights. The first is the choice of historical subjects in the genesis of human rights. Generally, there is a careful selection of an elite lawgiver or activist. The second strategy is the provision of a teleological account of the emergence of human rights. Whether this is a transcendent metaphysical account or an immanent historical teleology, its theory of progress remains theological. The final strategy I will suggest is the reduction of the heterogeneity of particular movements so that they mirror current conceptions of human rights (or at least an idealized version of current practice). I want to suggest that these three strategies are often put together in various fashions and lead to a smothering of any of the radical demands that have been asserted through human rights. The conventional rendering of human rights is thus pacified. What is thinkable through human rights is made safe for the modern state.

To even begin to think a different radical and non-metaphysical human rights, it is necessary to challenge these narrative techniques. Thus, having set out the manner in which the possibilities of human rights are closed by a selective historiography, I will spend the second half of the chapter exploring one instance of this: the silencing of the Haitian Revolution and the privileging of the abolition of slavery. I will develop this through Mutua's insightful analysis of the structuring of the human rights imaginary around the quasi-colonial triplet of victim, rescuer and oppressor. Events such as abolition fit neatly into this imaginary, as a bourgeois elite takes up the norm of humanity in the name of a blighted other. Whereas the violent and destructive days of the Haitian Revolution do not fit this at all, because here the victims violently take up 'humanity' and rupture the ontological construction of the 'west'.

Three strategies of pacification

The first strategy is the selection of the subjects of human rights history; in other words, the characters chosen retrospectively to bring human rights into existence. The traditional narrative suggests a succession of European patricians, nobles, gentlemen and, finally, international bureaucrats. Human rights is written into the mouths of these privileged subjects. There are many examples of this strategy, but I think Orend uses it most blatantly. He says:

> But by the medieval period we see, clearly, claims of rights and entitlements on the other side of certain duties. The king has duties not just to God and to his subjects, the nobles said, but to us as well: duties to stay off our lands, to allow us to travel, to tax us only in reasonable amounts, to have us thrown in jail only after a fair trial, and so on. And if the king has duties to do such things for us, they concluded, then we must have rights that he do such things. We have justified claims – authoritative entitlements – to the performance of such duties. In short, they said, we have rights.[5]

Orend speaks from the mouths of the nobles, he takes on their subject position – the 'us' of the paragraph seeks to identify the author and reader (presumably the human rights believer) with those nobles. He asks us to identify, at each point in the progression, with the person who uses the idea to expand those who have rights: 'as each inferior class rose, acquired more influence . . . [it] could use the language of rights against the one who used it last, as part of their own designs to pole-vault into better social standing and a higher standard of living.'[6] The nobles or patricians originate an exclusive idea of rights, each group merely 'widens' the concept of rights. However, the fundamental premise of this assertion is false. It is based on a double process: firstly, the rights highlighted (from the nobles of *Magna Carta* to the 'proletariat' of economic and social rights) are rendered the same as the rights claims that are made today, differences are sacrificed.[7] But, secondly, other traditions that are a little more difficult to find, recognize and explain are ignored. Human rights is presented as the natural property of an elite.

Against this careful selection of the historical subject of rights, commoners do not simply come to rights in the early to mid-19th century, rather, their position within rights and their utilization of rights is fundamental. Peter Linebaugh's *The Magna Carta Manifesto* gives us a good, albeit basic, insight into a very different tradition of human rights. Orend's rendering of *Magna Carta* is highly conventional. The nobles simply demand their rights and the king is forced to cede them.[8] Linebaugh challenges this by actually examining *Magna Carta* itself. Crucially, there is not one but *two* great charters. *Magna Carta* cannot be disassociated from the *Charter of the Forest* (hereinafter, the Charter), the all too often ignored second great charter of King John. The Charter maintained rights to commoning, along with disafforestation and protection of land from afforestation. Afforestation was the process by which land was excepted from the common law and came under the King's supreme control: 'To disafforest meant to remove from royal jurisdiction; it did not mean to clear or cut timber or destroy the trees.'[9] Linebaugh suggests that the Charter provides an insight into one of the key politico-economic questions of the time. For instance, he carefully reads chapters 47 and 48.[10] The forest is significant for both the King and the commoners. Afforestation, or the privatization of the forests was central to King John's ability to make war in the Holy Land, because, once afforested, the land could be sold on, thus raising capital. Against this, the forests can be seen as 'a hydrocarbon energy reserve'.[11] They were the spaces in which commoners could forage for food, kindling and building materials. Thus, Linebaugh suggests that *rights* were asserted against the King's privatization of these areas. The two great charters provide us with a curious mix of subjects, but what is clear is that this is not simply a story of nobles and kings. Linebaugh argues that today these two great charters of King John should be understood as a manifesto for a different imagination of rights. He highlights four demands: 'The first one calls for the abolition of the commodity form of wealth that blocks the way to commoning. The second one gives us protection from intrusions by privatizers, autocrats, and militarists. The third one warns us against false idols. The fourth renews the right of resistance.'[12] From the two great charters, he argues, resistance to modes of accretion of wealth and power are inscribed at the heart of human rights.

When Orend suggests that rights are just 'widened' he utterly betrays the multiplicity and heterogeneity within the genealogy of human rights. What Linebaugh very briefly sketches is just the tip of the iceberg. There are 'other' subjects of rights:[13] from Winstanley's right to wasteland;[14] through the (probably fictional) pirate utopia of *Libertalia*;[15] to the various slave revolts.[16] These other subjects have a very different imagination of what (human) rights were and could be. Linebaugh's central argument is that the significance of *Magna Carta* must be seen as an ever changing manifestation of radical demands for equality and social justice. However, this radical possibility is elided from the popular human rights narrative. The result is that Orend can assert that the common man gains historical subjectivity (defined by their entry as a subject of human rights) only from the beginning of the 19th century. Very clearly, this initiates a political trajectory for rights that places reform, gradual development and ultimately the 'providential hand of progress' at its heart. By excluding other rights assertions that are less familiar to our ears, human rights begin as a nobleman's discourse and essentially continue to maintain a patrician trajectory. The form (of limitation) is given by the nobles and even when the plebeian elements use it to 'pole-vault' into a better social position, they only expand those subjects of rights, they do not alter the form itself. Our current discourse, which tends to privilege international elites, is rendered necessary and immutable precisely because of its historical antecedents.[17]

The second strategy of human rights 'church history' is closely associated with the first. It begins from the current success of human rights in the international sphere and looks back over world history picking out the clean and pure moments of bourgeois morality: the end of the slave trade, the limitation of government, the rule of law, etc. These are then isolated and portrayed as crucial antecedents to modern human rights. This strategy tends towards an entirely closed teleological sense of the emergence of human rights – all of history has been leading up to this moment. It is determined by a certain necessity – human rights are historically and/or naturally mandated. This is achieved in one of two manners. Either tele-ology functions in a simple historic sense or it becomes a metaphysical assertion of certainty. Let me take each in turn.

The 'historic' teleology relies on a simple elision of the contingency of events and instead provides one clear and retraceable path. This narrative functions as a naturalization of the current state of things because there is but one path to this point without any other directions that rights might have taken. The 'progress' from *Magna Carta* to the UDHR is inexorable. The problem here is, of course, that this vision sees only one great history of the world. Certain elements must thus be privileged. Select any number of the major (and indeed minor) textbooks on international human rights law and you will see a similar history retold over and over again. It is through this *repetition* of world history as a 'human rights story' that human rights become positioned at the end of history. The contingency of current human rights is elided, along with the other traditions of rights not followed. The flipside of this is that the figures that are conjured forth in these narratives are cleansed.[18] Rights are only associated with the 'good' moments. So, for instance, the use of property rights by slave owners against the demands of abolition or rebellion are forgotten and, instead, abolition is the human rights cause of the day. This teleology is quite precarious and relies on a constant repeti-tion to secure its hegemony.

The second teleology is much more robust. In it, human rights are read back in time as evidence of a hand of providence or progress. With this vision, human rights are unchangeable because they are written metaphysically, expressing the hand of the creator or the naturalness of social peace and cohesion. Here we have a choice of two fundaments on which human rights are based: either a deity or a secularized humanity. These approaches to human rights are largely unshakeable as they rely on a religious certainty. The general narrative is that human rights are *discovered* rather than created by man.[19] The theological spirit of this understands human rights as (somehow) mandated by a higher authority, usually portrayed through a bastardization of medieval Christian theologians: human rights are written in (human) nature, which we discover through our right reason. The secu-larized, albeit still theological, option simply lops off the deity from this story. Instead of a deity writing human rights in (our) nature, humanity itself – by its very existence – becomes the supreme norm. The crucial element of metaphysical and historic teleological approaches to human rights is the placing of our contem-porary selves now, at the end of history. At this end, human rights have come about. Their full presence now can be read back into history – picking out those historical moments that resemble the now. This strategy at once demonstrates the naturalness of what we have now and the irrelevance of other histories of human rights. The gritty facts of prior accumulation, colonialism and slavery are placed outside the discourse. The effect is ultimately to render the current human rights *necessary*. They do not see the contingency and heterogeneity of events. This is shared in different ways by both forms of teleology, the difference being that one sees the hand of providence and the other sees historical necessity.

This leads me to the final strategy. Human rights histories seldom deal with the role of mass movements. However, when radical movements are considered, the tendency is to reduce them to 'human rights movements'. Lauren Gordon's rendering of Lenin is useful in explicating this. He says:

> Lenin ... spoke about human rights, but with extremely significant differences. He placed emphasis on social and economic rights rather than those of a civil and political nature, and focused on class and group rights rather than those of the individual, fiercely declaring that these rights could best be obtained through revolutionary communism rather than evolutionary and capitalistic democracy, and that the right of self-determination should apply not simply to Europeans but to the entire world.[20]

The key, of course, is that this is entirely correct. The problem is not that Lauren Gordon is misquoting Lenin who did indeed talk about rights both economically and in terms of self-determination. The problem is that he is seen *as a human rights thinker*. We are told that Lenin is interested in economic and social rights, along with self-determination. Importantly, Lauren Gordon sees nothing in Lenin that would force him to think differently about current human rights. He uses a variety of narrative techniques to prevent unsettling human rights by Lenin's inclusion: mass movements are rendered through individuals; radical claims are only asserted if they are irrelevant now (if they are relevant now, they need to be pacified); violence is elided from the struggles; the strategies for rupturing the political constitution of the time are pacified.

A good example of this tendency to reduce radical political demands to human rights movements can be seen in Haas.[21] To his credit, he sees the role of mass movements in the history of human rights. The democratic revolutions, the anti-slavery movement, suffragettes, trade unionists, and 'humane warfare' activists all reveal human rights through a variety of different agents. However, Haas neuters this insight by ascribing metaphysical status to rights – the second strategy. Thus, there can be no creativity in 'the masses', rather, they simply play their metaphysical duty by revealing the already given form. His treatment of the role of the trade union movement in particular is problematic: there he discusses 19th-century trade unionism without commenting on the various social utopian projections that were their fundamental motor.[22] By highlighting these movements without the radical horizon, he reveals the ideological function of current human rights practice. The radical heart of human rights is to be limited to its historical specificity. When the radicalism is no longer practical (gathering waste timber, manuring the wastes or bourgeois revolution against monarchy and colonialism), it is trotted out as a fundamental precursor to our modern practice. However, as we approach the modern day with trade unionism, its 19th-century radicalism is to be hidden or rendered irrelevant. For instance, Haas argues that two of the 'boldest assertion(s) of the rights of workers came in 1891' from Pope Leo XIII and his encyclical *Rerum Novarum,* and the German Social Democratic Party's *Erfurt Program*.[23] In doing this, Haas picks out the reformist notions of rights that best fit with today's pacified vision and suggests that they are the most relevant.[24]

The effect of this reduction of heterogeneous historical movements is that the radical is withdrawn. In doing so, human rights is handed over to the elite against whom the radical anti-slavery and trade union movements actually worked. In this, Bismarck becomes a human rights superhero when he split the radical and reformist left by offering the beginnings of a socialized state. Equally, the bourgeois supporters of anti-slavery become the human rights NGOs or activists. At the same time the slaves who violently revolted and radicalized one another become the objects of a sentimental discourse, cast aside when violent as unworthy of humanity, as I will discuss in the next section. The radicals who established the conditions in which we could settle for our current set of rights are cut from the narrative because ultimately human rights wish to lay claim to the left and right, 'to become neutral'. However, to 'become neutral', elements of the status quo must be accepted as eternal or at least pre-given. Only by cutting out the much more radical rights claims (i.e. radical economic equality or a freedom unrestrained by prior accumulation or an actual equality of race) can we accommodate those who were once on the other side (the capitalist who brutally suppressed unionization, the conservative slave owners, the great gentlemen who demanded their exclusive right to vote). Human rights as they now stand are the neutered shadow of their once multiple practices. They are reduced to the banality of legalism, individualism and statism. Yet, as I will argue throughout, there remains a radical remainder even after this withdrawal.

Slavery, the Haitian Revolution and abolition

> *Couté la liberté li palé cœurs nous tous.* (Listen to the voice of liberty that speaks in the hearts of all of us.)
>
> Dutty Boukman (1791)

Traditional human rights histories often talk of the French and American revolutions as crucial moments when 'human rights' are first brought into being; equally they mention the abolition of slavery as a fundamental moment in the emergence of the tradition. Curiously, however, these histories rarely mention the third revolution, one that combined both human rights with anti-racism. The revolution in Haiti, or St. Domingue as it was then known, forms part of an alternative narrative of human rights, closer to the modern rights 'to the city'[25] or 'of the poor'[26] than the rights asserted as defence of the Iraq War or even the (quasi-)juridical assertions of the Human Rights Committee or European Court of Human Rights. It suggests radical subjects of human rights, utilizing rights in the performance of their constituent power; it places property, race and slavery at the heart of human rights and not in the usual fashion.[27] It requires a very different thinking of rights and constituent power. This section will suggest that the absence of Haiti along with the overemphasis on abolition reveals much about the 'imaginal' structure of human rights. However, I will begin with a brief account of the events of the Haitian Revolution.

St. Domingue was the most productive French colony, remarkably peaceful until the momentous events of the 1790s. It was, however, riven with political divisions and it is these divisions that begin the conflagration. In particular, three slave-owning factions were important: the *grands blancs* (white large plantation owners), the *petits blancs* (largely professionals and smallholding whites) and the free *gens du couleur* (free slaves, both 'mulatto' and black).[28] These factions constituted the political community in St. Domingue, but the overwhelming majority of the population were the excluded slaves. The revolution on St. Domingue began in 1791. The French Revolution of 1789 and the disruption of the status quo of relations between the factions lead to the eruption of conflict. The three factions armed vast swathes of the slave population. Importantly, in the conflict the slaves began by fighting for their masters, thus this was not a simple anti-colonial war against the French Empire. However, the slaves soon saw that:

> if they could fight in separate causes for the antagonistic free sectors of the population, they could fight on their own behalf. And so they did. Violence, first employed by the whites, became the common currency of political change. Finally, in August 1791, after fighting for nearly two years on one side or another side of free persons who claimed they were fighting for liberty, the slaves of the *Plain du Nord* applied their fighting to their own cause. And once they had started, they refused to settle for anything less than full freedom for themselves.[29]

The slaves revolted, turning their weapons against their masters. Between 1792 and 1802 the war was waged with up to seven vying factions (the *grand blancs*, *petits blancs*, *gens du couleur*, slaves and continental French,[30] along with the invading Spanish and English). It is not the place of this volume to give a full and thorough summary of conflict with its many victories, defeats, treacheries and alliances, suffice to say as Knight summarizes in the broadest terms: 'As killing increased, power slowly gravitated to the overwhelming majority of the population – the former slaves no longer willing to continue their servility. After 1793. . . the tide of war turned inexorably, assuring the victory of the concept of liberty held by the slaves.'[31] The slaves shifted allegiance between the Spanish and French in order to maintain their tactical advantage. After an early attempt to negotiate a settlement only months into the revolt, which was rebuffed by the whites,[32] the slave forces radicalized and demanded: 'We are your equals then, by natural right, and if nature pleases itself to diversify colours within the human race, it is not a crime to be born black nor an advantage to be white.'[33]

Fick places Haiti's momentous events of 1791 in the context of the French Revolution:

> For nearly three years between 1789 and 1791, the slaves of St. Domingue witnessed the revolts of the propertied classes. The white colonists began by claiming their rights and demanding the abolition of the economic and commercial restrictions laid upon them by the *Ancien Régime*. They were followed by the *diffranchis*, who demanded an equal footing with the whites. New forces had burst open in the colony. Talk of 'liberty, equality and fraternity' fell upon the receptive ears of domestic slaves, who interpreted these slogans in their own way as they perfunctorily served their white masters.[34]

The causality appears to be straightforward. The domestic servants, not least Toussaint Louverture,[35] read the works of Enlightenment and the great masses of slaves heard the egalitarian words of the French *métropole*.[36] They (mis)understood the meaning of the idealistic phrases. It was a misunderstanding, of course, because the ideals of the revolution were hardly meant to apply to women and Jews, let alone slaves! However, the slaves *knew* that they were to be excluded from these declarations; theirs was not a mistake of ignorance. Thus, when they took up the words, they did so out of a *purposive misunderstanding* of the implicit logic and therefore they do not represent some sort of *tabula rasa* on which the enlightenment norms were projected, but rather active, thinking subjects who resisted 'enlightenment' with its own norms.[37] Thus, our causality is not straightforward. The revolutionary words travel west where they are mixed with the resistant traditions of the subjugated of the colonies.[38] Echoing the anti-humanist critique that opened the chapter – enlightenment humanism saw little contradiction with the existence of almost industrial levels of slavery. More than any of the great thinkers of the enlightenment, it is the violent and allegedly irrational slaves that present us with the truth of rights.

However, it is more interesting than a simple transplant of French ideas into Haiti. Laurent Dubois suggests a deep mixing of political ideas, using the story of an 'insurgent' captured and executed a few weeks into the conflict:

> When they searched his body, they found in one of his pockets pamphlets printed in France, filled with common-places about the Rights of Man and the Sacred Revolution; in his vest pocket was a large packet of tinder and phosphate and lime. On his chest he had a little sack full of hair, herbs and bits of bone, which they call a 'fetish'. The law of liberty, ingredients for firing a gun, and a powerful amulet to call on the help of the gods: clearly a potent combination.[39]

This is a powerful syncretism: the rights of man, western weapons technology and the fetish. Grovogue argues that: 'Reflecting their own historicity, slaves deployed the linguistic artifice of rights to signify not only their own humanity but also to underscore the uniqueness, inherence and permanence of their own representations of human faculties and capacities.'[40] Thus, the French 'Rights of Man' undergo a process of translation once they leave the shores of France. As the subject enunciating these liberties change, their very content and significance alter. This is never clearer than when the property, which the rights themselves are supposed to protect, *speaks*. The 'rights of man' with their absolute protection of property (not least slaves) are therefore pitched against the 'rights of man' with their absolute protection for liberty.[41] More than any of the other revolts (England, America and France), Haiti presents us with the revolutionary truth of this time. 'At the time of the French and American revolutions, few of the constitutionalists asked themselves how property was acquired and enjoyed.'[42] Haiti does this by presenting the actual revolt of the objects themselves. Haiti is a slave revolt, as such it is 'the property' itself that is challenging the 'property system'. Trouillot argues that 'the Haitian Revolution thus entered history with the peculiar characteristic of being unthinkable even as it happened.' He explains: 'The unthinkable is that which one cannot conceive within the range of possible alternatives, that which perverts all answers because it defies the terms under which the questions were phrased.' The Haitian Revolution thus challenged the 'ontological order of the West and the global order of colonialism.'[43]

However, it is not merely this straightforward – Haiti does not present us with a simple 'human rights revolution'. History resists grand narratives. It is deeply problematic to reduce the multiplicity of political thought circulating to a single narrative, especially when it comes to constituent moments. Let me stress this point: *Haiti is not (simply) a human rights struggle.* There are many different and conflicting political ideas circulating at that time of which a nascent human rights is but one. The assertion of rights is mixed with other traditions, it is used to annunciate different demands, it is used in internal and external conflicts by the (ex-)slaves. Interestingly, the rights asserted in the Haitian Revolution are at once deeply similar to current thought but also radically different in form and content. Rights were both a weapon against the existing international and national colonial order and also a projection of what might occur after the violence had subsided. They were both a political rupture and a projected social pacification.

One problem for the way I have portrayed the events thus far is the fact that some slaves – particularly in the early days of the revolution before news of the execution of the King in the *métropole* – did not refer to the republican tradition but rather either pronounced new kings or claimed to defend the French one.[44] This would seem in direct conflict with the republican tradition from which the French assertion of rights comes. There are a variety of reasons for this. There were persistent rumours both in St. Domingue and previously elsewhere in the Caribbean that the King had announced the freedom of all slaves which the rulers were simply not putting into effect. Equally in St. Domingue in 1791 rumours abounded of a three day a week holiday for slaves that was being ignored by the local government.[45] In fact, Fick argues that this rumour was repeated explicitly in the meetings of the leaders in the run up to the revolution.[46] Dubois says: 'Not unlike the peasant rebels in France during the Great Terror of 1789, the slave insurgents of St. Domingue invoked a powerful and distant figure – who they rightly understood might have the power to counteract the assemblies of the colony – against the all-too-local enemies.'[47] Equally, as contemporary reports note, it was not uncommon for the slaves to use the divisions on the whites' side, to aid their own cause. 'The insurgents . . . evoked the king in pursuit of concrete political goals that were in the local context, quite revolutionary.'[48]

However, there are accounts of slaves electing 'kings' of their own number. Dubois suggests that this is highly likely to reflect a form of political syncretism with the people of the Kongo who before being captured as slaves had fought a bloody civil war over various 'authoritarian' and 'democratic' governmental forms:[49]

> Such traditions in which many of those enslaved in St. Domingue would have participated. Indeed, the Kongo might even 'be seen as a font of revolutionary ideas as much as France was'. As with so much of the insurrection of 1791, the only evidence we have of the transcultural development of insurgent political ideologies is extremely fragmented but the naming of 'kings' among the insurgents likely involved a transcultural dialogue between European and African visions of leadership and government.[50]

Thus, we find what we might consider the political theories of the conflict (republicanism vs. royalism) aligned in apparently contradictory ways. But the apparent monarchism of the slaves does not deal a fatal blow to my argument here. In fact, it supports it. I am *not* saying that in a moment of vision, the slaves of St. Domingue rose up with a perfectly formed image of rights. This would be the same mythmaking that I earlier critiqued in Haas or Lauren Gordon. Quite the contrary, my argument is that the human rights discourse is fashioned in the fire of conflict and dispute. It is the manner in which rights are mixed with other theories, the manner in which they are put together *differently* that is crucial. There is a multiplicity in human rights and this multiplicity tends to get lost when we have the authoritative UDHR in our hands. What is missing from the traditional accounts of the human rights history is this internal conflict. It is pitched as us and them: the good, enlightened and universal humanitarians versus the disordered, uneducated and evil brutes. The Haitian Revolution presents a messy and confused story for human rights. When the slaves of St. Domingue frame their demands through rights, that is, in the words of their oppressors, they steal this language and make it their own.[51] And with that theft, a reversal occurs. The subject of rights is the slave become man, violently striking at the heart of the then political/ property system – colonialism and slavery.

What then is different about Haiti, why have I used it to introduce the radical in human rights? In his introduction to the writings of Louverture, Nick Nesbitt hits the nail on the head: the rights of man:

> offered a previously inconceivable opportunity to upset the (symbolic) economy of the 18th-century world-system. In their very emptiness, these concepts harboured a latent operative efficacy. The signifier 'general liberty' thus opened a gap or interval in that century, a gap inherent in the inadequation between the slaves' political exclusion and the 'universal' rights of man. To witness the politicization of Toussaint L'Ouverture and the Haitian Revolution today is to initiate a genealogy of the process of political subjectivation – an inquiry essential to any conceivable progress towards emancipation.[52]

The gap that Nesbitt describes is fundamentally important, because this is the possibility of rights – to open a schism between the governmental figuring of what is and the social imagination of what might be. 'The Haitian revolution confirms not merely the possibility but the actuality of alternative modernities, complete with formulations of universal human rights.'[53] The second crucial insight of Nesbitt's brief note is that human rights had a crucial place in the context of constituent subjectivation. Boukman's 'voice of liberty' spoke *from the hearts of the slaves*, informing them of the necessity of overthrow, informing them of their constituent *potentia*. Like Winstanley, as I will briefly examine in the next chapter, the Haitian slaves materially instantiated a different and radical human rights designed to rupture the given state of the situation.

Introducing a letter from Louverture to Laveaux, Nesbitt strikes on a hidden understanding of rights that the leadership of the revolution (by this advanced stage) sought to repress:

> For the rebellious workers [of the plantations], freedom arises instead [of from Toussaint's universal rule of law] through a shared communal experience of suffering such as that they have shared with Dutty [their leader against whose removal they had revolted] which has no necessary connection, and is even inimical, to large-scale plantation labour.[54]

Radical notions of rights – that is, demands for a different being-together – constantly emerge in constituent moments. In this instance, it is through the shared and mixed experience of resistance to the plantation economy that the demand for radical politico-economic change is enunciated. What I have tried to do in this section is draw attention not to the content of the rights demanded by the slaves, but to the use of rights as rupture and demand. The danger with the eternal focus on the content of rights is that their purpose is missed. They become a matter for standard setting and policing. This focus has the tendency to look for rights being effectively implemented by a government. The point with Haiti, however, is that rights are used for many purposes, not least as a tool of radical change. Rights are picked up by the slaves and mixed with their own political traditions in order to rupture the political constitution of the time. We can see a version of rights that is borne from and tightly bound to the constituent. This is an association that modern historians of human rights tend to overlook. To draw out the significance of this elision, I will compare it to the manner in which the abolition movement is lionized.

Evans suggests that: 'Those engaged in the human rights movement – government agencies, international organizations, and non-governmental organizations alike – perceive themselves as politically neutral modern-day abolitionists whose only purpose is to identify "evil" and root it out.'[55] The trope of abolition is crucial. It establishes Mutua's threefold imaginal structure of the victim, rescuer and oppressor. Instead of the active subjects of the slave revolts, the traditional human rights histories emphasize slavery in the context of the (British) abolitionist movement (with its international (white and middle-class) subjects rescuing poor black people).[56] I suggest that this reveals how the radical subjects of resistance and rights are withdrawn from the narrative, while the radical sense of rights is increasingly hidden. The histories of human rights place that movement in the bourgeois attempt to end the slave trade. Lauren Gordon is exemplary.[57] He says: 'It is hardly surprising that the first systematic efforts to protect humanity and defend justice should focus on the tragic fate of those condemned to slavery.'[58] He goes on to describe the manners in which 'a small minority of *thoughtful* men and women'[59] heroically refused to be swayed by the arguments of natural superiority and the vested interests of the day. Rather, they were 'prepared to make the critical mental leap of imagining a world that did not exist and seeing slaves not as property, but as living and suffering human beings.'[60] These heroic visionaries set up NGOs, Lauren Gordon tells us. It is clear from his narrative that his readers, who have already invested themselves in human rights, are to identify with these bourgeois liberal humanitarians.

This identification very clearly reveals a structure that we find throughout the human rights oeuvre, not just in the history. Mutua argues that human rights are structured in their imagination of the world. 'The grand narrative of human rights contains a subtext that depicts an epochal contest pitting savages, on the one hand, against victims and saviours, on the other.'[61] Mutua describes this as a threefold and compound metaphor. The first aspect is the idea of the savage, that is, the violent and destructive oppressor. The state, he tells us, is a 'classic savage, an ogre forever bent on the consumption of humans.'[62] The savage monster of the state is only too happy to embody the most violent and destructive aspects of human being, thus it falls to human rights to discipline the beast. But, of course, the state is not the only savage. Its collection of power makes it one of the most dangerous.[63] It is complex; behind the state lie political cultures that create the possibility of the worst states: juntas, theocracies or one-party states.[64] However,

I would go further than Mutua. As distinct as his metaphor is, I would suggest that the savage, victim, saviour (or oppressor, victim, rescuer as I prefer) is actually an imaginal structure.[65] It is a tendency to fit characters and situations into pre-given forms and figurations. In this extended sense, the savage or oppressor is not merely the state, but any character that is deemed evil. The state is merely the typical mode of delivery of evil; as an imaginal structure, it is the actual evil itself that is important.[66]

The second aspect of Mutua's metaphor is the victim who is the motor to the whole machine. I have argued elsewhere that the victim of horrendous violation is written at the heart of the modern human rights movement.[67] This is immediately apparent if we look to its inaugural document, the Universal Declaration of Human Rights 1948 (UDHR) and particularly its preamble. The preamble of the UDHR opens by positioning human rights at the foundation of freedom and justice and is supplemented with the warning that 'disregard and contempt for human rights *have resulted* in barbarous acts which have outraged the conscience of mankind.'[68] In this brief suggestion, the Universal Declaration poses an ethereal and haunting threat: appalling events (the Holocaust, Second World War and the various other hideous violations of the time) have occurred because human rights were not respected. At stake in this association is nothing less than the very authority of the politics itself, its moral and political weight. *An attachment is written at a fundamental level of human rights to the innocently wronged.*[69] However, the UDHR's inscription of horror in the face of the Holocaust and the Second World War, importantly, links human rights to the possibility of justice with which the declaration opens. The message is straightforward: manmade suffering will happen unless human rights are respected. Thus, respect for human rights is the possibility for an end to manmade suffering and pain. The final aspect of Mutua's metaphor is the 'saviour or redeemer, the good angel who protects, vindicates, civilizes, restrains, and safeguards. The saviour is the victim's bulwark against tyranny. The simple, yet complex promise of the saviour is freedom: freedom from the tyrannies of the state, tradition, and culture.'[70] The importance of this metaphor cannot and should not be underrated. It is a crucial structuring lens through which complexity is resolved.

If we look back at the human rights historiography of the abolition movement, we can find this structure at play. Take, for instance the classic 'brand' of the British abolition movement, its seal, entitled 'Am I not a Man and a Brother' (1787). On the seal (designed by Josiah Wedgwood), an African man in profile kneels with his manacled hands thrust forward in supplication. The function of the 'brand' was precisely imaginal. It aimed to brand the subconscious with an image, in clear black and white, of a passive non-threatening slave. These are not the slaves who had revolted in Jamaica, neither would they be the Haitians who would rise four years later. This is a Christian image that positions the British in the patriarchal position of power (saviours, bringers of light and religion (alongside slavery)), with the helpless slave dependent on their mercy. The supplicant slave kneels, presumably before a white master. But this is the power of Wedgwood's brand – it presents a stark choice to the British: decide whether to be (or become) saviour or savage, rescuer or oppressor. In terms of Mutua's metaphor, this image of the slave presents us with the good victim who raises his hands in supplication, not in anger. The image of the pleading slave on his knees reflects on us now, the slave was required to undertake the submissive posture in order to legitimate the order of the humanitarian. The victim is the most important cog in the wheel, the very object of the system. As regards the victim's (or object's) subjectivity, it was that of the passive and suffering human–animal. The image of the passive slave proposed by the abolitionists is very clear,[71] as is the negative imprint of the violent slave.

Abolition was a very complex process in which a variety of factors played quite crucial roles.[72] It lies beyond this work to engage with it in any real sense; the reason I raise it here is to throw into relief the human rights silence on Haiti and other slave revolts. To do this, let me suggest a multiplication of the readings of abolition. However, first, it is important to note that:

> To disregard [humanitarianism] completely . . . would be to commit a grave historical error and to ignore one of the greatest propaganda movements of all time. The humanitarians were the spearhead of the onslaught which destroyed the West Indian system and freed the Negro. But their importance has been seriously misunderstood and grossly exaggerated by men who have sacrificed scholarship to sentimentality and, like the scholastics of old, placed faith before reason and evidence.[73]

It is no surprise that the British moved firmly towards abolition only when they had lost the bulk of their American colonies. They maintained different colonies elsewhere, in Africa, Asia and Australia, but these did not require slaves in the same way that the plantation economies of the southern states required. Australia became the site for the transportation of convicts and both the African and Asian colonies and zones of influence had readymade populations to be subjugated. They banned the slave trade in 1808 and slavery in the British Empire in 1834. This gap (1808–1834) is important – the international trade is first challenged and only then is slavery itself threatened.

While much is made of the costs to the British,[74] there is also much to be said for the advantage that they gleaned over their competitor nations. For instance, Eric Williams, in his momentous *Capitalism and Slavery*, argues that Pitt the Younger's retreat (in 1792) from a strong abolitionist position can be ascribed to the destruction of St. Domingue:

> Faced with intense French competition in the world's sugar market, Pitt's plan in 1787 was twofold: to recapture the European market with the aid of sugar from India and to secure an international abolition of the slave trade. The effect of this would be to ruin St. Domingue, which produced the bulk of the French supply. If international abolition could not be accomplished then

>British abolition would suffice for the French were so dependent upon British
slavers that even a unilateral abolition by England would seriously dislocate
the French economy.[75]

Williams argued that after the revolution on St. Domingue had destroyed its
productive capacity, there could be no great benefit gleaned from abolition.
Equally, when the *grand blancs* invited Pitt to take control of the French half of
the island, it became crucial to maintain the slave trade. While Williams has been
thoroughly challenged in the manner in which he puts forward Pitt's motives,[76]
there is at least enough in the broader calculations to contradict Lauren Gordon's
lyricization of abolition, seen in the first half of this chapter.

Geopolitical machinations of the European powers aside, there are other notable
non-moralistic reasons for abolition. It is clear, for instance, that Voltaire, Hume
and Adam Smith all opposed the slave trade but not from a moral position. In *The
Wealth of Nations* Smith said:

>The experience of all ages and nations, I believe, demonstrates that the work
done by slaves, though it appears to cost only their maintenance, is in the end
the dearest of any. A person who can acquire no property, can have no other
interest but to eat as much, and to labour as little as possible. Whatever
work he does beyond what is sufficient to purchase his own maintenance,
can be squeezed out of him by violence only, and not by any interest of
his own.[77]

In crude economic terms, the slave trade was terribly wasteful. It was all too often
more expensive to ship someone across the oceans (with all of the loss of 'cargo'
implicit in this) and then house and feed them on a plantation. You could pay
'free' labourers much less than it cost to transport, buy and maintain a slave.
This was Smith's utility-based opposition. Trouillot says that 'behind the radicalism of Diderot and Raynal [the French abolitionists] stood . . . a project of
colonial management. It did indeed include the abolition of slavery, but only in
the long term, and as a part of a process that aimed at the better control of the
colonies.'[78]

There were many political positions within the abolition movement. The point
of multiplying the reasons for abolition is not to sully the purity of the British
motives, but to reveal the human rights historiography as ideological in its
rendering of abolition and to throw the absence of slave resistance in it into relief.
By failing to discuss the multitude of reasons for abolition, by failing to engage
with the multiplicity of slave resistance where the victim becomes an active agent
of his own liberation, human rights make a very specific rendering of its subject.
Human rights looks to Clarkson, for instance, because he 'should have' sided with
the conventional notion that slavery was either natural or necessary. People who
'betray' their own powerful side and thus 'discover' the humanity of the other
subjected side are the human rights heroes: the rescuers. However, all too often

the rescuers are those who keep their hands clean. Slaves who resisted their own oppression, thereby violating the political constitution of their time, are elided because they are not morally pure. They are sullied by self-interest and violence. Crucially, those who use rights to resist their oppression present us with a different history of human rights. They present different subjects with different imaginations of how rights can and should be used. In Lauren Gordon and many others, we find the reduction of the complexity of abolition to a moral self-evidence. When this is placed alongside the elision of slave revolts, I argue that the imaginal structuring through historical narrative is revealed. Human rights history is purified.

To close this chapter, let me suggest three aspects of human rights history that must become crucial if we are to think of human rights without petty moralization. First, it is necessary to maintain a cold and critical stare on relations between property and rights. This cannot be understated, as it follows the relation between social utopia and natural rights. The fundamental problem of privilege or more accurately prior accumulated property is not something that is usually considered a major human rights issue. Bloch puts forward this argument in order to suggest that we need to escape the distinction:

> Social utopias and natural law had mutually complementary concerns within the same human space; they marched separately but, sadly, did not strike together. Although they were in accord on the decisive issue, a more humane society, there nevertheless arose important differences between the doctrines of social utopia and natural law. Those differences can be formulated as follows. Social utopian thought directed its efforts toward human happiness, natural law was directed toward human dignity. Social utopias depicted relations in which *toil* and *burden* ceased, natural law constructed relations in which *degradation* and *insult* ceased.[79]

However, he is not entirely correct to say that the two remain completely separate. There are a few instances where the two 'strike together'. I have already suggested *the Charter of the Forest* and, in the next chapter, I will look briefly at the writings of Gerard Winstanley. The second element that must become central is the construction and use of 'humanity'. The shifting figurations of humanity along with the questioning of the often mystifying uses that it is put to, is of critical importance to challenge our current naturalized sense of the human. However, as will become apparent in Chapters 7 and 8, there should be no uncritical approach to 'humanity' as if it were some sort of ultimate civilizing term. Finally, the question of the subject(s) of human rights subsumes the two previous aspects. In this chapter, I have sought to challenge the traditional narrative of human rights by positing the need to understand the heterogeneity of its history. I have suggested a variety of different subjects and sought to challenge the traditional figurations. In the next chapter, I will focus on the manner in which the radical withdraws in human rights. I begin with Locke's right to revolution, demonstrating that even in what appears to be a truly radical enunciation of rights we find the clear evidence of the withdrawal of the radical. I will suggest that modern human rights is constituted by the completion of this withdrawal. The second half of the chapter argues that the structuring of human rights through individualism and statism seals out radical possibilities by metaphysically predetermining the discourse.

Chapter 3

The withdrawal of the radical in human rights

> If anyone says or writes that practical reason must henceforth be based on the rights of the individual and the individual alone, he invalidates his own proposition if he doesn't incite his audience to make this statement true for themselves. Such a proof can only be lived, grasped from the inside. That is why everything in the notes that follow should be tested and corrected by the immediate experience of everyone. Nothing is so valuable that it need not be started afresh, nothing is so rich that it need not be enriched constantly.
>
> Vaneigem, *The Revolution of Everyday Life*[1]

Rights do not belong solely to the liberal tradition. Far from it, they have been a strategy or technology of many different and radically conflicting political theories. As I suggested in the introduction, the association with authoritative demand and limitation need not be hegemonic. There are instances where the relation between the constituent and human rights seems to go beyond the traditional figuring of 'revolution in order to establish rights' as the French and American revolutions are usually explained. Through Haiti, I suggested in Chapter 2 that a different thinking of rights could be seen in the performance of constituent power. However, it was and remains too early to begin to examine this in a thorough fashion (that will have to wait for Chapter 9 and the idea of right-ing). For now, I want to suggest that it is possible to see a process of the 'withdrawal of the radical' in the emergence of human rights. I will open by looking at one crucial instance of this from the history of human rights; Locke's right to revolt. The first part of the chapter, therefore, briefly traces this right within the *Second Treatise on Government*, underlining the withdrawal of the radical at precisely the moment at which it appears to be most clearly enunciated in the discourse. With the withdrawal established through Locke, I will look to modern human rights where there is virtually no radical politics left. In fact, only a trace remains in the international texts. This remnant will be traced in order to underline a different possibility of rights (other than statism and individualism) even in the Universal Declaration of Human Rights (UDHR). The second part of the chapter sets out the two axes along which my critique of rights lies, as well as the themes that will need to be dealt with in my return to rights. I will detail the critiques of statism and individualism, which are the symptoms of a metaphysical malaise. Heidegger's critique of humanism is used to deepen the analysis of rights, in order to understand the metaphysical malady. I hope briefly to set out a Heideggerian position that provides the backdrop for subsequent chapters.[2] The critiques of statism and individualism open the possibility of 're-treating' the closure of the political (qua the space of being-together) implicit in the metaphysical closure of human rights.[3] Ultimately, these fault lines of critique (individualism, statism and the humanism that underlies them) will become the focus of the rest of the book.

The withdrawal of the radical

Locke's *Second Treatise* is often set up as a foundational text for human rights, not least because it was so influential in the build-up to the American and French revolutions. As such, it initially appears to be a good instance of the radicalness of rights. I will suggest that the opposite is the case – that Locke performs a classic example of the withdrawal of the radical. He begins by setting himself the task of explaining why there should be private property, given that God gave the Earth to Adam and his posterity in common. This argument rests on the assertion in §27 that 'though the earth, and all inferior creatures, be common to all men, yet every man has a property in his own person: this no body has any right to but himself.'[4] Crucially then, man is a possessive entity as it owns its own personhood. Property is not simply the commodities that one produces, consumes and alienates. Rather, one owns one's very self: life, liberty and estate.[5] By his labour, man rightfully appropriates that which is in common, but this appropriation rests essentially on the conception of the person as the possessive individual.[6] Private property rests on the personal possession of one's 'properties' or faculties. Equally, civil society and the social contract are based on the same foundation: 'The great and chief end, therefore, of men's uniting into common-wealths, and putting themselves under government, is the preservation of their property.'[7]

Locke suggests a broadly conflictual model of history while simultaneously pacifying certain elements. He distinguishes the political constitution from the social contract. When the government oversteps the bounds of its permitted power, the people may overturn it. But, this is not a return to the state of nature. The societal agreement remains as it is, based on the coincidence of interest because of property relations. Locke goes beyond the Huguenot position for justifying revolution.[8] According to him, the people do not have to wait until tyranny is thoroughly established: to do this

> [i]s in effect no more than to bid . . . [the people] first be slaves, and then to take care of their liberty; and when their chains are on, tell them, they may act like freemen. This, if barely so, is rather mockery than relief; and men can never be secure from tyranny, if there be no means to escape it till they are

perfectly under it: and therefore it is, that they have not only a right to get out of it, but to prevent it.[9]

There is a right to revolt '[w]hen [the legislative] endeavour[s] to invade the property of the subject, and to make themselves, or any part of the community, masters, or arbitrary disposers of the lives, liberties, or fortunes of the people'.[10]

However, all is not as it seems in this. Kain asks:

> Would the propertyless have a right to revolution against the government and their properties in order to set up communal property, equal property, or at least to reduce the degree of inequality in property? It is quite clear that this would not be legitimate. It would violate the law of nature which guarantees the right to unequal property.[11]

This is not simply a limitation on the right, rather it is a failure of Locke to conceive of the subjectivity of wage labourers. A quote from *Considerations of the Consequences of Lowering of the Interest and Raising the Value of Money*:

> For the labourers share, being seldom more than a bare subsistence, never allows that body of men time or opportunity to raise their thoughts above that, or struggle with the richer for theirs . . . unless when some common and great distress, uniting them in one universal ferment, makes them forget respect, and emboldens them to carve to their wants with armed force; and then sometimes they break in upon the rich, and sweep all like a deluge. But this rarely happens but in the mal-administration of neglected, or mismanaged government.[12]

To this Macpherson tells us that there 'is the assumption that maladministration consists not of leaving the poor at bare subsistence, but of allowing such unusual distress to occur as will unite them in armed revolt'.[13]

Kain is correct to say that '[i]t never occurs to Locke that in the normal course of events the poor concern themselves with anything but bare subsistence. When they do, it does not occur to . . . [him] that it may be for some legitimate reason. It is a problem of mismanagement.'[14] The poor do not think beyond their station, beyond subsistence. There is no class conflict for Locke: revolution is a matter for the like of his patron, the Earl of Shaftsbury. Macpherson again:

> Now the question who are to have the right to revolution is decisive . . .: the right to revolution is, with him, the only effective test of citizenship, as he made no provision for any other method of exercising the right to turn out an unwanted government. Although he insists in the *Treatise* on the majority's right to revolution, it does not seem to cross his mind here that the labouring class might have the right to make revolution. And indeed there was no reason why it should have crossed his mind, for to him the labouring class

was an object of administration, rather than fully part of the citizen-body. It was incapable of rational political action, while the right to revolution depended essentially on rational decision.[15]

The labouring class lay beyond the realms of rationality. Because it was without property it was also beyond the social cohesion that formed the basis for Locke's belief in the possibility of dissolving government but not society.

Locke's conception of the right to revolt is fundamentally prefigured by the question of property. This precondition sets property metaphysically beyond revolution. So to understand the significance of the tract, we must begin to understand it not as a radical move, but rather as an early attempt at the withdrawal of the radical in rights. By placing property above revolution, we can see why revolution falls away from subsequent human rights discourse. It pacifies revolution by pre-setting the juridical (something that I will return to through the Abbé Sieyès in the next chapter). Locke's right to revolution must be understood at once as the gradual coming to acceptability of a radically different sense of rights, but also as an attempt to limit a mixing of the social utopia and rights traditions. Locke is, after all, writing in the period directly after the English Civil War, where thinkers such as Gerard Winstanley proposed exactly this mixing.

Property played a crucial role for Winstanley. Unlike Locke's later defence of property, Winstanley asserts that ownership itself was the cause of evil. For Winstanley, God was immanent in a material sense, not as a figuration of stasis but of change. Instead of the possessive individual, we find primitive communism; instead of the God of stasis in the protection of unequal property, we find the immanent deity of creation; instead of the demand that the subject of politics is the propertied gentleman, we find the radical levelling assertion of equality of even the basest of the world.[16] Winstanley stands for a thinking of natural law that rejects the re-pacifying of agonism, which Locke's closure of the right to revolution entails.[17] This should not be underestimated. The concept of the commons returns to rupture the naturalization of conceptions of property that we find in this era. While Winstanley's primitive communism tells us little about current times, its importance lies in the fact of its existence. It is crucial that in a time associated with the naturalization of early capitalistic relations, we find natural law as the expression of a radical anti-capitalist resistance. Natural law is not simply the manner in which the emerging middle class reimagines itself, it represents a site of political thought of all shades, without closure. It is not simply the realm of the conservatively religious, the accumulative classes or the sovereign.

There is, of course, another sense in which Locke's work is useful in thinking the radical in rights. Foucault argues that what we find in Locke (among others) is a very different historiography to what went before. Instead of history as the legitimation of the state (Roman-style history) and the right to rule of the sovereign, we increasingly find history as the legitimation of struggle. This new historical discourse begins:

to demand rights that have not been recognized, or in other words, to declare war by declaring rights. Historical discourse of the Roman type pacifies society, justifies power, and founds the order . . . that constitutes the social body. In contrast, the discourse I am telling you about, and which is deployed in the late sixteenth century, and which can be described as a biblical-style historical discourse tears society apart and speaks of legitimate rights solely in order to declare war on laws.[18]

Foucault explains that the figure of this type of rights 'is not that of legislator or the philosopher.' There is no sovereign that could establish himself 'between adversaries at the centre and above them, to impose a general law on each and to found an order that reconciles.' Rather he explains, this different right that emerges with Locke is 'a right marked by dissymmetry, the founding of a truth linked to a relation of force, a weapon-truth and a singular right. The subject that speaks is a warring – I won't even say a polemical – subject.'[19] I quoted this at the beginning of the last chapter in order to underscore the difference in rights; on one side the legislator and on the other, the warring subject. Beyond the pacification of a right to revolution by establishing a society bound by property, Locke's rights are not legitimacy granting devices or at least that is only part of their operation. They are at once the creation of a warring rights subjectivity, but also the reassertion of a pacifying property. Crucially, these two are indissociable from one another. This is the difference of human rights that I suggested in Chapter 1.

Modern human rights (post-1945) come to completion with the withdrawal of the radical. Yet, with any claimed totality there always remain traces that challenge the implied closure. Thus, even as I assert that the radical is withdrawn from modern human rights, we can find remaining traces, even in the heart of modern human rights. In fact, the Universal Declaration of Human Rights (UDHR), albeit only in the preamble, contains precisely such a trace. The preamble is a strange (uncanny, improper) place, at once both a fundamental element and relegated to the introductory, the preparatory, the justificatory. In the two Covenants (the *International Covenant on Civil and Political Rights* and the *International Covenant on Economic, Social and Cultural Rights*), this partial inclusion of a preamble is explicable. As a legal document the explanatory or justificatory pretext aids subsequent judicial construction as well as explaining the sovereign power (of the signatories) to agree on the Covenant. However, what is preambulary to a declaration; is the preamble somehow not declared? The preamble is preliminary – it is liminal. In fact, it is the very site of the Declaration's self-authorization. It traces the limits of the Declaration, it is the moment at which a clutter of assertions become a 'declaration' (with all the historical weight of the form behind it).[20] The UDHR itself specifies this self-constituting of the declaration in the preamble when it asserts that 'the General Assembly proclaims this Universal Declaration of Human Rights as a common standard of achievement for all peoples and all nations.' The preamble must be given the significance it demands as the margin of the Declaration; it is where we must look if we are to find the limits of the document. 'Limit' here is not meant in the sense of 'shortcoming', but, rather, in the philosophical sense of the point at which the Declaration comes up against its other and from this touching derives its essence.[21] 'The limit is not negative: it traces an identity – and this tracing excludes itself from what it traces out, simultaneously carrying along with it the identity outside itself.'[22] At these limits, the Declaration and what is declared itself begins to come into view. This preliminary moment allows us to think the *proper* (*eigentlich*, *proprié*) of human rights, especially given that the preamble is somehow improper (liminal) to the Declaration.

The particular sentence in the preamble that reveals the hidden constituent reads thus: 'Whereas it is essential, if man is not to be compelled to have recourse, as a last resort, to rebellion against tyranny and oppression, that human rights should be protected by the rule of law.'[23] There are a number of points to be made about this. First, this is no open constituent power – but this should not surprise anyone. We are, after all, looking for a *trace* of the constituent. Revolution is posed as the *last resort* of human rights, the *'final'* human right. This replicates the second French Declaration of the Rights of Man and the Citizen (1793), which clearly states the relation: 'Resistance to oppression is the consequence of the other rights of Man.'[24] By placing the constituent last, as the last resort (even the last right), the constituted order of human rights is placed before the constituent. The result of this is conservative, in the traditional sense of the word: where the constituent comes after the constituted, where resistance is the last right, the only revolution is one designed to *reinstate* what had been undermined. Only when human rights are violated is resistance justified, according to the UDHR. By placing revolt as the final right, the power that resides with people is a last resort against tyranny (defined as gross and systematic violation of human rights). The constituent power must reinstate once more the human rights already violated. This is the theory of the UDHR, at least. However, it is clear from the many revolutions scattered throughout history that once the transgressive practice has begun and is learned, it is much more difficult to stifle the radical impulse to change. I will argue in the next three chapters that this sense of the constituent is what we might call a 'closed' or a dialectical notion of constituent power in the crudest of senses. Returning to the UDHR, the wording of the preamble reveals the addressee of the declaration in this paragraph. It is phrased as a warning to states; subscribe to human rights ideals, treat them as public right or your people will rise against you! This logic entails a temporality of prevention, in which the very newness of the future itself is to be guarded against.

Against this reading of the preamble, it may be argued that Article 30 destroys this trace of the constituent. Article 30 reads: 'Nothing in this Declaration may be interpreted as implying for any State, group or person any right to engage in any activity or perform any act aimed at the destruction of any of the rights and freedoms set forth herein.' However, this is a strange article in itself. It comes at the end of the substantive rights and so marks an end or limit, but this limit is marked from within the 'substantive', unlike the preamble. Article 30 demands that the text be taken as a totality, it demands that we synthesize any contradictions. Thus, the text *is to be read as one*. It is not a bundle of historically contingent associations, with a minefield of contradictions and conflicts. Rather, it is a single document with every right *always already* synthesized with every other right. This is precisely the old logic (or myth) of the Common Law, where the judges are seen as simply iterating laws that already existed out there in the ether. Article 30 hides the true nature of the Universal Declaration. In a positivist fallacy, it demands that the UDHR is a closed text that simply has to be applied. It denies that interpretation is creation. Yet, the indeterminacy thesis, whether taken in a limited or in a broad sense is generally accepted.[25] The UDHR, like all texts, is open and is full of contradiction. It is an ideologically schizophrenic document, made up of layer on layer of different philosophies, politics, cultural values and ideologies. Unfortunately, this is not the place to engage with this layering, suffice to say that the UDHR is the product of its time. It emerges from a complex genealogy and in that genealogy the radical (the constituent) has been gradually withdrawn.

The UDHR proposes revolution as the final human right: after tyranny and oppression, a people will rise against the oppressors and reinstate human rights. However, even as this 'final' right, constituent power is still too much for the discourse. When the Declaration is legalized into the two Covenants, the (more open) recognition of struggle against injustice morphs into the recognition of the (closed) right to self-determination. As the 'final right' of the UDHR, the form and content of resistance is kept (fairly) open. However, once it is constituted as self-determination, it becomes limited and hedged in on all sides. The subject of resistance is named as a people and the end of resistance is stipulated as the determination of a people's political status and their pursuit of economic, social and cultural development. This description of the people strips it of any potentiality to be otherwise – the self of self-determination is always already pre-constituted,[26] which as Christodoulidis points out is not truly self-determination.[27] Self-determination is rendered as the right to the self-rule of 'blue-water' colonies.[28] The subject of this right is a people to whom is given a stable territorial, racial, ethnic or national meaning.[29] Each of these groupings demands the production of a common and closed community around some aspect of identity.[30] Human rights focus almost entirely on the possession of rights by individuals and so the 'we' involved in struggling for rights is elided. The fact that the only article that addresses itself to a collectivity is also the only common article in the International Bill of Rights is read as signifying that it is exceptional. This exceptionalism reads as such: the logic of universality does not apply to the common article, *because it is common*. Instead, it is a right whose operation is historically and geographically relevant only in the decolonialization movement of the second half of the last century.

All that is left of the creative fire of the constituent is the ash in the hearth. The constituent is undermined. However, it is the manner of this that is important. The excess (of resistance against domination) is pre-structured in the Covenants: collectivity is bought forward and dealt with by placing it in relation to the *telos* of a state. The right to self-determination is all that remains of constituent power in human rights law. The originary excess is redrawn and neutralized – a people will only suffocate, entombed in the calcified sarcophagus of self-determination – the radical possibility of its form utterly withdrawn. This is where, despite many points of agreement, I would depart from Bill Bowring's work.[31] He would see a radical potential in *international human rights law*. He argues for what he calls a 'substantivist' account, by which he means 'that human rights are real and provide a ground for judgement, to the extent that they are understood in their historical context, and as, and to the extent to which, they embody and define the content of real human struggles.'[32] However, the extent to which Bowring determines these 'real' human struggles by already extant international norms is precisely the problem. Against Bowring, then, there is not a continuity between the use of human rights as the form of revolutionary struggle and modern international human rights law. Rather, a more statist and individualist (as we will see in the next section of the chapter) human rights comes to a point of completion with the ECHR and the Covenants. All that is left of the other more radical ideas are traces.

Anyone who positions the UDHR as the ultimate assertion of a universal truth facilitates the reduction and negation of other traditions of human rights. These other traditions, some of which Bowring quite rightly draws attention to, remain (as a trace) within the discourse because of the utterly hegemonic account given by international human rights law. While the potentiality of human rights can give form to 'real' human struggles, international human rights law is over-determined by the withdrawal of the radical, the elision of the creative fire of constituent power. *Modern human rights law comes into being only through the utter withdrawal of the radical.*[33]

Statist and individualist metaphysics

I have argued thus far that the radical has withdrawn from human rights and with it the possibilities of that discourse become increasingly limited. Perhaps the two most telling aspects of this withdrawal of the radical in human rights are the apparent 'naturalness' of statism and individualism. I will show how these two critiques are crucial to understand current human rights, but are also merely symptomatic of a much more difficult problem, the operation of an underlying metaphysics of the subject. In this section, I will use Heidegger's critique of humanism in order to draw out and explore the two classical critiques of human rights (individualism and statism). This metaphysical structure, which includes individualism and statism, pre-structures modern human rights in a way that holds off and suspends radical possibilities.

Let me begin with statism. The state forms the very horizon of meaning of human rights. Whether judge, administrator, legislator or police, the state forms the very *telos* of human rights struggle.[34] This is particularly manifested in two figures: the refugee and the revolutionary. As Arendt showed over 50 years ago, the refugee (or stateless person) throws the rights of man into question by bringing forth the distinction between the rights of *man* and the rights of the *citizen*.[35] Arendt shows that there are in fact no rights of man, but only rights of the citizen. Unlike 'man' (whatever its definition), the citizen is fundamentally constituted in relation to the state. Precisely when people are most in need of their rights, when they are cast from their home and their community, we find them without protection. When a person has no right accruing due to citizenship, they have no rights at all. The refugee represents a disquieting element not just for human rights but for nation-states 'because, by breaking the identity between the human and the citizen and that between nativity and nationality, it brings the originary fiction of sovereignty to crisis.'[36] The refugee unhinges the link between 'the human' and her rights:

> No paradox of contemporary politics is filled with a more poignant irony than the discrepancy between the efforts of well-meaning idealists who stubbornly insist on regarding as 'inalienable' those human rights, which are enjoyed only by citizens of the most prosperous and civilized countries, and the situation of the rightless themselves. Their situation has deteriorated just as stubbornly, until the internment camp – prior to the second World War the exception rather than the rule for the stateless – has become the routine solution for the problem of domicile of the 'displaced persons'.[37]

The camps at Calais and across Europe testify to those who are literally on the outside of law: '[A]s soon as people were stripped of everything except their humanity . . . it became hard to recognize them as human.'[38] Yet human rights seems so often given over to a sort of hyperbole. The UDHR, for instance, appears to project itself as the cure to all evil: unless human rights (of which the Declaration authorizes itself as the core text) are respected, terrible things will happen . . . *again*. The question that Arendt extends is whether, in fact, such a view is anything more than mere idealism.

The other side of this statism is that there is no space for a right of revolution in the international covenants. There is no scope for being-against-the-state, because we understand implicitly that the state is the be-all and end-all of the human rights movement. Indeed, anything other than statism would be ridiculous given that it is states (and their representatives) that write and ratify international human rights declarations and instruments. However, this has not always been the case. Article 10 of the New Hampshire Constitution enshrines a very different tradition: 'The doctrine of non-resistance against arbitrary power, and oppression, is absurd, slavish, and destructive of the good and happiness of mankind.' This is not simply a contractarian nod, it is a fundamental refiguring of human rights where the people rather than the state is the ultimate horizon. There are multiple traditions in the genesis of human rights, but I have particularly emphasized two (very broad) camps: the statist conservative mode positions natural or fundamental rights as a manner of pacifying revolutionary movements without sacrificing wealth, position and even social structure; and the 'bottom-up' mode would demand recognition, equality and liberty.[39] Human rights, by its emplacement in the *international* sphere, enshrines the former statist model, thereby short-circuiting the New Hampshire-style horizon of the revolutionary people. The state is placed at the end (both *telos* and *finis*) of human rights – becoming the determinant of the horizon of possibility of the movement. By bringing the human rights struggle within the law, the radical sense of resistance is withdrawn. Human rights becomes the linchpin of the constitution and with this it is not surprising that 'the juridical limits of human rights closely coincide with the concerns of elites.'[40]

However, this problem of statism is symptomatic of a deeper problem that is epitomized by the universal standard setting so crucial in international human rights law. Martin Heidegger's basic proposition was that western philosophy, for over two millennia, continually asked the wrong questions, focusing on 'What is the nature or essence of man?' Simply put, human rights is merely the latest answer to this traditional question. Heidegger tells us that, historically, there have been many answers:

> Marx demands that 'man's humanity' be recognized and acknowledged. He finds it is 'society'. 'Social' man is for him 'natural' man. In 'society' the 'nature' of man, that is, the totality of 'natural needs' (food, clothing, reproduction, economic sufficiency) is equably secured. The Christian sees the humanity of man, the *humanitas* of *homo*, in contradistinction to *Deitas*. He is the man of the history of redemption who as a 'child of God' hears and accepts the call of the Father in Christ. Man is not of this world, since the 'world', thought in terms of Platonic theory, is only a temporary passage to the beyond.[41]

Whatever the essence of man, whether society, reason, race or the 'dignity of the human', Heidegger suggests that the question being asked itself is problematic. The problem is that every time we ask 'what *is* the meaning of human being?', we set ourselves looking for something beyond being that would determine the meaning of 'humanity'. 'Every determination of the essence of man that already presupposes an interpretation of being without asking about the truth of being, whether knowingly or not, is metaphysical.'[42] With human rights there is very clearly an attempt, sometimes explicit and sometimes implicit, to find a value in people that transcends the individual. This is fundamentally metaphysical and, according to Heidegger, fails to ask the fundamental question as to the *being of beings*. The difference between the traditional human rights approach and question of the being of beings is crucial for this book. I will spend the rest of this chapter tying early Heideggerian philosophy to the critiques of statism and individualism.

The question for Heidegger is the being of beings. The first point to note is the *distinction* that he draws between being and beings. Being, in a very rough sense, is the state of everything that *is*.[43] Beings, on the other hand, are particular existents, entities in being. Thus, I am here in the sitting room on Saturday morning in front of the computer, the fox in my garden last night is presumably still about somewhere, the coffee is there in front of me, growing cold. Each of our beings is given in its there-ness (I'm here, the fox is somewhere and the coffee is there). However we each share being. Thus, Heidegger tells us that we need to distinguish being from all of the various beings-in-the-world. This is what he called 'ontological difference' or the difference between the ontological (being) and the ontic (beings).[44] Certainly it is only through everyday beings (me, the fox and the coffee) that we can understand being, but by just looking at beings, we can miss that fundamental level (being). When human rights asks what is the nature of man, it looks at human beings and finds in them an essence that functions as a transcendent value (dignity for instance) which legitimates protection. However, in so doing, it skims over being and even prevents further thinking on it.

Heidegger suggests that we might begin with the insight that being is always to be found in beings.[45] Everything that *is* is already be-ing. Being does not just appear in exceptional events, there are no convenient spontaneously combusting shrubs that would provide the means of revelation. There is no god or source of meaning beyond the world. Being appears in the everyday, but at the same time, it is constantly being obscured in/by the everyday. I will come back to this double movement in a moment, but for now let me just say one aspect of this obscuring/revealing of being will be the impossibility of any attempt to set some sort of final essence of man. The question posed earlier (what is the nature or essence of man?) does not even begin to understand the fundamental flux of being. Instead, the question itself begins by obscuring the question of being. Systems of meaning that find themselves capable of setting transcendent values are deeply problematic because they do not see being as such, but rather elements (man, race, the worker, society) of it that are elevated.

With this, Heidegger takes aim at the entire philosophical structure on which human rights rest. The essential method of modern human rights is juridification. Rights become defined by and through their judicial character.[46] Norms or standards are set broadly and universally, to be then applied and supervised. In a sense, this is the critique of statism; however, it goes much deeper. The very basis of this quasi-judicial system presupposes a fundamental association between humanity and the norm. The norm is understood as a basic rendering of the human (both in form and content). S/he must eat, live, drink, talk, associate, work, etc., and therefore have a right to do these things. These are renderings of the essence of humanity, just as 'society' or 'reason' in previous modes of thought portrayed humanity's being. Human rights pose a fundamentally metaphysical vision of the human. While these renderings may not be false,[47] Heidegger suggests that their understanding of man fundamentally obscures the ontological. It obscures the coming to presence of being, the becoming of the world and of man (whatever 'man' might mean after such a critique). With human rights, the exposition of man's essence as delimited in a number of given rights closes off the fundamental openness of the world. It completes the political – presenting the absolute end of politics in the givenness of human rights.[48] If we have discovered man's essence, all that can be left to us is to police its boundaries. However, this alleged 'completion' is, in fact, the destruction of sense through its calcification in eternal metaphysical assertions. 'The minute the question concerning the essence counts as settled, a door is opened to unessence.'[49] As soon as we have completely enumerated a common and universal higher *law* and we claim that this coheres fully with human nature or the dignity of the human being, we have calcified what it is to be. You can be sure that such a totalizing claim will produce modes of being that do not fit this universal law.

The critique of the standard-setting (statist) method of human rights seeps into the very basic structures of the movement. It is not merely the finding of an essence of what it is to be human that is problematic. The very rendering of the individual itself is radically called into question. This is the second critique of human rights; even when they propose to be 'communitarian', they remain individualistic in their outlook. There are many different figurings of the individual in rights literature and beyond. The problem of the individual is threefold: its inability as a grounding figure to account for community; its possessive nature; and its fundamental impotence in political struggle. Locke understands the relation between the individual and his rights best:

> In the *Treatise*, Locke declares the purpose of all social compacts to be the 'preservation of property' (§124) and further defines this 'property' as 'their lives, liberties, and estates' (§123). Since Locke identifies not just material goods and individual liberties but also life itself as 'property', the grounding for all right to property must be an inalienable property, namely, the property of one's own person: 'every Man has a *Property* in his own *Person*. This no Body has any rights to but himself.' (§27)[50]

Possessive individualism conceives of the existent singularity as a possessing subject that must be protected against other possessing individuals who might attempt to damage their property. Modes of being are thus entirely misunderstood, instead of events where being comes to presence, we are faced with reified properties.

Metaphysics, at least since Descartes, has focused on the subject (or the individual in many of the renderings). Descartes began with *cogito sum* (I think, I am). However, it was the *cogitans* (the thinking) that proves the *sum* (the being). Thinking was thus rendered prior to being, Heidegger tells us. This poses subjectivity as the fundamental question that is taken up by subsequent philosophy, particularly epistemology. In a slightly awkward manner, Heidegger describes the reductive thinking of the subject or the manner that all human being is reduced to the question of the I or the self: 'We ask: "Who are we ourselves?" Each one of us is he himself, and as such he is an I-Myself, and thus is shown that We-Ourselves, as the composition, as it were, as the multitude of many I-Myself, as the multitude of separate Is, have thereby led the self back to the I.'[51] However, he says that this thinking of the subject is not just untrue (in that it does not get at the *being* of the self) but it is also incorrect (in that it does not even remain internally coherent):

> Certainly each one of us is an I-Myself; he is, however, precisely also formally a You-Yourself, not only in the other You who addresses him, but also by addressing himself (for example, 'You have done that wrongly' [said to oneself]). Each I is for this reason not only a You-Yourself, in which an I-Myself speaks, but also a We-Ourselves and You-Yourselves.[52]

Heidegger set himself up against this rendering of the subject, asserting that it is the error of modern philosophy. There is not a 'thinking subject' first who extends into the empty space of the world. Axelos summarizes:

> Thought in its modern stage . . . posits the *ego* endowed with the *ratio* and self-consciousness in the form of *res cogitans*, assigning as its field of activity the whole realm of *res extensa*. Human subjectivity becomes thus the (objective) foundation of what is. The world comprises the world of the subject and the world of objects, with Man as the (objective) Subject, an active knowing thing dealing with objects and grasping them in representation.[53]

Heidegger tells us that there is not the self and then all the others and a world that the subject may or may not know. Rather, when something comes into being, it is thrown into existence. It comes to being precisely *as a being-there*. The being of that entity cannot be separated from its there-ness. Its being is given in its there-ness, understood temporally, as we will see. Heidegger uses the term *dasein* (literally, 'being-there') rather than 'person', 'man' or 'individual' all of which are determined by metaphysics. The crucial factor about *dasein* is that once she *is* (i.e as soon as she is *in* being), she is *there*. Her there-ness is the manner in which her being is given. Each of our being(s) is given in our there-ness.[54]

Heidegger suggests that *dasein* (being-there) is not *just* constituted by its there-ness. There are a number of crucial aspects that are given in one's being-there. Particularly, he argues that once one is there, one is also 'with' and 'in-the-world'. Heidegger tells us that these aspects of being are equally primordial. By this he means that they are co-constitutive of the being-there. Instead of starting with the subject or the self, one's being-there is constituted *in an originary sense* by being-with others: 'The world is always the one I share with Others. The world of *dasein* is a *with-world* [Mitwelt]. Being-in is Being-with Others.'[55] Jean-Luc Nancy returns to this idea, as we will see in Chapter 7. He suggests that to be is to share being. *Partage* (to share) is at once to share-in (to partake) and to share-out (to divide) being.[56] The world is not a collection of objects and subjects, but rather it is understood as a web of relations in which beings share being.

Heidegger argues that being-with is fundamental to *dasein*, it is part of its originary constitution. One is there and with other *daseins* and things in the world:

> The basic structure of being-with cannot be reduced to or explained from anything else. The articulated whole of being-myself-with-(another-self) cannot be melted down into an 'inarticulate', isolated 'I', which then somehow finds its way to another *Dasein*, because with the disclosure of his own being as being-with, the being of others is already disclosed and understood.[57]

One is always already in-the-world, always already with others and always already there. Thus, the possessive individual as the fundamental unit of thought is a fiction. It is a way of misunderstanding being.

I have critiqued the individualism and statism (juridification of the essence of man); however, Heidegger's ontology is much more radical than the rejection of essence and the co-originariness of being-with. I have already suggested that the everyday plays a crucial role in *Being and Time*. Being is encountered in everyday existence, however, the everydayness of this encounter veils being. *Being and Time* attempts to discover how to be authentically. Heidegger suggests that there are manners of being that are authentic and ones that are inauthentic. *Dasein* is fallen, that is, it has lost itself (its understanding of being) in the everyday and does not see (its) being in its essence. In *Being and Time*, inauthenticity is rendered by the figure of *das Man* (translated as the 'they' or the 'one').[58] Heidegger argues that *dasein* is in a double bind – it forgets the question of its being by getting lost in the everyday, but it is in the everyday that being is to be found.[59] *Das Man* operates by way of a 'levelling down', concealing *dasein*'s possibilities, hiding the openness of being. The Heideggerian analytic attempts to rupture this levelling down by bringing forth the negativity that lies at the heart of *dasein* – death. By understanding that death is *dasein*'s ownmost possibility, that it is the only certainty in life, Heidegger hopes that we will struggle to free ourselves from the conformity and normalizing pressure of *das Man*. In Villa's words, death provides a 'shock treatment' for *dasein* to shake it out of its numbness.

Crucially, this is all in process. Being is coming to presence, it is being hidden and unveiled, *dasein* is constantly becoming in/authentic. There is no stability of being because it is constantly (be)coming. This is where the confusion about *das Man* emerges. Heidegger says:

> If we may express this existentially, such Being-with-one-another has the character of *distantiality* . . . But this distantiality which belongs to Being-with, is such that *dasein*, as everyday Being-with-one-another, stands in *subjection* to Others. It itself *is* not; its Being has been taken away by the Others. *Dasein*'s everyday possibilities of Being are for the Others to dispose of as they please. These Others, moreover, are not *definite* Others. On the contrary, any Other can represent them. What is decisive is just that inconspicuous domination by Others which has already been taken over unawares from *dasein* as being-with. One belongs to the Others oneself and enhances

their power. 'The Others' whom one thus designates in order to cover up the fact of one's belonging to them essentially oneself, are those who proximally and for the most part '*are there*' in everyday Being-with-one-another. The 'who' is not this one, or that one, not oneself, not some people, and not the sum of them all. The 'who' is the neuter, *the 'they'* [*das Man*].[60]

Dasein in its everydayness stands in subjection to others, its being has been 'taken over' by others. This 'taken over' means that '*dasein*'s everyday possibilities of being are for the Others to dispose of as they please.' *Dasein*'s loss of its being is fundamentally a loss of its everyday possibilities. Its possibilities have become necessities because it stands in subjection to these others. *Das Man* is a force on *dasein*, it represents *dasein*'s tendency towards inauthenticity.

This dispersal of *dasein*'s being – inauthenticity – is a loss of its possibilities, which are disposed of by these indistinct Others. They 'are not *definite* Others', this is not a class or 'race'. Rather, in this domination by Others *you become the Others*, to whom you belong by way of your subjection. The dissipation of your everyday possibilities, the refusal to take the decisive decisions with regard to your everyday being, means that you cede the responsibility for your being to the they. What is more, you hide your belonging to these Others by blaming them. You blame them for the fact that you act as they do. You are (the) they, you become a representative of *das Man* for other *daseins* and your inauthenticity is a force on others to follow you in this mode of being. Inauthenticity is thus viral.

This terminology of an almost mystic set of 'Others' is problematic in that it is difficult to comprehend what Heidegger is actually getting at. He reveals the question when he starts to talk about the manners of these 'Others'. Perhaps most important is the idea of 'publicness' which constitutes the 'dictatorship of the they'.[61] Heidegger gathers the three aspects of *das Man* (distantiality, averageness and levelling down) into 'publicness' [*Öffentlichkeit*],[62] which he can describe polemically:

> Publicness proximinally controls every way in which the world and *dasein* get interpreted, and it is always right – not because there is some distinctive and primary relationship-of-Being in which it is related to 'things' . . . but because it is insensitive to every difference of level and of genuineness and thus never gets to the 'heart of the matter'. By publicness everything gets obscured, and what has thus been covered up gets passed off as something familiar and accessible to everyone.[63]

However, Heidegger is not suggesting that we could conceive of a space that is purely inauthentic. Rather, we have a double bind, the everyday is where we find being but also where we get lost – the space of the (un)veiling of being. Thus, for Heidegger, *das Man* is part of the constitution of *dasein* and one pole in the play between the concealment and unconcealment of being. At this point it is useful to think again about the purpose of raising Heidegger's ontology in such depth. Essentially, Heidegger would say that because human rights fail to force us to think about being, they lead us towards inauthenticity. They lead us in this manner to give up responsibility for being, by simply accepting the given norms of our time. Crucially, what Heidegger adds beyond a different starting point is a thinking of time.

Heidegger attempts to explain an authentic mode of being through a conception of temporality. He tells us that temporality is not a thing, it '"is" not an entity at all. It is not, but it *temporalizes* itself.'[64] The question is thus, not 'what is time?', but rather 'what is it to be in time?' (which is nothing more than 'what is it to be?'). To understand *dasein*, it is necessary to see that its being is finite. Once she is, the only certainty is that she will die. Death itself is an end.[65] However, because death presents *dasein*'s 'ownmost possibility' (one's ultimate end is absolutely one's own, no one can die for anyone else), we discover temporality in our being-towards-death. By understanding the negativity or the nothingness of death towards which *dasein* rushes, we can begin to grasp the significance of its being-there. *Dasein* is being-there always *towards* its own demise. Heidegger introduces the term 'ek-sistence', saying that 'What man is – or, as it is called in the traditional language of metaphysics, the "essence" of man – lies in his ek-sistence.'[66] Man's essence is his existence. However, existence is not merely what he is, existence is a 'standing-out' (*ek-stasis*)[67] into the flux of being/time. Being is being-towards the future, it is not static. Thus (if you can still use the term), man's essence is always coming to presence.

Human rights utilize a temporality that Heidegger called 'prestruction' in his early work:

> Prestruction, a Latinate form of the German *Vor-bauen* which literally means building beforehand and in ordinary German means 'pre-cautionary', is a kind of fore-structuring. As a being of care and need, factical life takes precautions against the insecurity which everywhere besets it. Thus it builds a cultural world (*Umwelt*) around itself, which means that it is a kind of pre-forming. Factical life structures its life in advance with stable objects and projects, surrounds itself with an *Umwelt* that assures life a secure passage. Prestruction promotes the illusion of self-sufficiency, thereby allowing factical life to lose sight of its fundamental mental insecurity.[68]

'Prestruction' is thus the manner of being-towards the future in a precautionary mode, where risks are assessed and 'protected against'. This is an extension of the modernist subject, attempting to will the world out of his imaginations of what it should be.[69]

Yet the fundamental idea of human rights remains centred on the thinking subject which must be protected at once by and from the state. Heidegger's use of *dasein* is then useful in that it suggests to us the necessity of escaping the confines of the monadic individual obsessed with the risks to its properties. The possessive individual, premised on acquisition of connections, utterly fails to understand the ontological condition of being-together, which is part of the co-constitution of being-there. The challenge is to think human rights without resorting to the extant individualism or its simple inversion in some of the cruder socialisms, placing of society as the supreme value. Both of these render the subject of human rights in an utterly destructive fashion: on one side, 'man' is each alienated and willing subject, seeking to protect his possessions from every other hateful alienated figure; on the other side, is the haunting threat of society, embodied by a government, requiring subjection and sublation for the greater good; one man takes his place in a total war of all against all, the other takes his place in the totality of a greater good.

In the relation between the individual and state, the political horizon of human rights is determined. In this, the triplet 'property-protection-prestruction' reaches the crux of the matter – it is the mode of statism and individualism. The traditional subject of human rights is the possessive individual, one's property and properties are therefore the object of protection. The world of this subject is rendered as a zone of threat in which the individual must be protected against the malign influences that would destroy his privileged position. In this, time is conceived through the notion of prior accumulated property (past), protection (present) and prestruction (future). The property-protection-prestruction triplet is crucial.[70] Property stands, as it does in Locke, at once for prior accumulation and one's properties as a human (voice, thirst, bodily presence). It is *privilege* that the radical precursors to human rights challenge. If property is the past of this temporal triplet, protection is its present. However, the 'individualism of universal principles forgets that every person is a world and comes into existence in common with others, that we are all in community. Being in common is an integral part of being self.'[71] This 'forgetting' is precisely the transforming of the in-common into common being. Expression, movement, association are all things that must be protected alongside and in the same way as stocks and shares or enclosed land and houses. Yet by overturning this understanding of the world through the lens of 'having' and replacing it with the more originary question of 'being', we begin to transform the sense of human rights. This is how, I suggest, we can reimagine the radical in human rights.

Human rights are metaphysical in their operation. They tend to reduce the multiplicity and creativity of existence down to a few pre-authorized norms. The everyday critiques of statism and individualism can be deepened to understand that which is most problematic in human rights: that is, the manner in which they seek to fix and enforce, through the normalizing force, a limited idea of humanity; and the manner in which they fail to understand the fundamental togetherness from which any ontology of human being must begin. It goes without saying that Heidegger's own politics, and the manner in which his ontology relates to that engagement, is deeply problematic. But these questions, especially relating to authenticity and the *Volk* will be dealt with in Chapter 7, when I return to the Heideggerian paradigm to think differently about constituent power and human rights (qua being-together and world creation).

I argue that the problems of individualism and statism, rendered through Heidegger's anti-humanism, suggest that it is not just that the radical has withdrawn from human rights and could somehow therefore be reinserted into the discourse. Rather, the central development of individualism and statism make human rights increasingly inimical to radical demands. They pre-structure radical demands, subjugating them to neutralized discourses that cannot challenge many of the most important and powerful nodes of power and domination. To begin to think human rights radically, therefore, it is a matter of 'beginning again', so to speak. Of withdrawing from the discourse that is entirely over-determined, and instead thinking a different strand of thought. Thus, for the next three chapters, I propose to discuss constituent power. I argue that an open constituent provides a non-foundational foundation for a different thinking of human rights. Or, perhaps better, it allows us to try to avoid foundations as such. A human rights that 'begins with' constituent power begins with nothing or, as I will argue in Chapter 8, begins with *the* nothing at the heart of being.

Chapter 4

The authority of change: Sieyès and Kant

> Studying constituent power from the juridical perspective presents exceptional difficulty given the hybrid nature of this power ... The strength hidden in constituent power refuses to be fully integrated in a hierarchical system of norms and competencies ... constituent power always remains alien to the law.
> Burdeau, *Traité de Sciences Politique*[1]

The focus of the book must now turn to the question of constituent power if it is to provide a basis for a different thinking of human rights. The next three chapters will begin to construct an 'open' constituent power. However, they will do so along the lines of critique set out in the last chapter. Constituent power provides a different thinking of human rights because it challenges statism and individualism. The starting point is authority. This is where traditional figurations of constituent power come closest to the conventional account of human rights. The conception of human rights as 'authoritative demands', for instance, posits an adjudicator who can deliver a decision in which the authority (of both the judge and the rights themselves) is (re)performed. The crux of this is the sovereign authority (or indeed international institutions vested with the authority by a sovereign power) vested in the judge as the legitimate mediator between the state, the individual and the law. In this mode, human rights becomes the very stuff of authority. As I will show in this chapter, authority is central to the classical thought on constituent power. However, the reliance on authority and sovereignty is much more difficult here. To think human rights in and through radical democratic theory, I suggest that we consider constituent power. This is because, as I suggest in this chapter, constituent power remains unauthorizable. In this unauthorizability, the possibility of a different human rights will begin to emerge.

Constituent power is fundamentally a principle of radical political change. However, much of the constitutionalist thought on the subject does not see the constituent in its essence. Loughlin suggests that constituent power 'helps us locate the source of modern political authority, and ... identify the base upon which the structure of the legal authority rests'.[2] The association between authority and the constituent is crucial, but it is not as simple as Loughlin seems to suggest. In the different temporal structures of authority and the constituent, we find the political and the legal. Thus, to understand authority as the defining feature of the constituent transposes an essentially political event into the legal. By rendering the constituent as a constitutional fact, the *possibility* of the constituent (its defining feature) is closed. This rendering of the significance of constituent power for the constituted creates a constituent-constituted dialectic. The sense in which this is dialectical is very crude; the given constituted order is negated by the successful exercise of constituent power, resulting in the new constituted order that is the negation of the negation. This vision ultimately leads to a fundamental mistake in the analysis of the nature of constituent power. It understands it as a closed event whose essence is to be found in the constituted order that comes after it. An open constituent power is not tied to any particular constituted form, it is not necessarily tied to constituting a state at all. In this chapter, I would like to establish this dialectic by examining the work of the Abbé Sieyès and Immanuel Kant, two classical authors of constituent power. I am particularly interested in the manner in which each in his own way implicitly closes the possibility of the constituent through the constituent-constituted dialectic.

Sieyès and the realization of the nation

The Abbé Sieyès proposed the fundamental alteration of the political and social system in France in the late 18th century. The confused public order of the time was to be replaced with a rationally organized political system. Unlike Kant, Sieyès was deeply enmeshed in the political struggle and therefore his writings are at once a description and an incitement. Sieyès explicitly sought to authorize the exercise of constituent power. The key to this is his idea of the 'nation',[3] which Schmitt understood:

> According to [Sieyès'] . . . theory, the *nation* is the subject of the constitution-making authority. Nation and people are often treated as equivalent concepts. Nevertheless, the word 'nation' is clearer and less prone to misunderstanding. It denotes, specifically, the people as a unity capable of political action, with the consciousness of its political distinctiveness and with the will to political existence, while the people not existing as a nation is somehow only something that belongs together ethnically or culturally, but it is not necessarily a bonding of men existing *politically*. The theory of the people's constitution-making power presupposes the conscious willing of political existence, therefore, a nation.[4]

The sense of 'nation' that both Sieyès and Schmitt mobilize is the antithesis of our meaning. Nation here is not ethnic or cultural belonging together but rather a political unity. For Sieyès, 'the first priority had to be for this maker or creator [the nation] to manifest itself, to appear. Everything was secondary to bringing about the crystallization of the nation as an active, independent power.'[5] Crystallization is the important term: Sieyès sees that the existence of the nation as the revolutionary subject is a matter of consciousness. This hangs on the double meaning of realization: the realization (qua consciousness) that the nation holds the world-making power *is* the realization (qua manifestation) of the nation. The nation was nothing other than the exercise of its own totality in constituent power.

Sieyès proposes that the substance and form of the nation can be analytically divided. The substance of the nation is its economic and social existence, the very body of the people. The form of nationhood, by way of contrast, is 'a common law and a common representation'.[6] This division is of the utmost importance because it is through this that Sieyès' thought becomes so effective in generating a revolutionary spirit. The formal prerequisite of nationhood is 'a common law and a common representation'. Such a definition was controversial at the time, as it rejected the recognized criteria of nationhood used by monarchy (i.e. the king, government, etc.). For Sieyès, '[p]rovided that [the nation] is endowed with a common law because there is an agency that is qualified to establish laws, the nation exists even before any government is formed, even before the sovereign is born, and even before power is delegated. That agency is the legislature itself.'[7] The fundamental formal (juridical) precondition of the nation then is the nexus between law and the agency to create law (legislature).

Alone, the juridical precondition of nationhood (law-legislature) would not be revolutionary. This aspect comes with the substantive precondition that Sieyès adds to the formal one. He argues that for a nation to be a nation it must take the form of law-legislature, but it must also have a certain substance: if a nation is to survive, 'if its survival and prosperity are to be not only a formal precondition for its juridical existence, but also a historical precondition for its existence *in* history', then it must exist in a certain manner. The substantive preconditions of nationhood are divided into two, what Sieyès calls 'works' and 'functions' and what Foucault renames 'functions and apparatuses'. Using Foucault's terms: the functions are agriculture, handicrafts, industry, trade and the liberal arts; and the apparatuses are the army, justice, the church and the administration:[8]

> It was precisely when men, or individuals scattered across the surface of the land, on the edges of the forests or on the plains, decided to develop their agriculture, to trade and to be able to have economic relations with one another, that they gave themselves a law, a State, or a government. In other words, all these functions were in fact effects of the juridical constitution of the nation, or at least its consequences. It was only when the juridical constitution of the nation was an established fact that these functions could be deployed. Nor were apparatuses such as the army, justice, and the administration preconditions for the existence of the nation; they were, if not effects, at least its instruments and guarantors. It was only when the nation had been constituted that it could acquire things like an army or a system of justice.[9]

However, these functions and apparatuses exist *before* the formal existence of the 'nation'.

It is through the difference between the substantive facts and the formal prerequisite that Sieyès becomes revolutionary. Between the two senses of nation, Sieyès mobilizes the righteous anger of those who are everything, but have been politically reduced to nothing. The functions and apparatuses are fundamentally an *historical* requirement, the conditions of the concrete existence of the nation:

> A nation can exist as a nation, and can enter history and survive through history, only if it is capable of commerce, agriculture, and handicrafts . . . [etc.] This means that a group of individuals can always come together and can always give itself laws and a legislature; it can give itself a constitution. If that group of individuals does not have the capacity for commerce, handicrafts, and agriculture, or the ability to form an army, a magistrature, and so on, it will never, in historical terms, be a nation. It might be a nation in juridical terms, but never in historical terms.[10]

Conversely, he posits the possibility of a collection of people that fulfils the functions and apparatuses but do not have the formal character of a nation – the juridical law-legislature couplet. He argued that while the Third Estate[11] was substantively the nation, it was not formally so. The 'crystallization' of the nation is nothing other than the becoming aware of the power of self-legislation, the constituent power. To become a nation the Third Estate had to become seized of itself and exercise its ownmost strength. The Third Estate is the totality of the body of the people and because it is the nation it should exercise its power over itself and not be ruled by the monarchy. In the meantime, because it does not exercise its constituent power, it has not gained the formal unity of self-legislating.

The Third Estate runs the 'private works': commerce, agriculture and handicrafts. They populate most (he says 19/20ths) of the 'public functions'; the army, church, administration and system of justice. Except for the most 'lucrative and honorific' of the public functions, the Third Estate is the entire substance of the nation, yet it is not formally a nation. He says, there is an absence of *common* laws, instead there are laws that apply to each of the different estates separately. Equally, there is no legislature, rather there is an 'aulic', courtly or arbitrary royal system of power.[12] Sieyès delegitimates the royal system and, instead, posits the Third Estate as *the* legitimate and entire nation. He sees himself as 'guiding the nation in its task of self-identification.'[13] Importantly for us, the 'self-recognition' of the Third Estate as *entire* nation is a form of empowerment, valorization or indeed a representational form of mythmaking. Foucault formulates it thus:

> Where, then, are we to find the historical core of a nation that can become 'the' nation? In the Third Estate, and only in the Third Estate. The Third Estate is in itself the historical precondition for the existence of a nation, but

that nation should, by rights, coincide with the State. The Third Estate is a nation. It contains the constituent elements of a nation.[14]

Or to put it in Sieyès words: 'The Third Estate comprises all that belongs to the nation; and all that is not the Third Estate, cannot be regarded as belonging to the nation. What is the Third Estate? Everything.'[15]

The Third Estate is the nation and political and public power belongs to it. The nation *is* constituent power. Thus, to show that the Third Estate is the nation is nothing other than revealing that it holds the power to insist that things should be otherwise. This is, quite literally, a rhetoric of (bourgeois) revolution. It would excise those in power from the system. 'For Sieyès, this process of national self-assertion was intrinsically an act of separation and repulsion. The nation could become itself only by distinguishing itself from what was alien to it and by sloughing off this 'foreign element'.[16] 'The Third Estate, or rather the nation, demands nothing less than to make the totality (*ensemble*) of citizens a *single* social body.'[17] The nation must take possession of itself, without those who do not share the unifying national interest, by meeting in a constituent assembly. The Third Estate is everything, it has been nothing, but it *only wants to become something*. It *is* the substantive nation, but it does not see its totality. It does not see beyond its own limited interests. 'Sieyès saw his task as raising the Third Estate to a true understanding of its historical mission as the dissolvent of existing political society and the embodiment of the nation.'[18] The Third Estate must not demand just to be 'something', it must become 'everything'. The major disjuncture that will only come after the bourgeois revolutions is the nature of action (i.e. direct vs. representative) and the trajectory of the 'everything'. Of importance to this latter point, then, is the 'end' of constituent power. Unsurprisingly, Sieyès saw a direct correlation between constituent power and constitutions. The (constituent) power of the substantive nation was to give itself law-legislature, that is, formal nationhood. There is no suggestion of a Negrean constituent power that is open and creative.[19] The operative relation is between two totalities: a substantive people (with its functions and works) and its *formal constitution in the juridical law-legislature nexus*. Sieyès projects the substantive totality in order to bring it towards the actual totality under a common law.

Ultimately, Sieyès' key to the exercise of constituent power is the gap between the resistant action (by a non-totality) and the projected idealization of the totality. However, when it comes to constituent power, this is also the gap between an action and its 'authorization'. The mobilization of this projected and ideal totality (the Third Estate is the nation, it is 'everything') is a manner of inciting revolution by authorizing the revolutionary actions of the nation. If the nation is everything then it is authorized to grasp *its own* power. Such a move is made *natural* in Sieyès. The nation is the power and the authority to give itself the form of state. However, this form of state is already determined by his formal definition of the nation as a common law and common representation. Constituent power is intimately bound together with constituted power. This is how Sieyès can *authorize* constituent power. The substantive nation finds its end (*telos*) in becoming itself, becoming both the substantive and formal nation. All that is required for Sieyès is to make the Third Estate aware of itself as the substance of the nation and the associated need to formally become the nation. This is a process of 'self-valorization' of the revolutionary subject. It asserts that it is the totality in order to authorize the revolutionary urge: 'We, the people, are public right.' If the Third Estate is the legitimate sovereign then the revolutionary illegality is displaced. It is not fundamentally wrong to revolt as the preceding ruler does not have public right on his side. *The claim to this totality* (as a justification) *sutures the tear between the revolutionary event and its authorization.* If the nation is everything, it is structurally and essentially bound to constituted power. If this 'We are everything' is true, then the king becomes an aberration, a monster who tears the nation from what is most proper to it (i.e. the exercise of its ownmost power, the power to rule itself). In this paradigm, the revolutionary Third Estate is only taking what is absolutely its own. However, the very question in revolution is *whether* the revolutionary should be subject to the power of the preceding constituted order. Sieyès conceals this question of the legitimacy of the revolutionary subject's actions. He makes the legitimacy of the nation/ Third Estate an *a priori*. The gap between the act and its authorization is sutured with the assertion that: 'The third estate is everything, it has been nothing, and (only) wants to become something.'

There is an implicit logic at work in this *a priori* assertion of the nation's legitimacy. On one side, it is given that the nation is the subject of sovereignty and, on the other, the Third Estate is the nation (or almost). Thus, it becomes *natural* that constituent power ends in the constituted. What is more, the form of the constituted is largely given by the logic of the constituent: the formal structure of nationhood, a common law and legislature. It is not difficult to see here that this authorization of the constituent is effectuated only by fixing the ends of the constituent in a teleological move.

Sieyès' conception of the 'power' of the constituent is crucial, especially when it is compared with more recent renderings.[20] Romance languages distinguish between two types of 'power'. The distinction stems originally from the Latin *potentia* and *potestas*. Both are translated into English as power, but *potentia* is better rendered as power in the sense of potentiality, capability, the power/ possibility to do or be something. *Potestas*, by way of contrast, is power over someone or something, dominion or rule. The translator's note from Negri's *Insurgencies* is useful here:

> I have translated the two Italian words *potere* and *potenza* as *power* and *strength*. Both Italian words would commonly be translated into English as *power*, but Negri's discussion rests heavily on the distinction between them. *Power*, for Negri, is always constituted power, and it often refers to the power shaped by and into existing State and political institutions. Strength, instead, is a radically democratic force that resides in the desire of the multitude and is aimed at revolutionizing the status quo through social and political change.

Strength is at the core of the concept of constituent power itself as the force that produces (but cannot be contained within) power and its institutions; constituent power is fuelled by strength. Negri stresses more than once here that strength, as well as constituent power, enables but is not realised in constitutionality.[21]

Negri argues that constituent power evokes 'the ungrounded and intrinsically disruptive strength of institutionally unmediated collective action: it is a form of power actualized through boundless and creative praxis.'[22] This multi-layered formulation can be taken apart a little. Constituent power as a *potentia* is portrayed by Negri as a collective 'strength' that is independent of constitutional form.[23] It is political, where such a formulation is set up in tension with the legal. Constituent power is the *potentia* of a group to be creative in relation to their political nature (the in-common), though this political nature is indissolubly linked with creativity in the social.[24] For Negri, constituent power is the fundamental creativity at the heart of all human political and social existence. Constituent *potentia* is fundamentally associated with the new, the possible, the future, etc. *Potentia* is essentially linked with the potentiality of constituent power, that is, with its possibility. However, Negri performs a sleight of hand here between *potentia* and *potestas*. Sieyès uses *pouvoir* (i.e. *potestas*) when he talks of constituent power. In Negri, this marks a major shift from Sieyès' thinking of constituent power that is intimately linked to the constituted, to an 'open' constituent power that does not set its ends in the constituted. Negri's insight effects a subterranean shift that goes unremarked in *Insurgencies*. It is no surprise then that he avoids the traditional thinkers of constituent power in that work, dismissing Schmitt and Kelsen in a paragraph each and largely steering clear of Kant and Sieyès.

Constituent power, rendered as a *potestas*, essentially ties it to authority rather than potentiality. Sieyès' formulation of constituent power as *pouvoir constituant* renders the creative capacity as a 'power over'. The people or nation has 'power over' itself that it must realize in Sieyès' given form (common law and legislature), rather than having the 'power to create' the world as it sees fit. Because of this formulation, Sieyès' can limit the constituent in his theoretical edifice. It is this limitation that facilitates Sieyès' *authorization* of the constituent. The association of constituent power with authority is largely antithetical to this creativity. *Authority is a force of the past manifested in the present.* The concept stems from the Latin *auctoritas*, which Arendt usefully addresses: 'At the heart of Roman politics, from the beginning of the republic until virtually the end of the imperial era, stands the conviction of the sacredness of foundation, in a sense that once something has been founded it remains binding for all future generations.'[25] The static origin is the liminal moment that grants authority; there is then a gradual augmentation of that foundation and it is this augmentation and not the origin that is the authority. Arendt tells us that this is evident in the semantics: *auctoritas* emerges from the verb *augere* 'to augment' and is to be distinguished from *artifices*. Where the former means to augment, the latter means to make or build.

Therefore, authority does not create but, rather, augments what is already formed. The relation between the *auctor* and *artifex* is not that of master and servant. Those in authority do not have power, rather, the relation is of senate to people. The *auctoritas* of the Roman senate is juxtaposed with the *potestas* and *imperium* derived from the people: 'Despite the subsequent powerlessness, the senate retained its authority, and, in the imperial period, it ultimately became the sole organ still able to confer something like "legitimacy" after the power of the Roman people perished in the Empire.'[26]

Arendt argues for a sense of authority untouched by power, violence or force. However, we need not concern ourselves with this argument here, suffice to say that she clearly sees the temporal nature of authority that is backward looking. For the Romans:

> [P]recedents of the ancestors and the usage that grew out of them were always binding. Anything that happened was transformed into an example, and the *auctoritas maiorum* became identical with authoritative models for actual behaviour, with the moral political standard as such. This is also why old age, as distinguished from mere adulthood, was felt by the Romans to contain the very climax of human life; not so much because of accumulated wisdom and experience as because the old man had grown closer to the ancestors and the past. Contrary to our concept of growth, where one grows into the future, the Romans felt that growth was directed toward the past.[27]

From its very basis in Roman thought, 'authority' rests on the sacredness of the foundation and the unbroken authority throughout the centuries.[28] Schmitt supports this view; 'sovereignty and majesty by necessity always correspond only to effective power. Authority, by contrast, denotes a profile that rests essentially on the element of *continuity* and refers to tradition and duration.'[29] Authority is temporally backward looking: its modes of existence are lineage, tradition and the sheer weight of history. Authority is something immaterial that haunts. The founding fathers in the USA demonstrate the manner in which the founding moment haunts the institution it creates. They exert a haunting 'force' on the present, a call for fidelity. This force is not the force that Arendt equates to violence and power, but it is a pressure, a weight bearing down on the present, a sense of *majesty*. Citing Victor Ehrenberg, Schmitt asserts that the word *auctoritas* 'denotes something "ethical-political", a "position oddly mixed together from political power and social prestige' that 'rests on supplements and social validity".'[30]

Sieyès associates the constituent with a line of authority. The nation holds the authority of power. Therefore, the revolution is not ruptural but forms a lineage or continuity. However, the problem with understanding constituent power through authority is that it frames it in terms of the wrong temporality (the past is the ultimate horizon rather than the future). While historicity is fundamental to any politics, setting the horizon of meaning as the past ultimately destroys the importance of constituent power. Rather, authority is better associated with the legal. The question of the 'authority of constituent power' is nothing other than the legitimacy of the moment without law, the moment between legal orders. The problem is Roman rather than Greek in its origin. It is not surprising that the ancient deity that represents the problem of authority and constituent power is Janus, one of the very few truly Roman gods not originally borrowed from the Greeks. Janus is the Roman god of origins,[31] the two-faced god of beginnings and ends. After all, the foundation is always both a beginning and an end. This is why Janus is always looking backwards and forwards, backward towards the epoch just finished and forward towards the time just beginning. Early representations of him had one side of this two-faced head bearded and the other bare faced (although in later representations both sides were bearded). We may surmise that this is to do with youth and age: the youth is the face of the new, while the backward looking, bearded, aged face represents the waning epoch. Janus is the god of the liminal, the point of transition where something new emerges or morphs. He carries the key in one hand, ready to unlock the door and emerge. For us, Janus is often the model of contradiction – literally two faced. But Janus' contradiction is more essential, as a figure of origin he expresses the *paradox* of the new emerging from the old, the paradox of radical change, the paradox of law's origins.

Sieyès sutures constituent power and authority through the prior authorization of the nation. This is the legitimate subject of the constituent because it is nothing, but by rights, it should be everything. With this, the paradox of the constituent is glossed over. Crucially, despite his proximity to Sieyès', it is Kant who clearly sees the problem with authorizing revolution.

Kant and the abyssal heart of the constituent

Kant's rejection of the right to revolution begins to re-open the suture between the revolutionary act and its authorization, but it also implicitly questions Sieyès' link between constituent and constituted power. Essentially, revolution is abyssal, it does not necessarily find an end (*telos*) that would *a priori* authorize it. Kant's position on revolution is a curious one, if not actually paradoxical. He is sometimes simply equated with an anti-revolutionary position and certainly his rejection of the right to revolution is explicit and well known. However, his thoughts are actually far more complex. In his unpublished notes, Kant justifies resistance and even revolt in certain circumstances that violate an original social contract: the people 'cannot rebel except in cases which cannot at all come forward in a civil union, e.g. the enforcement of a religion, compulsion to unnatural sins, assassination, etc.'[32] There are other stories that hint at his favour for radical change also: he was locally called the 'old Jacobin'; when he submitted an essay in 1793, his editor expressed the relief that he was not going to support the French Revolution; and a rumour circulated that he was to travel to Paris as an advisor to Sieyès.[33] However, his rejection of both the legality and morality of revolution is to be taken not as an outright refusal of constituent power or as a falsehood uttered out of political necessity, but rather as what Simon Critchley calls (after Benjamin) a plumb line of responsibility. To see this we must understand Kant's three various positions:

> [1] revolution was unconditionally wrong; [2] yet if it succeeds the government it establishes is a legitimate authority to which its citizens owe their obedience; and finally [3] our enthusiasm for the French Revolution, even our wishful participation in it, is an outward sign of the presence of a moral disposition in our nature, from which we may derive hope for our moral progress.[34]

He points (*from inside the constituted order*) to the limit of the constituted order: that the political state of things could be *utterly* otherwise. This is not to say that stasis is the necessary condition of the constituted order, many (if not all) constituted orders are internally dynamic. Rather, the constituted order finds its *limit* in the possibility of change that is not internally regulated by the system. Each of Kant's three positions stops or starts on the boundary of *pouvoir constituant*. They bring forth the absolute gap between the violence of constituent action and the absence of any form of authorization of the violence. Let me deal with each of these separately. As we will see, at each position the question is clearly one of authority and responsibility.

First, Kant proposes that revolution is wrong: 'All resistance against the supreme legislative power, every kind of instigation to bring the discontent of the subject into active form, every kind of rising which becomes a rebellion constitutes the highest and most punishable crime in the commonwealth for they destroy its very foundations.'[35] The reason why 'there is no right to sedition, much less a right to revolution' is that conceptually it is a contradiction in terms: there is no subject capable of exercising such a right! Speaking from within a constituted order, all assertions of a *right* (conceived of as relation between state and subject) to revolution are rent apart conceptually. For Kant:

> [I]n order for the people to be able to judge the supreme political authority with the force of law, they must already be viewed as united under a general legislative Will; *hence they ... may not judge otherwise* than the present chief of State wills.[36]

The 'already' is key to understanding Kant's position. The people must be constituted as the general will before they can judge political authority with the force of law. However, the general will (constituted by the people) is represented by the government. Therefore, as Christodoulidis says, 'to oppose the government is to oppose the general will. And to oppose the general will ... is to dissolve the juridical condition among human beings and thus to return to the state of nature.'[37] But, of course, there is no 'the people' in the state of nature. For the people to oppose the general will, it must be constituted through the general will: 'The people . . . cannot speak *as* a people until they have a voice. Anything – such as the revolutionary voice – that erodes the mutual constitution between the juridical relation and the general will is a reversal to the state of nature where there is no possibility to represent the people because there is no people.'[38] I will call this the circularity of the people/general will. Thus, for Kant, there is no right to revolution. It cannot be right to revolt because there is no people who can embody such a right. There is no people which is not already constituted by the general will, but the general will is the object of revolution. Importantly, then, the unity of the people (which occurs under and through the general will) is the subject of constituent power, but this constituent power may not occur in its revolutionary form within the system, thus revolutionary constituent power is unauthorized.

The circularity of the people/general will provides us with a starting point for Kant's second argument on revolution. He suggests that any successful revolution that constitutes a new order deserves just as much obedience as the previous one, in spite of the fact that its revolution was not right. The temporality of these positions is important. The first talks of the future revolution or, indeed, one that is past and failed, neither of which has the authority that is gained by success. The second position focuses on the successful revolution always already past. This post-revolutionary constituted order deserves the same obedience because it has constituted a new general will. There is a specific political content to Kant's first two positions; he is writing in 1793, after the French Revolution, but with the threat of a counter-revolution in the air. Politically, he says that any attempt to reinstate the monarchy is immoral, because revolution is wrong and the new state has right.

Theoretically, the key to these positions lies in the limit event of the constituent or 'revolutionary people', i.e. the very moment when a new state/order is constituted, almost a revolutionary *interregnum*.[39] Logically, there must be a threshold or limit moment where the anarchic and disordered power of the people constitutes the *new general will*. This is the moment of the auto-authorization of the people where it gives itself right. This threshold moment lies at the moment of self-authorization, the moment that the revolutionary people become 'the people' by constituting a new general will. However, it is an *impossible* moment on the reasoning of the previous thesis because the circularity of the relation between the people/general will does not allow any space for change. There can be no people who have not already been constituted by the general will that constitutes it. Thus, according to Kant, 'the revolutionary people' is an impossible but necessary threshold between constituent and constituted. The revolutionary people represent a rupture in the circularity of people/general will. To think this moment of change, it is necessary to posit the people, while at the same time denying its existence because of the absence of the general will. This is the impossible threshold moment of *change*, which I will come back to again in Chapter 6 through Derrida's *Declarations of Independence*. I must stress that this is an *impossible* moment; the new is instituted; the non-presence of the people manifests itself; the constituent moment is closed along with the old constituted order. Therefore, the revolutionary people is this threshold of the constituent and constituted order. Insofar as we accept that the people is a unity, such an aporetic understanding is necessary. The first two positions, while seeming to provide us with a clear rule, in fact, do little more than approach the circularity of the social contractarianism of the people/general will thinking of constitutional theory. However, the final position complicates the entire process.

Kant's final argument is that the enthusiasm for revolution is a sign of our moral nature and is proof of historical progress. This is revealing because it explicates the constitutive tension between the first two positions by approaching that impossible moment of the revolutionary people. Let us not forget that Kant is not just enthusiastic about the revolution, rather he draws proof of our moral nature and of progress from such enthusiasm. Foucault points out that Kant in 1798 takes up an old question that he had previously addressed in 1784 namely: 'What is this *Aufklärung* [enlightenment] of which we are a part?' However, in 1798 it is now the question 'What is the revolution?' Kant's reasoning regarding progress is clear: to find whether there is a constant progress for mankind, we must:

> determine whether there exists a possible cause for this progress, but once one has established this possibility, one must locate a certain event that shows that the cause acts in reality. In short, the attribution of a cause will be able to determine only possible effects, or, to be more precise, the possibility of an effect; but the reality of an effect will be able to be established only by the existence of an event. It is not enough, therefore, to follow the teleological thread that makes progress possible; one must isolate, within history, an event that will have the value of a sign.[40]

The sign shows us the existence of the permanent cause. The sign must be three-fold, *rememorativum, demonstrativum* and *prognosticum*: 'It must be a sign that shows that it has always been like that (the rememorative sign), a sign that shows that things are also taking place now (the demonstrative), and a sign that shows that it will always happen like that (the prognostic sign).'[41] Thus, we know that it is not just a particular event, but rather the sign of something metaphysical. He tells his readers that it is no great event:

> Do not expect this event to consist of noble gestures or great crimes committed by men, as a result of which that which was great among men is made small, or that which was small, made great, nor of gleaming ancient buildings that disappear as if by magic while others rise, in a sense, from the bowels of the earth to take their place. No, it is nothing like that.[42]

It is not the revolution then because, for Kant, this 'merely inverts things' and 'if one could carry out the Revolution again, one would not do so.'[43]

What is meaningful, what has the value of a sign of progress, is the '*sympathy of aspiration [for the Revolution] bordering on enthusiasm*':[44]

The revolution as a spectacle, and not a gesture, as a focus for enthusiasm on the part of those who observe it and not as a principle of overthrow for those who take part in it, is a *signum rememorativum*, for it reveals that disposition that has been present from the beginning; it is a *signum demonstrativum* because it demonstrates the present efficacy of this disposition; and it is also a *signum prognosticum* for, although the revolution may have certain questionable results, one cannot forget the disposition that is revealed through it.[45]

For Foucault, at this moment when revolution is situated in enlightenment, we are at an origin. The two questions that Kant formulates ('What is *Aufklärung* [Enlightenment]? And What is Revolution?') are 'the two forms under which Kant posed the question of his own present.'[46] What is more, Foucault claims that they continue to haunt much of philosophy, dividing it in two, between the piety of those who wish to keep the *Aufklärung* living and intact ('Such a piety is of course the most touching of treasons')[47] and the philosophical question of what is to be done with 'the will to revolution'. The latter question, the 'other face of the present' that Kant encountered is, the revolution: the revolution was 'at once event, rupture, and overthrow in history, as failure, but at the same time as value, as sign of a disposition that is operating in history and in the progress of humankind.'[48] It is an ontology of the present quite distinct from the analytics of truth posed by *Aufklärung*. Kant does not just blindly affirm constituted power against constituent power, but rather in a complex manner asserts that the very 'will to revolution' is the sign of progress:

> Revolution is the sign of a disposition to govern ourselves freely ... While the time of arrival of revolution 'must remain indefinite', the possibility of deferral does not undermine the moral disposition to progress it brings forth. This is because the latter relates to a certain anticipation of something to come, an opening to the future that is already at work despite the absence of any guarantee of its fulfilment.[49]

Arditi links this to Benjamin's references to the Messiah, 'at least to the extent that they both call for a collective effort to *provoke* an arrival rather than simply await it'.[50] With this, Kant approaches a very interesting position, whereby it is the *will to revolution* that corresponds to constituent power in its *potentiality*. It is the *potential* to change the world that proves our moral nature. Yet again the abyss opens up here: while revolution may not instantiate the threefold sign, 'sympathy of aspiration' for revolution (Foucault's 'will to revolution') provides us with our proof of progress.

While one may have grave concerns for the enlightenment promise of moral progress, we can see clearly that Kant's position is not simply against revolution: 'The moral aspirations of mankind are not satisfied by punctilious obedience to the powers that be.'[51] Thus, instead of understanding Kant's threefold position as an outright rejection of revolution and constituent power, I argue that it should be read as a rejection of any already given rightness of revolution. Legitimacy is granted only once the revolutionary moment is closed around a newly instituted order. The determining question here is of legitimacy and right. While Kant's position is quite complex, we can see a fundamental tension within his conception of constituent power, between the illegitimacy of revolution and the 'enthusiasm' of the will to revolution. This tension goes to the very heart of my argument. There is something within constituent power that resists the transposition from the political to the legal:

> Deprived of a legal-moral foundation, but not of historical legitimacy or political-institutional productivity, the revolution is stubbornly resistant to something that is at the heart of Kant's enterprise: the subsumption of politics under the moral law. For the revolution defies all notions of foundation . . . The Kantian conception of politics and the philosophy of history underlying it are thus taken to their limit, which is, at one and the same time, the point of theory's greatest advance and the boundary beyond which the whole edifice collapses. With Kant, philosophy settles in for a very long crisis.[52]

As Kouvelakis sees, Kant cannot account for the actual enactment of constituent power, because it resists any legal determination short of Sieyès' mythmaking. Kant's position(s) are utterly determined by the project of showing the universal moral *law*.

There is an abyss between constituent revolutionary action and its authorization. Authorization here must be understood as the legitimation or *possibility* of legitimation of revolutionary action. Korsgaard supports this by a close textual analysis of Kant: the duty not to revolt is a 'duty of justice', which means that 'others may coercively require your performance. To say that something is a duty of justice is to say that its violation is punishable.'[53] It is legally wrong because there can be no right to revolution. It is also morally wrong to revolt because of the nexus between government and people through the general will. The moment of revolution is abyssal. Kant says: 'Revolution under an already existing constitution means the destruction of all relationships governed by civil right, and thus of right altogether. And this is not a change but a dissolution of the civil constitution; and a palingenesis, for it would require a new social contract on which the previous one (which is now dissolved) could have no influence.'[54] At stake in constituent power is nothing less than *palingenesis*, the utter rebirth of society, but this is fundamentally a problem for Kant.

The abyss of revolutionary action is fundamentally the same as the gap that Sieyès quietly attempts to suture. For revolutionary purposes, Sieyès mobilizes the *différance* between the nation that is substantively everything and the sovereign self-legislating nation. The Third Estate is everything and so must exercise its totality to become everything. The closeness of Kant's abyssal crisis of subjective enthusiasm and the event of revolution and Sieyès' two nations lies in an assumption of absolute responsibility, *a salto mortale*. Constituent power resists the legal and remains in each instance an un-auto-authorizable leap in which all is risked. The '"*Salto Mortale*" . . . entails a risk (which is what makes this leap "perilous", *mortale*); its results are not guaranteed in advance; it arrives without warning; in short, it is *always* untimely.'[55] This untimeliness coupled with the absence of any auto-authorization is the fundamental insight of Kant on revolution. Where Sieyès *in media res* mobilizes the rage of the excluded from power, Kant engages in the enthusiasm of the spectator.

While there are many ways of authorizing constituent power,[56] I argue that they all miss its nature. In the next chapter, I will deal with Sorel, Benjamin and Bataille who see that the crude dialectic that seeks to tie constituent power to a new constituted order ultimately misunderstands what is at stake. The constituent is unauthorizable. Thus, I hope my idea of a very different human rights is beginning to emerge, even if what such a 'human rights' might look like is not yet clear. A human rights shorn of its pre-constituted authority would be *radically* different, but I want to approach it very carefully and slowly. Thus, for now, I have established the manner in which traditional theorization of the constituent mistakes it as authority creation. The constituent-constituted dialectic closes the possibility of constituent power by positing an already given end point. The next chapter will look at three thinkers who develop different non-teleological understandings of constituent power.

Chapter 5

An open constituent power: Sorel, Benjamin and Bataille

> Anger is the political sentiment par excellence. It brings out the qualities of the inadmissible, the intolerable. It is a refusal and a resistance that with one step goes beyond all that can be accomplished reasonably in order to open possible paths for a new negotiation of the reasonable but also paths of an uncompromising vigilance. Without anger, politics is accommodation and trade in influence; writing without anger traffics in the seductions of writing.
>
> Nancy, 'Compearance'[1]

Kant and Sieyès introduced a constituent power that was fundamentally linked to the constituted order that it instituted. This thinking of the constituent was at base concerned with the status of constituent power *for the constituted order*. In this chapter, I propose to look at three heretical thinkers of constituent power: Sorel, Benjamin and Bataille. In their engagements, we find very different notions of an 'open' constituent power. I want to engage properly with radical politics in order to challenge the relation between the individual and the state. In the question of force (legal) and violence (illegal), we find a very different subjectification. Sorel, Benjamin and Bataille reach for a subject that is collective but has no substance at its heart, that is, an event. However, it is important to note that what links each of the engagements is *failure and rejection*. Each of the authors later rejects his writings on these means without ends: Sorel turned away from the engagement on violence, Benjamin's *Critique of Violence* was part of a greater opus on the political which he destroyed and Bataille's early work on political sacrifice was later discarded when he realized its proximity to the fascist use of violence. Importantly, then, each of these authors fail. This section is thus both a consideration of an open constituent power but also the beginning of a turn away from politico-legal terminology. Each failure brings forth the concepts and themes that will later become crucial.[2]

Reflections on violence

Sorel is a much maligned theorist, who mobilizes a deep and constant concern for overturning capitalist modes of being-with. His association or at least proximity to certain French fascist or proto-fascist groupings is well known.[3] He is often portrayed as a blood-thirsty and violent revolutionary, largely because of a misreading of his most controversial text, *Reflections on Violence*. Despite suggestions otherwise, his writings never turn to associate socialism with nationalism or the racism that is perhaps the *sine qua non* of fascism.[4] A key aspect in Sorel's thought is an idea of sacred violence that does not parallel the French Revolution's idea of a teleological founding violence. The problem he sets himself is how to begin the process of revolutionizing 'proletarian morality'. He rejects the necessary association of sacrificial violence with states (where he says it becomes pathological). Sorel actually envisions a very limited and restricted 'use' of violence in the process of creation:

> Historically, class conflict has been bloody because, more often than not, states and employers have used force to compel workers to be more productive, and because workers have sometimes resisted. Sorel links workers resistance, which he calls 'proletarian violence' to strike activity, but does not assume that such militant collective action is necessarily violent. When strike violence does occur, Sorel anticipates the death of workers, not of bourgeois.[5]

As such his theory of violence is, in fact, a form of victimology. He sees that violence will be used *against* the workers and, in this, there will be inevitable death. This death was then to be used to bolster the 'myth of the general strike'. The sacrifice of a few workers through the force of the bourgeoisie provides martyrs for the socialist movement. The victimology imagines the self-valorizing process inherent in seeing those with whom you share a solidarity being targeted by a collective enemy. A quick look to Luxemburg's examples in *The Mass Strike* sees the affective truth of this proposition:

> In Kiev . . . [on] July 23rd, an incident occurred which gave the signal for the general strike. During the night two delegates of the railwaymen were arrested. The strikers immediately demanded their release, and as this was not conceded, they decided not to allow trains to leave the town. At the station all the strikers with their wives and families sat down on the railway track – a sea of human beings. They were threatened with rifle salvoes. The workers bared their breasts and cried, 'Shoot!' A salvo was fired into the defenseless seated crowd, and thirty to forty corpses, amongst them women and children, remained on the ground. On this becoming known the whole town of Kiev went on strike on the same day. The corpses of the murdered workers were raised on high by the crowd and carried round in a mass demonstration. Meetings, speeches, arrests, isolated street fights – Kiev was in the midst of the revolution.[6]

It is through the death of the few that the new proletarian morality is valorized. However, the violence done unto the proletariat is only the beginning of the process.

The death must be incorporated into the workers' movement through what Sorel calls the 'myth of the general strike'. This is not the same as the myths handed down from antiquity.[7] Laclau tells us that the myth becomes a regulatory principle: it 'allows the proletariat to think the *mélange* of social relations as organized around a clear line of demarcation; the category of totality, eliminated as an objective description of reality, is reintroduced as a mythical element establishing the unity of the workers consciousness.'[8] The myth mediates between the sacrificial death and the people: 'The myth of the general strike conveys a transcendent, redemptive meaning to martyrdom; martyrdom in turn gives the myth of the general strike an affective capacity to inspire revolutionary action.'[9] The myth gives narrative to the martyrdom and the martyrdom gives affect to the narrative. Each one strengthens the other by sublating[10] death into the process of creating a new morality. While Goldhammer argues that there is no sublation in Sorel, that he leaves the class struggle open in the moment of crisis that will guarantee its morality, this morality itself represents a deeper sublation. The death of the martyr is subsumed into the transcendent myth. The struggle comes up against the finitude of its particular members and this negation (death) is negated through the transcendent myth of the general strike. Nancy describes the communist sublation: 'Generations of citizens and militants, or workers and servants of the States have imagined their death reabsorbed or sublated in a community yet to come, that would attain immanence.'[11] In Sorel, this absorption does not occur in the statist sublation of the community under the state as we saw in Sieyès, rather it occurs in the form of a new 'proletarian' morality. This is the transcendent truth of the movement, which, as I will show in Chapter 7, tends towards 'immanentism'.

Sorel's thought is anarcho-syndicalist and does not adopt the constituent-constituted dialectic that is found in the traditional liberal and republican thinkers of revolution. Rather the symbolic substitution involved in affective identification with a martyr, in the myth of the general strike, changes the 'proletarian morality'. The general strike and its myths and martyrs are, therefore, a moral education of the proletariat:

> Violence, myth and morality anchor Sorel's revolutionary thought because they alter human behaviour. To capture this dynamic interaction of different elements of revolutionary violence, Sorel uses the word 'sublime'. . . . [like those of the French Revolution who] often described their violent acts as sublime when they wished to draw attention to bloodshed's capacity to regenerate the decadent moral beliefs of the aristocracy.[12]

Thus, while Sorel rejects the French Revolution on the grounds that it is essentially a revolution of the state with terror at its end, he nevertheless associates deeply with the revolutionizing of morality that occurs in the mobilization of the sublime violence of sacrifice. For Sorel, the sublime of revolutionizing morality occurs only in proletarian self-sacrifice.

Isaiah Berlin maintains that Sorel's conception of violence in the *Reflections* is 'never made clear'.[13] It is clear that it is opposed to 'force', which in the normal narrative is understood as authorized or legitimate (state or police) violence. Because of Sorel's revolutionary political affiliations this traditional dichotomy is reversed. 'We should say, therefore, that the object of force is to impose a certain social order in which the minority governs, while violence tends to the destruction of that order.'[14] Violence, that is proletarian violence in Sorel, destroys or at least corrodes the sedimented, class relations.[15] 'Any attempt to place proletarian violence in the service of the authority of the state risks Jacobinism. The effectiveness of violence risks Jacobinism. The effectiveness of violence rests largely, but not exclusively on its capacity to undermine bourgeois values, which permeate every aspect of the workers social, political and economic lives.'[16]

To sum up, Sorel's violence is limited to self-sacrifice of the proletariat at the hands of the bourgeoisie. He views this limited form of sacred violence as regenerative. Using Vico's sense of *ricorso*, he argues that the decadent morality of France at the time had to be violently interrupted by the newly regenerated revolutionary morality. Through the myth of the general strike, the martyrdom of the proletariat's heroes would be mediated. 'Perhaps no violent social act inspires more "sublime compassion" than martyrdom because it gathers communities around a sacrificial death of immense positive, symbolic importance. The sublimity created by martyrdom serves to sacralize the moral beliefs at the core of the anarcho-syndicalist movement.'[17] The community of sacrifice is gathered by such an event. It gathers in the 'sovereignty of the proletariat', around the sublime mythic narrative. Sorel does not take us far beyond the constituent-constituted dialectic. He proposes an open creation of myth, but the problem itself lies in the very myth form. The collection, accretion and agglomeration of sense in this myth of the proletarian general strike is designed to provide a transcendental narrative into which one sublates one's suffering and struggle. I will show in Chapter 7 that this is the model that Nancy attacks in the *Inoperative Community*. For now let me concur with Laclau and Mouffe: 'in Sorel the horizon of the promise is somewhat closed-off when he proposes the *class* unity of the subject or community to come.'[18] Instead of this creation of mythic narratives, we must think instead of the very transformation of the sense of the world itself. We must think about 'transformation', 'the political' and about the role of rights in all of this. However, for now, I propose to follow how Benjamin takes up this discourse.

Critique of violence

Benjamin's *Critique of Violence* (hereinafter the *Critique*) directly and enthusiastically refers to Sorel's *Reflections on Violence* (hereinafter the *Reflections*), but the relation is not as clear as it may seem initially. It is true that Benjamin's concept of divine violence shares much with the general strike, which, despite all the talk of violence, is essentially *non*-violent in its outlook. However, as I will show, the two authors do not share the same concerns. Benjamin rejects Sorel's theory of the myth and sacrifice, instead emphasizing the fragmentary manner in which the past returns to haunt the present. Myth totalizes the past in a coherent (mythic) narrative, through which death and violence is subsumed and stabilized. In Sorel, it is therefore no surprise that morality is created as a result of the operation of myth. Morality requires this stabilization of meaning but it is clear from the end of the *Critique* that Benjamin is not interested in this. However, this does not mean that he only pays lip service to Sorel. Rather we find a process of fragmentation in his writing on the *Reflections*. Benjamin tears the work apart, drawing some elements together while quite clearly setting others aside. This methodology mirrors his philosophical and cosmological thought:

> 'All creation entails destruction, or as Benjamin says overtly, "Construction" presupposes "Destruction".' The theme of destruction is a bedrock of Benjamin's philosophical-theological-aesthetic impulse. He shares the theme of creative destruction with Freud – seen in the 'death-drive' and its movement towards homeostasis – and the Dadaists and surrealists – with their destruction of limits between art and life, public and private. For Benjamin, destruction lies at the heart of creation and to get to truth, boundaries imposed at creation must be taken apart. Shiava- or Dionysus-like, the cosmos is perpetually destroyed and recreated in an on-going dance. Although the cosmos is formed through separateness, those very divisions are impermanent and could always be restructured.[19]

Past successes have led to our current situation. Thus it is from the ruins of the past that we can rethink our future. But this future is not to be constructed through myth, rather in the instability and uncertainty of the to-come. In a way, the methodology of this chapter follows Benjamin's concern with past failures. I will examine three failed notions of an open constituent power, in order to rework the idea of an open constituent power. Benjamin destroys Sorel's fundamental association of myth and the to-come. He fragments the *Reflections*, but in this process of destruction and resituation something distinct and new emerges. Myths must not be simply replaced with rational thought, neither can they be rewritten as better myths, they must be destroyed from within. The stability of meaning that is gleaned from the sublation of death in the mythic narrative is to be challenged, but more of this in coming chapters. Benjamin takes Sorel apart, moving elements around, exploding concepts and motives while all the time keeping an eye to the creation that emerges from this fragmentation.

Benjamin starts with the distinction between force and violence that is crucial to Sorel. The possibility of this authorization of violence is the subject of the *Critique*: 'The question that concerns us is, what light is thrown on the nature of violence by the fact that such a criterion or distinction [of sanctioned and unsanctioned violence] can be applied to it at all, or, in other words, what is the meaning of this distinction?'[20] Benjamin's subject is *Gewalt*, which in German is both violence *and* its authorization. The question is, what is the meaning of the fact that violence is sanctioned, that violence can become 'force' in the sense of state violence. Skipping swathes of what is a very complex essay, Benjamin sets forth two forms of authorized violence: the law-making (*rechtsetzende – Setzung* also means 'settle' or 'posit' so it literally could be translated as law settling or law positing)[21] and law preserving (*rechtserhaltende – Erhaltung* means maintenance, conservation or preservation) functions of violence. Law-preserving violence is the violence (understood in the broadest of senses) exercised by constituted order to protect and preserve the order. Law-making violence, by the same token, is the violence exercised in the revolutionary foundation of the state, however, this violent origin is *continually manifested within the constituted order*. This is the dialectical notion of constituent power that I put forward in the last chapters. The dialectic of constituent power and the law is thus between law-positing and law-preserving violence:

> [A]ll law – unlike justice – is dependent on a positing (*Setzung*), and no such positing manages without violence – without a violence that, with this positing, impedes, denies and compromises itself. The self-obstruction and corruption of positing and law-imposing violence become apparent every time such a violence seeks to preserve itself. By turning from positing to preserving law, it must also turn against hostile forces of positing and thus indirectly against its own principle – the principle of positing itself. In order to remain what it is – violence of law imposition – law-imposing violence must become law-preserving, must turn against its original positing character, and in this collision with itself, must disintegrate.[22]

There is a dialectical rise and fall of law governed by the higher law of 'historical change'. The content of this higher law is that all positing must 'expose itself to another positing'.[23] In this, the constituted always ultimately succumbs to the constituent that must betray its pure violence by preserving itself.

Benjamin cites the death penalty and police violence as two examples of the combination of law-making and preserving violence in the constituted order. With the continued use of the death penalty, 'the origins of law jut manifestly and fearsomely into existence'.[24] The retention of the death penalty literally manifests the law-making or positing function: 'in the exercise of violence over life and death more than in any other legal act, law reaffirms itself'.[25] Thus the law-making and preserving functions are manifested in the death penalty, however, a more 'spectral' manifestation of co-presence of law-making and preserving power is found in the police.[26] The police haunts the modern state with the violence of law, released to manifest its presence at the blunt edge of a cosh or truncheon. Constituted order manifests itself through authorized violence, asserting the order's origin and its preservation.

In terms of the dialectical relation between law-making and law-preserving violence, it is important that Benjamin wrote this text at least partially in response to Schmitt's *The Dictator*. Schmitt's conception of constituent power is seen as entirely outside constituted power, which is reliant on constituent power for its content and legitimation.[27] Benjamin wishes to associate constituted and constituent power, but not as other to one another, but rather flip sides of the same coin. Against these he presents the 'general strike' as a manner of non-violent or divine violence, a pure means that does not take law as its end. The law-positing or law-making violence is an already deteriorated form of 'pure violence'. Schmitt's constituent power is shown to be fundamentally part of the constituted order. But through the mediality of 'pure violence' (which has no teleology) Benjamin posits an outside or beyond the constituted order, which, as Hamacher shows, is before any positing:

> Pure violence does not posit, it 'deposes'; it is not performative, but afformative. If the pure violence of de-posing exists even beyond the sphere of law, this pure, and thus non-violent, non-instrumental violence may at any time – if not universally at any time – break through the cycle of laws and their decay.[28]

The afformative occurs before or within the performative – it is its condition. 'Afformations do not belong to a class of acts – that is, to a class of positing or founding operations [performatives] – they are nevertheless, never simply outside the sphere of acts or without relation to that sphere.'[29] Afformatives allow something to happen, they are the condition of performatives. Hamacher claims that pure violence is such an afformative. 'Deposing is a political event, but one that shatters all the canonical determinations of the political – and all canonical determinations of the event.'[30] Divine or pure violence is thus the absolute deposing that lies at the heart of 'positing' but that positing must betray. The betrayal never occurs more so than in the slippage from the singularity of the deposing to the universality of the law. 'Singularity for Benjamin is a determination of justice – indeed, its determination *par excellence* – and thus a determination of pure mediacy. Laws require universality, but their claim to universal validity is founded on a logic of subsumption that views each individual situation only as a case under the law, disregarding its singularity.'[31] Pure violence is singular because it is unique in each instance. It is singularly just in each instance without subsumption into law.[32]

The general strike is pure means, because unlike the limited strike it has no end or goal other than the shattering of canonical determinations of the political:

> While the [the limited strike] . . . is violent since it causes only an external modification of labour conditions, the [general strike] . . . as pure means, is non-violent. For it takes place not in readiness to resume work following external concessions and this or that modification to working conditions, but in the determination to resume only a wholly transformed work, no longer enforced by the state, an upheaval that is this kind of strike not so much

causes as consummates. For this reason the [strike] . . . is law-making but the [general strike] is anarchistic.[33]

The debt to Sorel here is clear. In the hands of the state 'violence' becomes 'force', it is authorized as law-making or preserving. However, the general strike, in the eyes of the state, is absolutely violent because it attempts to set aside the very essence of the constituted order. Whereas the limited strike is merely extortionate, that is within the bounds of an immediate law-making violence, the general strike 'clearly announces its indifference toward material gain through conquest by declaring its intention to abolish the state; the state was really . . . the basis of the existence of the ruling group, who in all their enterprises benefit from the burdens borne by the public.'[34] This sense of 'divine violence' is a direct transliteration of Sorel's proletarian morality that is always open. Sorel refuses to close the struggle through the ultimate synthesis of the proletarian/bourgeois dialectic. There is no end in Sorel, only the perpetual revolution of morality, no utopia where morality will no longer need violence to regenerate. The closure of the bourgeois/proletarian dialectic would close Vico's circular history by opening the regenerated morality back up to decadence.

For Benjamin, however, it is *precisely* mythic violence that is the problem. At this point Benjamin marks a difference with Sorel. Where Sorel's violence was mediated by the myth of the general strike, for Benjamin it is the general strike that interrupts the stabilization of the meaning of violence by myth. Thus, Benjamin removes the stability that Sorel insists on. It is no longer a question of proletarian morality, but rather of divine violence. Mythic violence is the establishment of a law guilt. It at once seeks to establish law through the instantiation of its violence (and with it the subject bound by guilt), while at the same time, in the moment of the law's violent instantiation, 'it specifically establishes as law not an *end* unalloyed by violence, but one necessarily and *intimately bound to it, under the title of power*. Law-making is power-making, and, to an extent, an immediate manifestation of violence.'[35]

Against the law-making of mythical violence, Benjamin opposes the idea of divine violence which is, in every way, its antithesis: 'If mythical violence is law-making, divine violence is law-destroying; if the former sets boundaries, the latter boundlessly destroys them; if the former is bloody, the latter is lethal without spilling blood.'[36] Where mythical violence through guilt is subject-creating violence, divine violence purifies that guilt of its relation to law. However, to get to this purity one must traverse the abjection of violence. Here again, we find both an engagement with Sorel and his rejection. Divine violence cannot be deployed in the myth of the general strike because it is bloodless, it is not sacrificial. Benjamin, therefore, rejects the very mechanism of providing a stable meaning to death that we find in Sorel. There is no myth of a general strike into which the death of the proletarian victim can be sublated. He contrasts the myth of Niobe[37] to the biblical story of God's judgment on the company of Korah, where Korah is bloodlessly swallowed by the earth. This violence strikes the Levites without warning, without guilt, and annihilates them. The bloodless nature of the violence is key for Benjamin, as the blood is a symbol of mere life. In a very dense and difficult passage Benjamin asserts that the:

> dissolution of legal violence stems ... from the guilt of more natural life, which consigns the living, innocent and unhappy, to a retribution that 'expiates' the guilt of mere life – and doubtless also *purifies the guilty, not of guilt, however but of law*. For with mere life the rule of law over the living ceases. Mythical violence is bloody power over mere life for its own sake, divine violence pure power over all life for the sake of the living. The first demands sacrifice, the second accepts it.[38]
>
> Divine violence does not strike at the body or the organic life of the individual, but at the subject who is formed by law. It purifies the guilty, not of guilt, but of its immersion in law and thus it dissolves the bonds of accountability that follow from the rule of law itself.[39]

Divine violence strikes at the legal division of subject and living being. The very mechanisms of sacrifice in law-making violence are subtly undermined by rejecting the transcendental absorption of a stable meaning of death. That Benjamin's divine violence is 'bloodless' must not go unnoticed – it is, after all, in the abject cleansing through the blood of the sacrificial victim that an execution becomes a sacrifice. There is no blood in divine violence, no purgation of sins. Thus, the escape from guilt, the purification from law is not a legal rejection of responsibility, but rather a deeper assertion that beyond law and its subjection is the realm of life that is crushed by legality. This realm of life is freed by the divine violence. Let us remember that this is in conversation with Sorel: Benjamin is rejecting Sorel's myth and sacrifice but in a similar form of anarchism he keeps the dialectical process of destruction and creation open – 'messianic completion never comes to a close.'[40] 'Justice – the singular, not prior to, but *in* its imparting – is the manifestation of a sociality free from the imposition of legal positings – the manifestation of a freedom itself.'[41]

Importantly, it is at this point, in the context of a discussion of divine violence, that Benjamin posits the idea of *Rechtschnur*. He indirectly approaches the Kantian categorical imperative: 'Act only according to that maxim by which you can at the same time will that it should become a universal law.' Rather than this principle of universalizability, Benjamin asserts that each situation is to be wrestled with in its own context. I will come back to this again at the end of Chapter 8 with Nancy's idea of 'creation *ex nihilo*'. Benjamin proposes that the commandment – 'Thou shalt not kill' – is to be considered a *Rechtschnur*, what Critchley calls a plumb line.[42] He sees that the possible extension of divine violence will bring forth the counter-argument that it gives 'men even lethal power against one another'. However, this, he argues cannot be conceded:

> For the question 'May I kill?' meets its irreducible answer in the commandment 'Thou shalt not kill.' This commandment precedes the deed, just as God

was 'preventing' the deed. But just as it may not be fear of punishment that enforces obedience, the injunction becomes inapplicable, incommensurable once the deed is accomplished. No judgment of the deed can be derived from the commandment. And so neither divine judgment, nor the grounds for this judgment, can be known in advance. Those who base a condemnation of all violent killing of one person by another on the commandment are therefore mistaken. It exists not as a criterion of judgment, but as a guideline [*Rechtschnur*] for the actions of persons or communities who have to wrestle with it in solitude and, in exceptional cases, to take on themselves the responsibility of ignoring it.[43]

'Thou shalt not kill' is not an absolute prohibition and a criterion of judgement, but rather a guideline. This does not justify or excuse murder, but rather reserves judgment for God. 'The commandment, for Benjamin, has no police force. It is immoveable, it is uttered, and it becomes the occasion for a struggle with the commandment itself.'[44] 'Thou shalt not kill' is not law with its crushing guilt, but rather it is the plumb line that tests the straightness of responsibility. Justice is, in each case, singular.

What is it that divine violence strips from the relation of life and law? Benjamin talks about attempting to find a place outside law from which to critique the authorization of violence. This space, this 'outside' is divine violence. From this *impossible* outside, critique is possible: it is impossible because it is a projected space, on the final page Benjamin says it is less important for man to recognize divine violence when it manifests itself, 'because the expiatory power of violence is not visible to men.'[45] Thus, while the sacrificial vision of Sorel, with its transcendental stabilization of sacrifice in proletarian morality is expunged, there remains in violence something of the sacrificial. This is its divine element. Yet this is ultimately beyond us, beyond that which is visible to men. According to Benjamin, we must see that violence is of the utmost weight and the decision to kill can only be taken in the weightiest of circumstances. This is not an irresponsible assertion, as it is seen from some sides, but rather in its revolutionary call it accepts responsibility absolutely. It is not, as is at times suggested, a mystical pacification. Rather, it is the assertion of life without the calcifying guilt of authority. It is sacrificial violence where the guilt (although perhaps not the responsibility) of the sacrificer is expunged. Most importantly, it is an interruption of the notion of (ontological and political) production:

Benjamin's political theory is a theory of pure means that neither present . . . nor produce . . ., and that neither posit nor are the act of positing itself . . .; Benjamin's political theory of pure means which do not posit but depose, which do not produce but instead *interrupt* production, is not only thematically about a revolution, but itself effects a reversal of the perspective of classical political theory: it no longer defines politics by reference to the production of social life and its presentation in the 'moral organism' of the state, but by reference to that which subverts the imperative of production and self-production, which evades the institutions of its implementation and suspends the paradigm of social self-production.[46]

Benjamin's divine violence strikes against the model of production found in Negri. Equally, it strikes against the violence that Fanon's colonial people level at the colonizer.[47] Ultimately, this violence is supposed to produce a new man. Benjamin's pure violence is not productive, nothing new emerges to become the new static essence. There is no prime mover creating something from nothing. Rather, the becoming of life is manifested by striking against the calcifying guilt of authorized violence and guilt. The strike is a negativity that is manifested as pure means in the political.

The dark night of revolution-without-end

Let me now move on to Bataille. The biographical link between Benjamin and Bataille is well known. Benjamin attended the College of Sociology lectures, they knew one another in Paris in the 1930s and Bataille famously hid Benjamin's text on the Paris Arcades in the *Bibliothèque Nationale* when Benjamin fled the Nazis to Spain. But, as Michael Weingrad shows, there was little or no agreement between them theoretically. The fundamental similarity of the project of attacking enlightenment of both the College of Sociology (Bataille, Klossowski, Leris and Callois) and the Institute of Social Research (Adorno, Horkheimer, Benjamin, etc.) did not attenuate their differences. Klossowski says that Bataille was 'at variance with him on every position, [but] listened to him with fascination'.[48] Nevertheless, we are not interested in the proximity of Benjamin and Bataille, but rather in what they can tell us about an open constituent power. There is no direct connection between Benjamin's *Critique of Violence*, which was written in the early 1920s, and Bataille's work on sacrifice, coming at least a decade later. Nevertheless, in some senses at least, Bataille offers us a clearer vision of a sacred violence, where Benjamin only hazards cryptic messianic suggestions.

In Bataille, there is a radical move away from the dialectical relation between constituent power as the act of foundation and constituted power as that which is founded. In his early work, he sets out a relation between a radical thinking of sacrifice and the political – a sacrificial political (anti-)foundation. Sacrifice for Bataille is a manner of approaching and achieving radical change. In this, he is quite different from Kelsen, Schmitt, Sieyès and Kant, because he sees violence as a pure means. It is a manner of effectuating change without positing a resolution, without establishing any new order. His use of sacrifice is not novel, given that it is traditionally connected with political foundation:

A subcategory of violence, sacrifice is etymologically an act that renders holy or sacred. If rendering sacred entails a process of setting apart from the quotidian or profane, then sacrificial violence is a paradoxical practice: it is a form of violence capable of breaking and forming distinctions or erasing and drawing boundaries. This definition is counter-intuitive because the modern view of violence exclusively associates it with breaking down of social distinctions, chaos, mayhem, disruption, anarchy, loss of control, and the like. In contrast, sacrificial violence involves a double movement; it transgresses limits in order to inscribe or reinscribe them.[49]

The sacrificial violence of foundation, of constituent power, is at once a marking of beginning and end, like Janus' backward-forward looking duality. The key in Bataille is that while sacrifice is revolutionary, it is also entirely *useless*:

> In seeking a revolutionary role for sacrifice, Bataille theoretically unmasks the great danger in using sacrificial violence to found new regimes: it generates authoritarian politics whose stability requires further bloody sacrifices. This realization breaks the continuity of the discourse on sacrificial violence by severing the historical relationship between violent revolutionary acts and political foundation.[50]

Quite early on in his writing, Bataille sees that sacrifice and a notion of the sacred is fundamental to the political being of fascism. However, he attempts to rupture the necessity of this link.

Bataille challenges the vision of sacrifice as productive of new foundation and limit. Rather, for Bataille, sacrifice is both *effective* and *useless*. The use value of violence itself is thus the object of his critique. In this, his work steps beyond Benjamin, who takes the utility of violence as a given, while the authorization of violence is questioned. The Place de la Révolution/Concorde in Paris is central to the Bataillean imagination of sovereignty, community and politics – as it is where the revolutionaries executed the king. The king, in his majesty, his authority and his power was sacrificed for the founding of the new political community. This is the very essence of revolution for Bataille: 'As a result of the revolution, divine authority ceases to found power: *authority no longer belongs to God but to the time whose free exuberance puts kings to death, to the time incarnated today in the explosive tumult of the people.*'[51] This explosive 'free exuberance', the moment of sacrificial transgression of that majesty and authority destabilizes the political. However, the people does not return this stability, the people remains the acephalous figure that André Masson draws for the cover of the journal *Acéphale*. However, as Bataille shows, after the Place de la Concorde, there can be no return to the unifying sovereignty of the king. The sacrifice of the king means that the people will forever be headless. In Bataille, we find a '"will to loss" that refuses all gain in terms of profit or power'.[52] The head is gone, the place of authority is *permanently empty*. All attempts to place a uniting sovereignty are ultimately false attempts to recapitate the acephalous body politic.

Fundamental to Bataille is the concept of uselessness, unrecoverable loss and waste, which ruptures the means–ends logic of sacrifice where the loss itself becomes unrecoverable. In this, sacrifice loses its role in foundation because it cannot produce authority. The regicide does not recover a new authority for the people, rather, the sacrifice leaves politics in a constant state of turbulence; always looking for its lost head but incapable of firmly attaching it once more. In the Kojèvean world of the end of history where 'the dialectic has finished with its work and negativity is unemployable, violence destroys without conservation. Unrecoverable loss thus becomes the leitmotif of all sacrificial violence without sublation.'[53] Violence in Bataille loses its productive element that had guaranteed its utility for the political thought that preceded him. In an irruptive exposure, violence brings each one up against the hard negativity of death and accursedness and with this comes the fragmentation of the self that replicates the headlessness of the people after the execution. Accursedness is brought to us in its most radical manner in the negativity (the no-thing) of death and not-being. It is our finitude that we expel from our consciousness, all aspects of our accursedness are expelled – death, faeces, blood, corpses, dead skin, hair, nails and other excrement. It is our ego-ideal in the terms of psychoanalysis that is disrupted by sacrifice. It destabilizes the purity of the self by bringing not-being, death and accursedness directly to the subject.[54] The accursed share is human existence, each singular being takes a share of the accursed.

Authority is of the utmost importance to Bataille. The debates between Kant and Sieyès all come down to revolutionary authority: 'Republicanism, monarchism and anarcho-syndicalism all presuppose the possibility of authority, even if they posit radically different embodiments of it. Bataille's concept of sacrifice gives rise to a community in which the act of foundation never coheres.'[55] Instead, the community is destabilized around the unrecoverable loss. In response to this and as an attempt to recover the head, fascism would then continue to sacrifice victims in order to attempt to stabilize the community. War is thus the ultimate conclusion of fascism, which becomes a suicidal/self-sacrificial politics:

> So murderous power and sovereign power are unleashed throughout the entire social body. They were also unleashed by the fact that war was explicitly defined as a political objective – and not simply as a basic political objective or as a means, but as a sort of ultimate and decisive phase in all political processes – politics had to lead to war, and war had to be the final decisive phase that would complete everything. The objective of the Nazi regime was therefore not really the destruction of other races. The destruction of other races was one aspect of the project, the other being to expose its own race to the absolute and universal threat of death. Risking one's life, being exposed to total destruction, was one of the principles inscribed in the basic duties of the obedient Nazi, and it was one of the essential objectives of Nazism's policies. It had to reach a point at which the entire population was exposed to death. Exposing the entire population to universal death was the only way it could truly constitute itself as a superior race and bring about its definitive regeneration once other races had been either exterminated or enslaved forever.[56]

By exposing the entirety of the state to death, German fascism attempted to create the community of absolute unity. This sacrificial politics has what Bataille calls a 'right' (as opposed to left) understanding of sacrifice. This understands sacrifice in the same way as the French revolutionaries understood it – that the exceptional event would found the new authority. Yet, since the revolution, we know that all that is left after sacrifice is the headless body of the people.

Variously, both Marx and Negri suggest an ontology of producing humanity. Each in his own way proposes the role of making and acquiring things as central to our existence. Bataille rejects this and supplements it with the principle of *unproductive expenditure*. This places waste rather than gain at its core. There is no utility with unproductive expenditure. There is nothing ultimately produced. Instead, we have a pure means, pure and continuous production with no final product. This becomes Bataille's great addition to the literature. The proletariat is the excrement of capitalism, it is 'the part of no part',[57] which reconfigures humanity in its violent useless destruction. It cries 'We have been nothing, let us become everything.' Yet it is not this straightforward. In the great night of revolution, the proletariat does not purify the world and become the single unity, it does not become everything. There is no purification, where with the sacrifice of the bourgeoisie, the proletariat passes through the night to daylight. Instead, everyone is plunged into the *great night* of revolution without closure, where each one is transformed ontologically.[58] In this great night politics is revolutionized, the proletariat is ontologically transformed through unproductive expenditure of an 'all-consuming human potlatch'. This is a 'left' sacrifice:

> As Bataille claims, communication between sundered beings emerges when they lose themselves in a sacrificial experience, thus permitting a communality unfettered by rational discourse or socio-political ideals. The social unity that results from unproductive sacrificial violence is thus rooted in the emptiness created when human beings confront what is beyond the scope of their humanity. The empty, headless space left by the regicide of Louis XVI is identical with the self-subversion initiated by participation in social expenditure. Both sacrifice and sacrificed are lost.[59]

Unproductive expenditure ruptures the very sense of usefulness just as it ruptures the rationalizations produced continually by the self. Sacrifice destroys the sense of the subject as a single unitary self just as it destroys the sense of the people as a collective subject. There can be no unified body of the people because after the sacrifice there is no unified self. The logic of the sacrifice of Place de la Concorde is taken to its ends in the frenzy of a new politics.

In *The Psychological Structure of Fascism*, Bataille develops the sense of homogeneous and heterogeneous. Homogeneity, primarily a form of the profane, 'describes societies structured by production, rationality, specialization, organization, conservation, predictability, and preservation. For Bataille, these terms characterize modern Western bourgeois society, which excludes anything that does not conform to its homogenous structure.'[60] In other words, Bataille sees rational, risk-averse liberal society as fundamentally structured by the 'making-safe' of the world (homogeneity). Thus, we should not read homogeneity in a multicultural sense where it corresponds to ethnic sameness. Rather, Bataille's insight is much deeper. The hallmark of liberal society is the contract that establishes a general equivalence among men and things. Thus, commensurability among elements of a contract is the key here. It develops a system of order(ing) that is quite close to Ranciere's 'distribution of the sensible' and Nancy's *glomus*, which I will look at in Chapter 8: 'Depending on whether the state is democratic or despotic, the prevailing tendency will be either adaptation or authority. In a democracy, the state derives most of its strength from spontaneous homogeneity, which it fixes and constitutes as the rule.'[61]

Homogeneity is to be distinguished from heterogeneity: where the former is focused around a certain common law or measure under which all are commensurable; the latter is bipolar – combining both repulsion and compulsion:

> [Heterogeneity] encompasses everything that is unproductive, irrational, incommensurable, unstructured, unpredictable, and wasteful ... Bataille offers five descriptions of heterogeneous elements: (1) taboo and mana; (2) everything resulting from unproductive expenditure, including excrement, eroticism, and violence; (3) ambiguous phenomena that are simultaneously attractive and repulsive; (4) excess, delirium, and madness; and (5) any reality that is affectively forceful or shocking.[62]

Politically, heterogeneity is associated with the disordered. Thus, where the rule of law and capitalist forms rely on the possibility of common measure or homogenous order, the heterogeneous is disordered by nature. Police violence, the ad hoc violence of the fascist mob or revolutionary violence are all heterogeneous. But Bataille divides the heterogeneous into two: the imperative and the subversive. The imperative or sovereign heterogeneity is constructed in a hierarchical manner with authority stemming from 'above'. There are two instances of this imperative heterogeneity: on one side, the violence of the police who patrol the borders of liberal homogeneity; and, on the other side, the fascist or monarchist state, which relies entirely on the whim of the leader/king. Modern liberal states set the heterogeneous violence of the police and army to work defending the boundaries of the rational homogeneity. In that instance, sovereign violence hides behind the rational/legal façade of liberal states. However, the king or fascist leader performs a very different form, according to Bataille: 'The king or the fascist leader (as imperative heterogeneity) is in a way excluded from the homogeneous activities of society, but he dominates that society and embodies it.'[63] Fascism takes the heterogeneity of society and orders it along the lines of the army that is 'hierarchy and discipline in the service of death'.[64] It is the dream of unity through sacrifice, through war and exclusion and final solutions.

Subversive or revolutionary heterogeneity focuses not on the homogeneous, but on the abject itself. It is unproductive loss that results in the dissolution of self. Instead of forming limits and authority, it begins only around the transgression of limit and authority. Revolutionary violence is entirely 'useless', it does not produce an end but, rather, is pure mediality. Bataille emphasizes the *Lumpenproletariat* in these texts, whom he believes are the key to setting loose the 'the disintegration of all the structures guaranteeing the homogeneity of the social edifice'.[65] The *Lumpenproletariat* is the excremental excess of the excremental excess of capitalism. This doubly excluded collection is the most abject of the abject. For Bataille, they embody revolutionary heterogeneity because they have not succumbed to the organization of the proletariat and the rationalization of the struggle.

In revolutionary abjection, the proletariat would be submerged into the great night of the violence of sacrifice without gain, without use. In this, a new humanity is created, one that is ultimately connected and touched by the abject. The 'sacrificial community does not repair, restore or regenerate. It is incapable of establishing, founding and inaugurating. It "begins" with the violation of the limits that make politics possible and tragically it must exist in a permanent state of violation':[66]

> Bataille is not a writer of radical breaks because these breaks are violent gestures of division and purification. To destroy all complicity with what has gone before would involve purifying ourselves of the past. The break is dominated by a belief in a new pure state, a new pure human nature (for example, Che Guevara's 'new socialist man'). Bataille's violent class rhetoric of the 1930s does call for the destruction of the bourgeoisie but it is not clear that he means mass physical destruction. He is not a writer of purification but a writer of the principle of contagion and contamination.[67]

Contagion and contamination occur in the sacred; they are the process of revealing the abject nature of our humanity.

In this chapter, I have given three examples of an 'open' constituent power. This is a constituent power that is not simply tied to whatever constituted order that it seeks to found. With Sorel, there is the sense of a community of struggle, a community that has no pre-given essence, but rather is in a constant state of generation. It is an effect of the struggle, rather than given beforehand. With Benjamin, there is an idea of an a-nomic action, a challenge to the idea of authorized legal violence. Instead, he suggests a divine violence, which is beyond the to-and-fro of law's constituent-constituted dialectic of authority. His sense of divine violence is beyond use. This meshes with Bataille, where there is the attack on use and utility in a radically anti-capitalist fashion. As I will show in Chapters 7 and 8, in a strange sense, this mirrors Heidegger's attack on Descartes' calculative thinking. However, what links each of these three, beyond the radically open constituent power, is the sense in which each project fails utterly. The reason I have used them is not to suggest that their projects could be translated into human rights, but rather to raise the possible outlines of a radical politics of human rights that begins from an 'open' constituent power. In a sense, this will begin in the next chapter, where I deconstruct the traditional subject of constituent power: the people. This continues in the following chapters, where I attempt to weave together the attack on utility, the sovereign (or immanentist) sense of community and the question of law.

Chapter 6

Differing the people: Derrida and Rancière

[I]t is not that easy to think of the sovereignty of the people because it is impossible to present the people as given before the making of the people. This is always the problem of 'constitutive power'.

Nancy, 'On Finitude and Sovereignty'[1]

For modern democratic theory, the people holds sovereign power. The people is represented as a unitary actor, capable of making its will known. In democracy at least, it is seen as a 'free' agent capable of self-determining, that is both determining itself and for itself. In this sense, it is deeply connected to the nation-state which provides both the self to be determined and the politico-constitutional framework through which it determines for itself. As I explained in Chapter 4, liberal democratic theory tends to understand the raw power of the people through a banal dialectic. The sovereign people is supposed to be directly represented in government. According to this theory, the 'constituent power' of people is the power and possibility of that collective subject to make its will known, either through the representational mechanisms of the constituted order or else in a more direct manner. In this latter manifestation, constituent power is the power and possibility of altering the very *basis* of government, it is the principle of radical political change. Thus, to some extent, the people within traditional democratic theory represents the most radical potential of constituent power. This chapter seeks to address itself to the 'event' of the people in its most radical sense, that is, during constituent power. It starts, however, from a fundamental dissatisfaction. There is never any unity to the people within the constituent moment. In other words, I would like to suggest a little heretically that the people in its constituent moment should not be conceived of as a fully present and self-aware entity, in the process of self-determining.

To begin, I will look briefly to three relatively distinct but related strands of thought about the people, beginning with Kelsen and Schmitt, then Virno and Negri, and finally the jurisprudence of Hans Lindahl. This opening section is designed to foreground the problem of the people's unity and suggest that there are other possibilities to Schmitt, Negri and Virno's substantialism. Equally, it suggests that while Kelsen's analytic clearly folds the constituent into the constituted, Lindahl's reworking of this begins to get at a sense of the people that is not fully present to itself. In the following sections, first using Derrida and then Rancière, I will supplement Lindahl, outlining two different approaches to the people. In particular, I am interested in deconstructing the people, thinking it in a deferred and differed sense. Yet the challenge of this deconstruction is to de-structure the people, without neutering its constituent power by forever postponing it. It is a multiple term, full of dissonance and echoes and it is precisely this dissonance that makes it politically productive.

A substantive or elided people?

It is useful to start with the debate between Hans Kelsen and Carl Schmitt because it mirrors the discussion in Chapter 4 of Sieyès and Kant, but also maps out the two trajectories in this chapter that I want to problematize. The disagreement between Kelsen and Schmitt is manifold, but of particular importance for any political theory of constituent power is the manner in which each sees the foundation or authorization of the constitution through the people. The authority of the constitution in both theories resides in very different figurations of the subject of constituent power. Carl Schmitt's work recovers the primacy of the constituent over the constituted, of politics over law. The key to this is asserting that '[t]he people, the nation [in Sieyès' sense], remains the origin of all political action, the source of all power, which expresses itself in continually new ways, producing from itself these ever renewing forms and organizations. It does so, however, without ever subordinating itself, its political existence, to a conclusive formation.'[2] The people may never bind itself forever. This primacy of the constituent over the constituted is achieved at the cost of creating a substantialist idea of the people, where the 'concrete existence of the politically unified people is prior to every norm'.[3] The people is that which lies behind the constituent, because it is what defines it as constituent. We can see that this is at once an acceptance of Sieyès' notion of the people's two forms of existence, but at the same time, a rejection of Sieyès' attempt to tie the people to one juridical form. Schmitt poses an act of self-rule by the collective subject of constitutions. In this act of self-rule the subject (the 'We') is 'immediately *present* to itself'.[4] This 'We' is the political constitution of the collectivity, prior to all legal constitutions: 'Schmitt argues that a political concept of the constitution precedes its legal notion, both chronologically and conceptually: prior to "having" a legal constitution, a state *is* a constitution, a *status*: the "concrete aggregate state [*Gesamtzustand*] of political unity and social order". This existential status, not a basic norm, grounds the validity of a constitution.'[5]

This political entity is a substantive presence and present to itself as 'the people'. Yet the problem immediately here is the actual 'concrete existence' of such a subject: what is the 'state' of the people that allows their political unification? Schmitt struggles with this in *Constitutional Theory* and ultimately fudges the issue: 'Even if they have a determinate will only in less definitive moments and express themselves recognizably, they are nevertheless capable of and in a position for such willing and are able to say yes or no to the fundamental questions of their political existence.'[6] Even this almost mystical explanation needs further caveat. He says 'The weakness is that the people should decide on the basic questions of their political form and their organisation without themselves being formed or organized. This means their expressions of will are easily mistaken, misinterpreted, or falsified.'[7] The people makes its will known when it pronounces on its form, yet what is the difference between the people pronouncing and something that just looks like the people?

Against Schmitt, Kelsen argued that there could be no 'concrete existence' of the people prior to legal norms, because the unity of the people is found only through the unity of the legal order. For Kelsen, each legal norm is authorized by a previous or higher norm which can be traced back regressively to the paradoxical *Grundnorm*. Constitutions for Kelsen lead back ultimately to the historically 'first constitution'. The 'assembly referred to in the historically first constitution, by adopting this constitution establishes itself – according to this constitution – as the Constituent National Assembly provided for by the constitution.'[8] This is the paradoxical self-creation at the heart of the constituted order:

> As Kelsen recognizes, self-empowerment is a contradiction in terms. Hence his analysis unveils a paradox at the heart of the law: legislation, in its most powerful manifestation, is the exercise of constituent power, an act that creates the first constitution without being empowered to do so; but because the law can only think of power as legal power, an act can only initiate a legal order if it is *retroactively* interpreted as an empowered act – the exercise of constituted power. Such is the function of the basic norm, the *Grundnorm*.[9]

Kelsen takes Kant's rejection of the authorizability of constituent power and makes it the core of his fundamental norm. The *Grundnorm* becomes the *Grundnorm* by establishing subsequent norms that rely on it for validity. The law empowers itself through a retroactive authorization, a process of attribution. However, as Schmitt complained, Kelsen 'collapses constituent into constituted power and politics into law, thereby hypostatizing the legal order into a self-grounding, self-serving, and self-sustaining system of rules'.[10] It is only in the constituted order that we can find the people. So there can be no sense of the people as the subject of constituent power.

Thus, we reach an impasse. Between Schmitt and Kelsen, just as between Sieyès and Kant, there is a differentiation over the substance of the people. A different move would be to follow the suggestion of the Virno and Negri (with and without Hardt) and reject the people entirely as a tool of constituted power. Curiously, Virno and Negri render the people in a substantialist fashion, but also as an effect of the constituted order. They unite the worst aspects of Schmitt and Kelsen through Hobbes. Both Virno and Negri accept the Hobbesean definition of the people and use it to distinguish the multitude. 'The two polarities, people and multitude, have Hobbes and Spinoza as their putative fathers. For Spinoza, the *multitudo* indicates a *plurality which persists as such* in the public scene, in collective action, in the handling of communal affairs, without converging into a One, without evaporating within a centripetal form of motion.'[11] The people then is that which is gathered together under the state, 'it is a reverberation, a reflection of the State: if there is a State, then there are people.'[12] Virno tellingly quotes from *De Cive*: 'The *People* is somewhat that is *one*, having *one will*, and to whom action may be attributed.'[13] Hobbes asserts that the people *is* the king (in monarchy) or the court (in aristocracy or democracy). Thus, while the citizens or subjects are the multitude, the sovereign *is* the people in whatever form of government. He then goes on to explain the base notion that the 'common sort of men, and others who little consider these truths' tend to understand by the people (I will come back to this later in the chapter). He says that they:

> [D]o always speak of a *great number* of men, as of the *People*, that is to say, the *City*; they say that the *City* hath rebelled against the *King* (which is impossible) and that the *People* will, and nill, what murmuring and discontented Subjects would have, or would not have, under pretence of the *People*, stirring up the *Citizens* against the *City*, that is to say, the *Multitude* against the *People*. And these are almost all the Opinions wherewith Subjects being tainted doe easily Tumult. And forasmuch as in all manner of Government Majesty is to be preserv'd by him, or them who have the Supreme Authority, the *crimen laesae Majestatis* [the crime of high treason] naturally cleaves to these Opinions.[14]

Virno says that for Hobbes, 'the multitude is anti-state, but, precisely for this reason, anti-people.'[15] He takes the Hobbesean line that the people converges into the unity of the state, aligning himself with Hobbes' dismissal of the opinion of this 'common sort of men'.

Negri's *Insurgencies* is a little more nuanced in this sense than Virno. It frames the problem; 'if the "people" is the subject of constituent power, it can be so only insofar as it first undergoes an organizational process capable of expressing its essence.'[16] This has escaped the cartoonish portrayal inherited from Hobbes and explains the fundamental process of the people – organization. Negri then goes on to say that to imagine ' "an ordering force that can be ordered by a multitude without order" would represent a contradiction in terms.'[17] The multitude cannot organize itself into a people because there is no 'ordering force' before the constituted order. Thus, he argues, it is a necessity that 'any definition of the constituent subject in terms of the people boils down to a normativist conception and a celebration of the constituted law . . . This normative conception confuses constituent power with one of the internal sources of law and the dynamics of its revision, its constitutional self-renovation. Briefly stated, constituent power is the people only in the context of representation.'[18] Thus, for Negri, the people is never the subject of constituent power because it presupposes a sort of representation, an ordering that determines the essence of the collective and sets that essence to work around the edges of the group. In other words, by organizing in such a fashion that an essence is produced, it becomes possible to say who is properly 'of' the group. It becomes possible to police the borders of the people, determining who is 'in' and who is 'out'.

Negri and Virno thus propose the multitude as the subject of constituent power, although their conception of the multitude differs quite substantially. For Hardt and Negri, the multitude is immanent, it is created through capitalist forms, particularly within their conception of empire. The multitude itself is a heterogeneous web of creative actors. Through its creative capacities, it communicates and collaborates, producing 'the common' that serves as a platform for resistance. The common itself is created within and often through the capitalist modes that it ultimately resists. The multitude is to be distinguished from the people in Hardt and Negri:

> The multitude is a multiplicity, a plane of singularities, an open set of relations, which is not homogeneous or identical with itself and bears an indistinct, inclusive relation to those outside of it. The people, in contrast, tends toward identity and homogeneity internally while posing its difference from and excluding what remains outside of it. Whereas the multitude is an inconclusive constituent relation, the people is a constituted synthesis that is prepared for sovereignty. The people provides a single will and action that is independent of and often in conflict with the various wills and actions of the multitude.[19]

For Virno, the people is the result of a centripetal force (pulling entities towards a centre or axis). The multitude, by way of contrast, is the result of a centrifugal force (pulling away from a centre or axis).[20] He argues that the multitude begins from the common and individuates from there. 'The unity that the multitude has behind itself is constituted by the "common places" of the mind, by the linguistic–cognitive faculties common to the species, by the *general intellect*.'[21] From this unity, it moves through individuation to the many, but the people starts from the individual and moves through the juridical to unity. However, as I have said, these portrayals of the people are ultimately taken from Hobbes and Spinoza. There is no sense that Virno and Negri want to recover this subject of constituent power. Rather, they are interested in expelling any sense of its utility, creating a straw man, against which they may define their multitude. Everything that the people is (sovereignty, constituted order, representational), the multitude is not.

Laclau critiques the stark dichotomy between the multitude and the people in Hardt and Negri, whose multitude is united only by its 'being against' empire. Laclau suggests that the ontological assertion of 'being against' is mystical and without critical purchase. The unity provided by the common of resistance is a 'gift from heaven', which oversimplifies the political process. If resistance is natural then there is no need for the political construction of the subject of revolt. Against the notion that the people is the closed unity that tends towards homogeneity, Laclau argues that the people is a political category. It is not the '*datum* of the social structure . . . [It] designates not a *given* group, but an act of institution that creates a new agency out of a plurality of heterogeneous elements.'[22] The fundamental construction of the people is therefore not a particular group defined ethnically or politically, rather the people is structured by a socio-political *demand*. The people is not a stable and pre-given unity. Rather, it is defined by the gathering of people around the iteration of a demand. Hardt and Negri (and presumably Virno) are too quick in denigrating and dismissing the people as an effect of the juridical formation of the state. They miss the possibility of such a term. However, the people remains problematic in its Hobbesean regalia. I suggest that we must begin to think differently about it and to begin this I will, perhaps surprisingly, begin with the contemporary jurist Hans Lindahl and his re-examination of Kelsen's model of the retroactive nature of constitutional legitimacy.

Lindahl's insight is a crucial starting point as, by giving a different account of the people, it opens a path to Derrida and Rancière's deconstructions of that term.[23] Temporality is of the utmost importance for Lindahl. He tells us that the people is not present to itself, but rather it exists only as a retroactive act of attribution: 'an act of constituent power gives rise to a legal order only retroactively – that is, when it is viewed as an act of constituent power.'[24] Thus, the people, for Lindahl is never present to itself, but rather can only be seen to exist after the fact. Lindahl argues that this retroactivity, when supplemented by a theory of reflexive identity, provides an ontology of collective action without Schmitt's substantialism:

> In effect, no collective self exists independently of the individuals that compose it because . . . acts of self-attribution are in each case individual acts. But the self to which they attribute these acts is a political unity, a 'We', the existence of which is not simply the summation of a manifold of individual acts of attribution.[25]

The people is never fully present to itself, he tells us. Instead, when people exercise 'their constitutional rights, they retroactively take up the first-person plural perspective of a "We" that has (already) enacted a constitution.'[26] In other words, the people (now past) is an effect of performing one's constitutional rights. In this, neither the people nor the person performing her constitutional rights is fully present to self. Rather, they are temporalized. The people of the constitution is never a closed unity, it can never be *fully* present, because it must again be re-performed in the future.

To give a material example of this version of the subject of constituent power Lindahl uses the example of Vittorio Agnoletto's intervention at the European Social Forum (ESF). Agnoletto, speaking for a revolutionary faction of the ESF, attempted to marginalize the non-revolutionary contingent (primarily NGOs) by saying that the ESF was a radical not reformist movement. The Charter of Principles of the ESF asserts that 'no one is authorized to express . . . positions that claim to be those of all the participants.' According to Lindahl this makes the ESF an 'open' forum, without the closure of a constituted order. Agnoletto is quite clearly in violation of this, when he attempts to 'close' the movement by defining it as revolutionary. The question for Lindahl is that for the ESF 'a space remains open only if no claim is made in the name of a whole; but without such a claim, no alternative political and legal order can be founded, by revolutionary means or otherwise. The price of "radical openness" in politics is the loss of constituent power.'[27] This analysis initially appears apposite. He says by way of explanation: 'Unless the multitude becomes a unity in action, unless it ceases to be a multitude and becomes a collective subject, it cannot constitute itself as a political community.'[28] He argues that Agnoletto's 'We' may be equated with the people:

> Crucially, Agnoletto's invocation of a 'We', when referring to 'our movement . . .', reveals a remarkable equivocity that goes to the heart of collective self-constitution. On the one hand, there is no first-person plural perspective in the absence of an act that effects a closure by seizing the political initiative to say *what* goal or interest joins together the multitude into a people, and who belongs to the people. Accordingly, Agnoletto's invocation fails not merely because there is no subject to whom his speech-act can be attributed, but because the author to whom the act would be attributed is authored by his attribution: 'there can be no "people" prior to the invocation of a will to them.'[29]

Yet, something jars in this analysis; in particular, it seems that this analysis reveals something about the conception of the people as a unity. Agnoletto's call does not attempt to close the openness of the constituent moment (here symbolized by the ESF), rather, he attempts to bring forth the constituent by opening the ESF to being-otherwise. Agnoletto attempts to change the movement. The constituent demands the impossible in order to change the very possibilities of the given situation.

Agnoletto's choice of words appears descriptive, but it is clear from the context that it is an attempt to *perform* change. When he says 'We', he does not close the movement, but calls others together in a manner that is different from what has already been established. However, the example is misleading because the ESF is already a constituted order, regulated by the norm: 'no one is authorized to express . . . positions that claim to be those of all the participants.' Agnoletto challenges this by the assertion of a 'We'. Thus (inverting Lindahl's use of the example), the ESF is not 'open' and unconstituted but rather already constituted. Agnoletto's assertion does not close the movement, as Lindahl suggests, but rather opens the constituent within the group. The forum is opened to being otherwise by Agnoletto. He calls forth change by attempting to summon the constituent mob. In the constituent moment, the people (qua totality) is *called-forth* ('We who are nothing, are everything') to overturn the existing order.

There is an important point here that goes directly to the heart of the problem of the people.[30] The *truth* of Agnoletto's assertion of the 'We' may only be seen once the constituent moment is suspended in the constituted order. Agnoletto's assertion could only be true if he succeeded in altering the very nature of the movement to make it revolutionary. That is, he must change the preceding constituted order. Let us imagine that everyone agreed when Agnoletto makes his assertion that the movement is revolutionary rather than reformist. If that had happened, then at the moment of agreement through retroactive attribution, the truth of Agnoletto's assertion could be verified. However, in the moment before this agreement there is the constituent. Agnoletto opens the constituent with his assertion that the group *could* be otherwise. He disturbs the settled order of the movement (that no one may speak for it); this is the opening of the constituent. As we will see, the constituent is defined by potentiality. The key to Lindahl's argument is that we are being asked to *recognize* the 'truth' of the people or to *know* the people. This 'problem of the people' is thus a question of knowledge/judgment within the constituted order, the question is how do we truthfully know the people.

This can be seen clearly in Lindahl – 'whether or not a collective subject exists politically can only be established retrospectively, from within the unity of a legal order: political unity does not admit a pre-legal existential judgment.'[31] Accordingly, the unity of the people can only be known/judged from within the constituted order. But this means that we are dealing with different questions, the question of 'knowing the people' is *epistemic*. Lindahl is asking *how we know or verify* the people. He is correct to assert that the *epistemic* question can only be answered in the constituted order. Yet, the question here is of the constituent in its own terms, that is, in the moment where the decision could go either way (a moment of potentiality), an open moment of disagreement, dissensus, or antagonism.[32] The crucial term in Lindahl's earlier assertion is 'established'. A collective subject's existence can only be *established* retrospectively. The moment of rupture is experienced not as establishment of a new order but as potentiality. Certainly, constituent power is fundamentally and indissolubly connected to the establishment of a constituted power. However, the constituted order that may follow the exercise of constituent power does not provide the essence of the constituent moment itself. If I might express this quite awkwardly: the constituent is constituent even if it does not ultimately constitute a new order.[33] I have already explained (in Chapter 4) the difference in the term 'power' between *potentia* and *potestas*. *Potentia* is a mode of 'power' that is intimately tied to *potentiality*.

Referencing Aristotle, Agamben shows that potentiality remains potential only for as long as it *may or may not be*:

Unlike mere possibilities, which can be considered from a purely logical standpoint, potentialities or capacities present themselves above all as things that exist but that, at the same time, do not exist as actual things; they are present, yet they do not appear in the form of present things. What is at issue in the concept of potentiality is nothing less than a mode of existence that is irreducible to actuality.[34]

The traditional philosophical position is that potentiality is fundamentally linked to actuality, but remains potential only for as long as it has not been actualized. In Book Theta of the *Metaphysics*, Aristotle says: 'what is potential can both be and not be, for the same is potential both to be and not to be' (*to ara dynaton einai endekhetai kai einai kai me einai*).[35] In other words, every potentiality is also at the same time an impotentiality. Its essence is that at once it must potentially be and potentially not be. If a potential becomes actual, it is no longer potential. Rather, the potentiality has been closed and the power to either be or not be has been decided in one or the other.

What does it mean therefore to say that constituent power is fundamentally and indisassociably linked to *potentiality*? Simply, it means that constituent power is the potential to constitute, but also the potential not to constitute. This the flaw of Sieyès' position from Chapter 4, where he attempts to demand the necessity of a particular form of government once the Third Estate manifests its sovereignty. Constituent power remains a *potentia* even if it does not constitute power. Thus, when a group asserts that it is the people, it opens the potentiality of constituent power. In their resistance, they hold both the possibility of constituting a new order and the possibility of failing. This sense of potentiality is very important then for the 'We' or the people. In Chapter 4, Kant showed that there is no transcendent law that would guarantee the constituent power before or during its exercise. Fundamentally, this means that revolution is a *salto mortale*, that an *uncertain* 'We' together leaps perilously, in the hope that its action will subsequently be seen as an act of the people. This assertion of a 'We' *claims* the status of the people, however, the truth of this assertion and the authority that stems from this truth, can only be found in the new constituted order that may or may not follow from it. The assertion of 'We, the people' is the opening of constituent power, it opens the already constituted order to becoming otherwise. It sets in motion a truth process that *may* bring about the conditions of its own verification. However, at the moment of iteration, the assertion of 'We, the people' is an open call; it is an '*inchoate performative*'.[36] I cannot emphasize this enough. 'We, the people' is always incomplete. In performing an 'I', one self-reflexively constitutes the 'I'. However, an inchoate performative cannot complete itself, it remains always partial. Nancy says, ' "*We*" is always in *statu nascendi*.'[37] The important question is not 'how do we know or verify that this is the people', but rather what is the nature of this community in *statu nascendi*?

At this point, I think it is useful to begin to develop this sense of the people in *statu nascendi* through two deconstructions. The first is a traditional Derridean deconstruction. It challenges the temporally static idea of the people as an entity out of time, there alongside the state as its secure foundation of authority. The

Derridean deconstruction proposes that the people is haunting and called-forth. In both, the to-come takes effect with the force of potentiality. The second deconstruction looks to Rancière's challenge that the people is not a stable and unitary entity, but rather contains within its folds a fundamental split between the people (qua sovereignty and power) and the people (qua the excluded, traditionally the poor).

Derrida and Rancière's deconstruction of the people

Derrida's deconstructive philosophy is well known. He is significant here as he facilitates a challenge to the pure presence of the people, whether this is in Schmitt's radical vision or in the sanitized people projected in the right to self-determination. However, the danger with any attempt to use his political writings is that one falls into an easy postponing of the political in the name of an endless deferral of the 'to-come'. This too often becomes a manner of suspending the political in the name of the 'ethical'. I want to resist this tendency, while still maintaining the importance of Derrida for a deconstruction of the people. To begin, I will suggest that the people haunts (with the possibility of its violent return). In this, the people is suspended, but comes to presence in the possibility of radical change. The second usage of Derrida is slightly more traditional, it looks to his early work in order to think about the moment of constitution of the people.

The people haunts. The Derridean deconstructive move from ontology to hauntology[38] is important: where ontology asks the question of being, hauntology questions the traces that collect around every closure or totality. Let me suggest initially that there are two aspects of the manner in which the people haunts: first, it haunts the present with the possibility of the people (qua constituent power). Like the spectre that haunts Europe in the *Communist Manifesto*, the people may always return and effectuate the injunction that things may be otherwise. Second, in the performative iteration of the people in the American *Declaration of Independence*, for instance, the people haunts with the possibility of successfully constituting a new order. Both aspects of the people are fundamentally hauntological. The people is not a full presence, but rather the trace of possibility to either come back or to repeat an iteration. Both versions of the people play around the calling forth of the projection of a totality, both question the manifestation of the people without resorting to a politics of presence.

To begin, therefore, it is necessary to have a sense of Derrida's hauntology. In *Spectres of Marx*, he addresses the inheritance of a revolutionary 'tradition'. For Derrida, like Lindahl, temporality is the very key to constituent power. The revolutionary tradition returns like a ghost to haunt the present with the possibility of radical change. However, Derrida is more radical than merely describing a haunting; hauntology parallels ontology. He tells us that the present itself is *anachronous*. Derrida is not merely reading a number of isolated texts; rather, he is exploring a broader assertion. He does this through a reading of *Hamlet* and in particular the speech: 'The time is out of ioynt [joint]: Oh cursed spight [spite], That ever I was borne to set it right.'[39] There are two aspects to this: First, that time (the present) could be out of joint (untimely or uncanny); and, second, that this untimeliness is connected to injustice. These two aspects are intimately connected. Hamlet is called to responsibility by the untimely return of his murdered father in an apparition. Using Heidegger's *Der Spruch des Anaximander*, Derrida questions the 'present':

> The present is what passes, the present comes to pass [*se passe*], it lingers in this transitory passage (*Weile*), in the coming-and-going, *between* what *goes* and what *comes*, in the middle of what leaves and what arrives, at the articulation between what absents itself and what presents itself. This in-between articulates conjointly the double articulation (*die Fuge*) according to which the two movements are adjoined (*diefügt*). Presence (*Anwesen*) is enjoined (*verfügt*), ordered, distributed in the two directions of absence, at the articulation of what is no longer and what is not yet. To join and enjoin. This thinking of the jointure is also a thinking of injunction.[40]

Time is out of joint. This is Heidegger's insight in *Being and Time*, that we are outside ourselves, always projecting into the future, being-there-alongside the present and being always already there of the past. These are the three ecstasies of time. For Heidegger in Anaximander's fragment, *Dike* should be translated not as right/justice but as 'joining, adjoining, adjustment, articulation of accord or harmony, *Fug, Fuge (Die Fuge is der Fug)*. . . *Adikia* to the contrary: it is at once what is disjointed, undone, twisted and out of line, in the wrong of the injust, or even in the error of stupidity.'[41] Thus, for time to be out of joint, to be untimely is intimately connected with *Dike*, with justice. To be out of joint is at once to be untimely and unjust. It is the very untimeliness which shows us the injustice (Hamlet's dead father is the untimely figure of injustice). That the time is out of joint shows us that '[t]he world is going badly . . . The age is off its hinges. Everything, beginning with time, seems to be out of kilter, unjust, disadjusted.'[42] Injustice calls from the past, it returns to demand action. We are haunted by the past and this haunting cannot be exorcized: 'a spectre is always *revenant*. One cannot control its comings and goings because it *begins by coming back*.'[43]

For Derrida, the ghost is a way of re-opening every attempted closure. The editor of *Spectres of Marx* opens the text with a direct reference to the 'closure' of communism of 1989. Derrida's long-awaited engagement with Marx, and politics in general, comes in the form of a discourse on traces and comes at a time when communism was being claimed to be 'exorcized' from the world. Derrida is suspicious of this closure and so follows the logic set out by Marx in the *Manifesto*. He demands that one can never be exorcized of one's ghosts. A ghost, a revenant, begins by coming back in an always untimely fashion. The ghost is the only one that cannot be killed. It cannot even be exorcized, because it will always haunt with the *possibility* of return. It 'never dies, it remains always to come and to come-back.'[44] This logic of revenance is of the utmost importance if we are to conceive of the people:

> At bottom the spectre is the future, it is always to come, it presents itself only as that which could come or come back; in the future, said the powers of old Europe in the last century, it must not incarnate itself, either publicly or in secret. In the future, we hear everywhere today, it must not re-incarnate itself; it must not be allowed to come back since it is past.[45]

The ghost is a tradition inherited from the past, but it is always to return, always to come. The people is this ghostly figure. It haunts constituted power with the possibility of its return.

On this view, the people is a threat to constituted power. It is not a stable, given, present, collection of all the people in a state which give legitimacy to the constituted order. In absolute contradistinction to Hobbes, the people is not the stable unity that emerges out of the multitude through the institution of sovereignty. This is an ideological fallacy necessitated by contractarian thought. The people is not vested in the king, but rather it is *the threat* of constituent power to the constituted. This is also different from Lindahl's paradigm, which places us in the time of constituted power, looking backwards and attributing ourselves to the constituent people. Lindahl's view allows us to see how the revolutionary mob becomes a people, it explains how a disparate grouping becomes the unity necessary to legitimize the new order. There is a self-attributive regression to the constituent moment where 'I' take up the 'We' of the constitution's creation. The people as a hauntological supplement inverts this. 'We' do not project ourselves backward, but rather the revolutionary people haunts us with the call to change, to action and to constituent power. The being of constituent power is in the possibility of the to-come. With Lindahl, the people is more than an agglomeration of the citizens and denizens, more than the subjects collected under sovereignty as per Hobbes. It is not simply the bare fact of a collection of individuals. The people is a spectral supplement. It is temporally displaced. Revenance is the mode of the people, it is always to come (back). The people is not the stable given unity under a politico-legal order, rather it is the ethereal call to constituent power, it is the promise that things could be otherwise.

This inversion allows us to view the revolutionary problem of authority differently. The people in their *constituent power* are spectral because we can only 'call them forth' in revolutionary practice, but the legitimacy that the people would convey is always uncertain, until the revolutionary moment has passed. Thus, we are never certain that the people is present (in its legitimizing of otherwise illegal revolt) until it has already gone, until the revolution has passed. Lindahl terms this the 'alegal':

> acts that create legal orders cannot themselves be a part thereof. Indeed, the founding acts of legal order are themselves *neither legal nor illegal* because

both terms of this binary opposition already presuppose a legal order as the condition for their intelligibility. Instead, foundational acts are *a*legal: they institute the distinction itself between legality and illegality.[46]

In Lindahl's sense, constituent power remains unintelligible to the legal order. This is the problem in Hamlet: should we believe the ghost, is it a good or bad spirit? It could be that it is an evil spirit playing on Hamlet's mental instability, or it could be Hamlet's dead father, an 'honest ghost'. There can be no warranty for the people: is it merely a disturbance or is it an exercise of the power of those who decide on the form of state?[47] The spectre of the people is always in doubt. Yet even when constituted, the people remains uncertain, never complete.

Perhaps more importantly when the alegal act of constituent power is normalized by the constituted order, 'the alegal foundation of a polity catches up with it from behind by announcing itself from up front – from the future.'[48] The people is called forth again in the struggle constitutive of political agonism:

> The *agon* refers, in legal terms, to the ever-present possibility of alegal behaviour, to a form of behaviour that is not merely disorderly by dint of being illegal, but which also contests the orderliness of the law itself by revealing the residual groundlessness of what that order calls (il)legality. In other words, struggle is the overt manifestation of the irreducible contingency of legal orders. Moreover, to the extent that in the foundation of legal order has a residual alegality that never entirely disappears, so also political struggle is ineluctable: no legal order can succeed in stabilizing itself definitively.[49]

The people is always to-come, always to-come back, always to return.

The second aspect of this temporality, is the manner in which the people is called forth in an exercise of a constituting moment. This is the liminal moment, the signing of the declaration which creates the people. I have looked at this through Lindahl's retroactive attribution, but Derrida's *Declarations of Independence* clarifies the moment of constitution beautifully. In a sense, many of Derrida's most political texts are variations on the theme that 'the revolution is not present to itself'. From the early *Declarations of Independence* (1976; hereinafter, *Declarations*) through *Spectres of Marx* (1993) and even in the later *Rogues: Two Essays on Reason* (2003), each demonstrates Derrida's constant and careful consideration of radical change. In *Declarations,* addressing the American Declaration of Independence, Derrida addresses the seminal question: '*who signs, and with what so-called proper name, the declarative act which founds an institution?*'[50] At the heart of the question lies the authority of the constitution. The problem for Derrida is who may sign this creation, how does the together establish itself as such: 'Who is the signer of such acts?' How can signatories be authorized to sign, and what makes their signature effective? This question is central if we are to consider the texts of revolution. Derrida begins by using Austin's distinction between a constative (descriptive discourse which conveys knowledge) and a performative speech act (which 'does what it says it does').[51] He claims that the intentional structure of the declaration is to perform that which is declared. However, this throws up the problem of the author/signer of this performative. 'The declaration which founds an institution, a constitution or a State requires that a signer engage him- or herself. The signature maintains a link with the instituting act, as an act of language and of writing. . . .'[52] The signatories sign both for themselves and 'for' others. They act and sign in the name of the 'good people' and by their *authority*. This performative speech act, the signing, calls forth the people and in this, it authorizes itself.

The people is called forth by the declaration, the signatories sign in the name of the people:

> [B]ut this people does not exist. They do *not* exist as an entity, it does *not* exist, *before* this declaration, not *as such*. If it gives birth to itself, as free and independent subject, as possible signer, this can hold only in the act of signature. The signature invents the signer. This signer can only authorize him- or herself to sign once he or she has come to the end, if one can say this, of his or her own signature, in a sort of fabulous retroactivity. That first signature authorizes him or her to sign.[53]

The people comes into existence, as the people, when it signs its name through the representatives. It is a 'fabulous retroactivity'. Yet how are the representatives representing something that does not exist? 'In signing, the people say – and do what they say they do, but in differing or deferring themselves through [*différant par*] the intervention of their representatives whose representativity is fully legitimated only by signature, thus after the fact of the coup.'[54] The people is performed, but this performance contains the *différance* of the signatories and the people. The people is performed but remains temporally and spatially other to the signature. The representatives, in 'fabulous retroactivity', legitimate their signature by their signature. *The people comes into being by being declared to declare.*

The people comes to presence, as the people, retroactively. This is very close to Lindahl's 'retroactive attribution'. However, while Lindahl's schema is concerned with the status of the constituent rupture for constituted order, in Derrida's *Declarations*, the people is a precarious supplement, there at the moment of signature. While the retroactive attribution in Lindahl does not provide a certainty, in the sense of guaranteeing the people, there is often an inevitability in its emergence. With Derrida, there is no certainty. We are dealing with traces and ethereal haunting presences. The people is a futural possibility at the moment of signature. It is called forth but it cannot be guaranteed by the Declaration. In this constituent moment, the people haunts. It is declared to declare, but there is no certainty that it will have declared. The revolutionary actor performs/shares (*partager*) the *possibility* and *potentiality* of the people. But in the constituent moment this remains a potentiality, which as we saw through Agamben previously, is only potential so long as it both may or may not be actualized. The Declaration depends on Lindahl's retroactive attribution to be true. This is what I described with Agnoletto's 'We'. There, Agnoletto set in motion a truth process that is ultimately verified or not. At the moment of its iteration it stands as a call to others to join him in the 'We'.

Importantly, Derrida's retroactivity does not deny a revolutionary subject before the signature, but rather rejects that it should be 'enclosed' as the people. The *assertion* of the people in the Declaration is an open call. As such, the people is never present to itself. The people, to the extent that it is conceived as a unity, is shared [*partager* – which also means divided up] between those who act together in its name, or better, those who perform its name and thus call it forth. However, it cannot be reduced to this alone, rather it is always supplemented temporally (both in its historicity: the haunting presence of those before – and in its *revenance*: that it is always to-come back). The people is the *sharing* by each revolutionary actor of the constituent *potentia* of the together, the community. But there is no enclosed totality here, the community is open to the becoming of the constituent. The question Derrida sees is really that of right, the people is nothing other than an appeal to right:

> There was no signer, *by right,* before the text of the Declaration which itself remains the producer and guarantor of its own signature. By this fabulous event, by this fable which implies the structure of the trace and is only in truth possible thanks to the inadequate to itself of a present, a signature gives itself a name.[55]

The Declaration is something of a fable, but it has the trace of truth. It becomes true when it is taken as truth after the fact, when it is continued to be performed in the independence of the colonies and in the foundation of its institutions. So long as we understand it entirely in terms of the present, the Declaration is a ridiculous fiction. But the present is inadequate to itself. Only when we temporalize the Declaration does the signature make sense. The signature authorizes itself after the fact. In the moment of signing the Declaration is the trace of the future authority of the Declaration. Yet Derrida argues that it is not even this simple. The Declaration is not just the moment that allows the fabulous retroactivity of the future. It is the moment of auto-authorization – the moment when the people come forth in their (ghostly) totality. The establishment itself, the performative element, is incomplete as it must be taken up along the way. Those who come after the Declaration must accept it as truth, the declaration of independence must continue to be performed.

The people is temporally different from itself, that is, it is never entirely present to itself. It involves a number of projections, returns, assertions and performances. The people could not, therefore, take possession of itself and in an auto-authorizing motion, guarantee its own action constituting a new authorized power. This fantasy is essentially an attempt to justify and authorize constituent power precisely by not thinking about its *openness*. Constituent power is 'open' because its conclusion is not determined in advance, nor is it somehow legislated for in its exercise. The myth of the fully present people is an attempt to close the constituent. It places constituted power as the necessary end of the constituent in a betrayal of the mediality of constituent power, as introduced in the last chapter. The *différance* of the people from itself is crucial.

A second deconstruction of the people is presented by Jacques Rancière's theme of the *sans-part*. However, to begin, I want to return to Hobbes. I suggested in the opening section that Hobbes explains his idea of the people by denigrating the views of '[t]he common sort of men, and others who little consider these truths'. These fools, he said, 'do alwayes speak of a *great number* of men, as of the *People*, that is to say, the *City*; they say that the *City* hath rebelled against the *King* (which is impossible) and that the *People* will, and nill, what murmuring and discontented Subjects would have, or would not have, under pretence of the *People*, stirring up the *Citizens* against the *City*, that is to say, the *Multitude* against the *People*.'[56] Through their silence, Virno and Negri join Hobbes in the denigration of this second opinion, instead, taking up Hobbes' version as that against which the multitude is constructed. Yet there remains a fundamental difference within the people that this dismissal gets at. Hobbes acknowledges another usage of the people, although he dismisses it. The passage actually hinges on whether there is a difference between the city and the king. The reason Hobbes must claim that the city cannot rebel against the king is that for him it marks a chain of signification: city–people–king. The city–people rebelling against the king is impossible only because of the identity of the king–people. This other understanding, a 'common sort of' understanding, associates the people with the city but not with the king. Where the king stands for unity, this understanding of the city implies a space of multiplicity, as well as the loose collection of those within its walls. Hobbes dismisses this other idea of the people and so it remains only a trace in his works, but I want to underline the difference.

Agamben sees this trace quite clearly. The people traditionally refers to the totality of those under the state (the Hobbesean view), but this must be supplemented, in what Agamben calls a biopolitical split, with the sense of the people as the poor or excluded 'common' people:

> [O]n the one hand, the *People* as a whole and as an integral body politic and, on the other hand, the *people* as a subset and as fragmentary multiplicity of needy and excluded bodies; on the one hand, an inclusive concept that pretends to be without remainder while, on the other hand, an exclusive concept known to afford no hope; at one pole, the total state of the sovereign and integrated citizens and, at the other pole, the banishment – either court of miracles or camp – of the wretched, the oppressed, and the vanquished.[57]

He distinguishes the two senses of the people through capitalization, while simultaneously fitting them to his paradigm of the *homo sacer*: the people (small 'p') is the suffering ordinary people or *zoe*, included in the political only by way of their exclusion: the People (note the capital 'P') is the people of sovereignty and power, it is *bios* for Agamben. 'The concept of people always already contains within itself the fundamental biopolitical fracture. It is what cannot be included in the whole of which it is a part as well as what cannot belong to the whole in which it is always already included.'[58] He argues that we can trace certain genealogies of the two concepts: the Roman distinction between the *populus* and the *plebs*, and the *popolo minuto* (artisans) and the *popolo grasso* (merchants) of the Middle Ages. From the French Revolution, where the People become sovereign, the *people* become an embarrassment, and so '[t]he economism and "socialism" that seem to dominate modern politics actually have a political, or, rather, a *biopolitical*, meaning.'[59] The goal of both is thus the elimination of *people* and the production of 'one single and undivided people . . . without fracture'.[60] However, this is always a false drive, he asserts, as where there is a *People* there must necessarily be *people* who are excluded. I will come back to the importance of this split in Chapter 8 when I deal with biopolitics; for now I want to propose the significance of this for a deconstruction of the people (equally I will discard Agamben's capitalization of the people as a means of distinguishing 'the ordinary people' from 'the people of sovereignty').

Rancière makes use of this split in the people in a radical fashion. The first point to note is his political framework, from which the sense of the people emerges: Rancière emphasizes that politics occurs not in the everyday micropolitics of Westminster or Washington, but rather in the disruption of the everyday course of things. This interruption is rare and revolutionary in its outlook. Hewlett explains:

> True politics exists when there is a popular uprising of a particular type, when the *sans-part* revolt and disrupt the status quo by asserting their right to be equal with all others. This direct challenge to the unjust status quo itself takes the form of a declaration of radical equality on the part of the excluded and is necessarily just.[61]

Politics, therefore, is not everyday, it occurs rarely when 'the part of no part' ruptures the everyday sense of the political and demands equality in a radical sense. Hewlett then quotes from Rancière:

> Politics exists where the count of parts of society is disturbed by the assertion of a part of those who have no part. It begins when equality of anyone with anyone else is declared as being liberty of the people . . . those who are nothing assert that they are collectively identical to the whole of the community.[62]

Rancière terms the everyday order the 'police'. This is the established order and should not be associated directly with a particular arm of the state. 'The police is not a social function but a symbolic constitution of the social. The essence of the police is neither repression nor even control over the living. Its essence is a certain manner of partitioning the sensible.'[63] It is the 'police' 'in the classical sense of the term, that is, prudent administration of interests of the governed by rational governors.'[64] The everyday politics of the police order is a process of counting, of managing who and what counts, and the manner in which they count. In the international realm, this can literally be seen with the strategic and legitimatory fixation of the west on the horrors of Halabja and the incessant counting of those murdered there. This is then to be put beside the refusal to count the Iraqi deaths since the beginning of the invasion and occupation and more recently the deaths due to Turkish incursions in northern Iraq. In this, the very same citizens are counted or not counted by the very order of everyday politics. The *demos*, the poor or the *sans-part* 'does not designate a socially inferior category', rather the 'one who speaks when s/he is not to speak, the one who part-takes in what s/he has no part in – that person belongs to the *demos*.'[65] The politics/police dichotomy is literally a process of valuing, a question of the *sens* (sense) of the in-common. The police determine what and who may be heard.[66] They operate to distribute the sensible. '[T]he distribution of the sensible sets the divisions between what is visible and invisible, sayable and unsayable, audible and inaudible. It functions like a Kantian categorical framework that determines what can be thought, made or done.'[67]

Everyday politics of the police order is an aesthetic distribution of what is sensible.[68] It should not surprise us then that it is the poor, the excluded, those who are only a part by means of their exclusion, that provide the interruption of the banality of the everyday. Politics (proper) is an exceptional event, it is not everyday:[69]

> The struggle between rich and poor is not social reality, which politics then has to deal with. It is the actual institution of politics itself. There is politics when there is a part of those who have no part, a part or party of the poor. Politics does not happen just because the poor oppose the rich . . . Politics exists when the natural order of domination is interrupted by the institution of a part of those who have no part. This institution is the whole of politics as a specific form of connection. It defines the common of the community, in other words, as divided, as based on a wrong that escapes the arithmetic of exchange and reparation. Beyond this set-up there is no politics. There is only the order of domination or the disorder of revolt.[70]

The *sans-part* are part of the system only in so far as they are excluded, a part of no part.[71] Politics, Rancière tells us, is the speech act of declaring that the *sans-part* is 'collectively identical to the whole of the community'. The conditions of comprehension of the *sans-part* are created in the political (revolutionary) moment of the performative speech act: '[S]ubjects must believe in their actions and statements and make them true by creating the revolutionizing criteria by which they are judged.'[72]

This is what I have been describing as the difference of the people. It is the revolutionary cry of 'We are nothing, let us be everything', it is the claim to the totality: '[I]n protesting the wrong they suffered, they also presented themselves as the immediate embodiment of society as such, as the stand-in for the Whole of Society in its universality, against the particular power interests of the aristocracy or oligarchy.'[73]

> The 'people' that is the subject of democracy – and thus the principal subject of politics – is not the collection of members in a community, or the labouring classes of the population. It is the supplementary part, in relation to any counting of parts of the population that makes it possible to identify 'the part of those who have no-part [*le compte des incomptés*] with the whole of the community.[74]

The people of sovereignty (or the police in Rancière) is supplemented by the people of politics. This supplement, like the Derridean trace, interrupts the given logics that it haunts. The people is thus the very name of the totality under the state, and 'the supplement that disconnects the population from itself, by suspending the various logics of legitimate domination . . . The "people" is the supplement that inscribes "the count of the unaccounted-for" or "the part of those who have no part".'[75] The subject of this politics is not the reified subject, not the 'proletariat, the poor, or minorities. On the contrary, the only possible subject of politics is the *people* or the *demos*, i.e. the supplementary part of every account of the population.'[76] The people is different from itself. The supplementary people opens once more onto the question of authorization and constituent power.

The people is defined in Hobbes as the collection of everyone in the sense that they *are* the sovereign. In international human rights the people is bound together (in a fusion with the concept of nation) ethnically, racially, by language or some such commonality. These naturalistic and positivistic conceptions neuter the people, rendering it the subject and object of sovereignty. As such, it is capable of both having its own borders policed and acting on itself to generate its own essence. It self-determines, in the most closed and empty of senses. This is the people, conceived through immanentism as I will show in the next chapter or of Agamben's biopolitical sovereignty as I will examine in Chapter 8. This people is rendered through the authority of the constituted order. However, as I have argued in the last two chapters, the constituent and constituted are different. The constituent must be understood in its essence, that is, as utterly distinct from the constituted. In Chapter 4, I argued that Sieyès and Kant folded the constituent into the constituted. In Chapter 5, I argued that the constituent could be seen in a very different, more open light through Sorel, Benjamin and Bataille. That is, as a 'means without end'. Here, I have argued that the people, in a differential sense, can be understood as both the 'people of sovereignty' but also as a claim of the not-all, as a displacement in temporality and presence. The people haunts, but this temporal deferral occurs through the difference of presence.

However, in this, much remains unthought. It is certainly very far from a thinking of constituent power *with* human rights. To take a banal example, human rights have always refused to understand rights through any prism other than the individual. Group rights are understood as a collection of individuals exercising their rights together. The starting point must always be the one, to which others are added. However, constituent power, by its nature, must always *begin* with two. It is a power of association. This is crucial. In human rights law, the right to association is never a right of the association, unless that association becomes a one (i.e. it incorporates or at least is regulated as an entity, like a union). The tension between constituent power and human rights lies at the very basis of their philosophical structures. The challenge, therefore, is to begin to think about both human rights and constituent power differently. I propose that one possibility is to use the philosophy of Martin Heidegger, and the (mainly) French post-Heideggerians to rework some of the grounding assumptions of human rights and constituent power. Therefore, to begin this task in the next two chapters, I propose to examine the ontology of being-together and the question of biopolitics and sovereignty.

Chapter 7

On being-together: beyond the subject of human rights

In order not to presuppose the subject [in the political], it will be necessary, [Nancy and Lacoue-Labarthe] claim, to problematize the very notion of the 'social bond'. For that notion has always been thought as a relationship among previously constituted subjects.

Fraser, 'The French Derrideans'[1]

In Chapter 3, I highlighted that the problem of the individual in human rights discourse remains critical although problematic. I argued that the 'possessive individual' of human rights tends to render the subject as a closed entity. The problem with the individual is fundamental. It cannot be solved by inverting a hierarchy of value from individual to community, society or state. The question of the individual is not simply a priority within a field of political choices, as though it is possible to decide whether one was on the side of the individual or the community. Yet this is how (neo)liberalism and (neo)conservatism demand that political theory be divided. The basis of the individual lies in the very question of the subject, that is, on a metaphysical level. To think differently about human rights it would be necessary to think again about the human *being*.

What makes human rights so enticing is at the same time what makes them potentially so problematic; the conjunction between the human *being* and the political. The closure of the subject renders human rights closed to the possibilities of human *being*. However, I argue that by engaging again with the ontological question of human there-ness, it is possible to think differently about this enticing conjunction. The challenge for this chapter is to engage with and set out a different thinking which escapes the atomistic subject while still seeking to think that conjunction between human *being* and the political. To this end, I propose to return to Heidegger and to supplement him with Jean-Luc Nancy. I want to develop and draw out the question of being-together as a 'starting point' for human rights. Importantly, this chapter should be seen as a continuation of the concerns from the deconstruction of the people, but also, as the beginning of a distinct connection between human rights and constituent power. In this chapter, I want to suggest that the ontology of being-together provides an alternative framework for thinking this connection. From it we can begin to re-treat the radical pole of human rights based upon the open sense of constituent power seen in Chapters 5 and 6.

Heidegger's *Volk*

At the end of Chapter 3, I underlined the problems of the metaphysics of human rights with two themes; the subject and temporality. For Heidegger these critiques of humanism were fatal. In the 'Letter on Humanism' he argued that humanism was philosophically over-determined and prefigured – that there remained no escape from the closure of the subject within it.[2] Alongside this critique, in Chapter 3 I also presented an exposition of Heidegger's different understanding of human being, which did not simply repeat the *res cogitans* and *res extentia* dichotomy so prevalent since Descartes. I will now draw on this in order to develop the sense of being-together that can challenge the hegemonic thinking of the individual.[3] I am ultimately interested in *mitsein* (being-with), but the problem with being-with is that it is the site of both authenticity *and* inauthenticity. In the everyday, being is forgotten. However, it is also in the everyday that being comes to presence. In togetherness, being is (un)veiled. The problem with *mitsein* is thus that it is structured through authenticity. In this section, I want to trace how this leads Heidegger to the deeply problematic figure of the *Volk*.

The question of inauthenticity is crucial in *Being and Time*. *Dasein* exists through a constant play of authenticity and inauthenticity. In Chapter 3, I explained that *dasein* begins as always already fallen, always already enmeshed in the inauthenticity of togetherness. In this everydayness, Heidegger suggested that *dasein* loses its way and forgets to ask the fundamental question as to the being of beings. He uses *das Man* to explain the manner in which we flee from asking of our being and thereby constantly fall into inauthenticity. The problem that Heidegger approaches with the figure of *das Man* is nihilism. It is the manner in which 'the light of the public obscures everything'.[4] This figure levels down all existence to a banal monotony in which sense itself is withdrawn. Based on this, some have leapt to suggest that by simply being-together we become inauthentic, whereas it is somehow from the 'self' that authenticity is revealed.[5] This is then read as necessitating a political individualism.[6] However, this reading of authenticity is deeply problematic. Heidegger remains clear throughout regarding the co-originariness of being-with (*mitsein*) and being-there (*dasein*).

Once we discount this selective reading, the question becomes about his sense of an authentic being-together. In the second part of *Being and Time*, we find the suggestion that this occurs in the *Volk*.[7] However, already here we are onto dangerous ground. In *Being and Time*, the *Volk* (the 'people', the 'nation', the 'folk') is understood through the triplet of 'heritage, fate and destiny'. Heritage is the existential awareness of one's tradition as significantly determining, to some extent, the makeup of the 'world' that one is 'in' as Being-in-the-world.[8] Fate is understood as a projection of death in its negativity that allows *dasein* to escape its inauthenticity. 'Only freedom *for* death gives *Dasein* an outright goal and thrusts existence into its finitude. Once grasped, the finitude of existence wrenches *Dasein* back from the endless variety of immediate possibilities presented to it, of contentment and care-free shirking, and brings it to the simplicity of its *fate*.'[9]

Heidegger then moves from fate – an individual projection – to destiny, which is similar to fate, except for the community or the people. It is at this point that de Beistegui pinpoints the fatal flaw. While fate and heritage are both ontologically grounded, destiny is not. Heidegger seems to ground destiny in being-with-one-another,[10] but he has already precluded this because being-together is generally overcome by *das Man*. He has not yet established the possibility of authentic being-together. Thus, the only other possible support for it lies in 'our resolute-ness for definite possibilities' (that is being-towards-death). However, as de Beistegui asks, how can a community share the horizon of death in the same way as *dasein*? I will come back to this later, but it is important to note that while *dasein*'s death is its only certainty once it comes to existence, a community's death cannot be presupposed in the same manner. Individual deaths within a community cannot be understood as of the same significance for the community. Besides, Heidegger cautions against understanding community as the sum of all individuals. De Beistegui argues that at this moment of moving from fate to destiny, the analysis 'head on, blind to the consequences, precipitates itself all too hastily, all too carelessly, in[to] the abyss of steely and *völkisch* rhetoric.'[11] He argues that there is a political rather than ontological grounding of the section,[12] asking a number of rhetorical questions that lay bare the lack of support for Heidegger's jump. In particular, the question of this community which Heidegger does not seem to support ontologically: 'Where does the unity of the "we" lie? Can we say "we" in the same way in which *dasein* speaks its own singularity through the "I"?'[13] These questions remain unanswered in *Being and Time* because they have moved too far from the ontological.

The concept of destiny is critical as it is our introduction to the *Volk*, wherein Heidegger suggests authentic sociality resides. Yet this is a move that the first half of the *Being and Time* seems to reject. In producing this authentic sociality – *Volk* emerging from *Man* – the community appears to coalesce around its authentic substance. This substance cannot be given in being-towards-death, it cannot be given in authentic sociality that is not ontologically grounded. Instead, it miracu-lously appears. Every question of responsibility seems to become fixed in a deter-minate relation with an origin. Later, Heidegger himself cautions against this tendency. In 1934 he lectures:

> [T]here is no gradual and steady crossing from the unessential into the essen-tial. Each one must leap for himself; nobody can be relieved from it, not even through the ever so genuine and indispensable community. Each must himself venture the leap, if he wants to be a member of a community.[14]

However, in the 1934 lecture course (which I will come back to later), Heidegger seems to demand acceptance of the absolute subjugation of all under the state.[15] He appears to see no major contradiction between maintaining the necessity of authentic decision, while at the same time determining the state as the ultimate horizon of the *Volk*'s historical being. This is astounding because surely this is precisely the 'taking it easy' that is so important in *das Man*.

In the *Introduction to Metaphysics*, despite no longer using the term *das Man*, Heidegger says that there looms 'like a spectre over all of this uproar the question: what for? – where to? – and what then?'[16] In other words, now that time is levelled down to nothing but 'speed, instantaneity, and simultaneity ... when a boxer counts as a great man of the people; when tallies of millions at mass meetings are a triumph'[17] being is nowhere in question. This is what Heidegger calls 'the dicta-torship of the public sphere'. Interestingly, Stuart Elden argues that 'the public' or 'publicness' as a mode of thinking is ultimately a result of the Cartesian form of thinking that is based in average intelligibility. He describes the three things that cause us to forget being: 'calculation [*die Berechnung*], acceleration [*die Schnelligkeit*] and massiveness [*Massenhaften*].'[18] Elden tells us that the first term is the vital one and forms the basis of a technological thinking. Heidegger describes this calculative mode of thought:

> All calculation lets what is countable [*zählbare*] be resolved into something counted [*gezählten*] that can be used for subsequent counting [*Zählung*]. Calculation refuses to let anything appear except what is countable. Everything is only whatever counts. What has been counted in each instance secures the continuation of counting. Such counting progressively consumes numbers [*zahlen*], and is itself a continual self-consumption. The calculative process of resolving beings into what has been counted counts as the explana-tion of their being. Calculation uses all beings in advance as that which is countable, and uses up what is counted for the purposes of counting. This use of beings that consumes them betrays the consuming character of calculation. Only because number can be infinitely multiplied, irrespective of whether this occurs in the direction of the large or small, can the consuming essence of calculation hide behind its products and lend to calculative thinking the semblance of productivity – whereas already in its anticipatory grasping, and not primarily in its subsequent results, such thinking lets all beings count only in the form of what can be set at our disposal and consumed. Calculative thinking compels itself into a compulsion to master everything on the basis of the consequential correctness of its procedure.[19]

There is a key etymological association between the German term for measure *Maß* (deriving from *messen* meaning to measure or gauge, but also associated with the masses) and the fascist term for conformity, *Gemäßheit*.[20] This term was used to signify 'the removal of dangerous elements as things are brought together around a fixed measure or norm.'[21] Heidegger implicitly critiques this provision of a single way of being, a single model for one's life. That is the manner in which *das Man* operates to remove one's ownmost possibilities.

It is this calculative thinking, which sees only equivalents, that is to be critiqued in traditional understandings of the people. Ordinarily, as I explained in Chapters 3 and 6, people are rendered *as the people* by some categorical reduction: the people is all of the citizens of a state (in different ways, Kant or Kelsen); or the people is nation understood ethnically (Common Article 1 of the ICCPR/ICESCR and in some ways Schmitt), or economically (Sieyès). The problem with this process is that it makes the being-together itself operative, thereby creating an enclosure of legitimacy. The people understood by this internal logic demands criteria whereby each person may be judged to be 'of the people'. As such, people are reduced to this simple categorization.

I will come back to this sense of the people again in the next chapter where it takes on increasing importance as a critique of the logics of sovereignty. To return to Heidegger's account, however, there are two issues at stake for a political questioning of *das Man*. The first is the sense of possibility (which publicness hides) and the second is the being-together itself qua the *polis*. Heidegger begins with a caution:

> One translates *polis* as state [*Staat*] and city-state [*Staatstaat*]; this does not capture the entire sense. Rather, *polis* is the name of the site [*Stätte*], the Here, within which and as which Being-here is historically. The *polis* is the site of history, the Here, *in* which, *out* of which and *for* which history happens.[22]

The *polis* is therefore, not a question of the creation of a stable organization of the state, it is something much more fundamental. In the lecture course on Heraclites and Parmenides in 1942–43, Heidegger suggests that the *polis* is the pole of being [*pelein*].[23] In an extremely careful reading, Fried suggests that 'the *polis* as pole and as *pelein* is not a constant, secure being, a permanent political and social order, upon which some secure, objectifiable horizon of intelligibility can be erected.'[24] The political is a pole of being, a space which might 'hold open for *dasein* the possibility of confrontation and dissolution in the understanding of its world.'[25] The political *is an open space of conflict where the possibility of community is maintained.* I have already suggested that the political is this sense of possibility as distinct from everyday politics. However, Heidegger's insight is more radical even than this. He argues that the current understanding of the political, with its emphasis on 'the public sphere' and 'average intelligibility' is actually part of the problem. The problem is not how best to politically organize society, but the understanding of 'politics' and 'society' themselves. Heidegger brings us to the necessity of conceiving of the with-world in terms of the possibilities of being-together. An authentic politics is beyond his analytic, but it is clear that a conception of the political, as a clearing, is crucial.

Nevertheless, we must not simply stop there. Villa is correct to say that 'the possibility of an authentic *mitsein* (being with) opens the way to a political reading of *Being and Time*.'[26] However, she also sees that we must go beyond Heidegger to begin to find this politics. When discussing *dasein*'s fallenness, Heidegger says; 'our existential-ontological Interpretation makes no ontical assertion about the "corruption of human Nature," not because the necessary evidence is lacking, but because the problematic of this Interpretation is *prior* to any assertion about corruption or incorruption.'[27] The ontological analysis precludes *a* politics, the most we can talk about is the essence of politics – the political (as the space for the possibilities of the with-world). However, this is not the end of the story. At the end of his 1928 lecture course on Leibniz, Heidegger suggests the idea of a metontology. It is important to explain that the metontological (or meta-ontological) is not somehow above the ontological:

> [It] is not a theory of being carried out onto the 'metalevel', but it is rather an ontology fuelled by constant metabolism between being and beings. Wherever this theme is mentioned a single famous Heideggerian claim is tediously cited: namely, that metontology alone is where philosophy would be able to work out the possibility of an ethics. True enough. But if we continue to refer only to this possibility, then we rely too heavily on the accident of what Heidegger mentions.[28]

Rather, Harman suggests that metontology holds out the possibility of everything from a psychology to a politics. It collapses 'ontology back into the specific regions of life that it initially tried to surpass'.[29] However, we must be very careful with this type of analysis. It cannot simply be put into the service of *a politics*, providing an origin or foundation for a particular programme. However, it can begin to allow us to understand the political more fully. With this we can begin to work through a left-Heideggerian metontological rendering of the political, but carefully.

Villa reads Heidegger with Arendt and finds two modes of politics in *Being and Time*: rupture and authority. The first role:

> would be to shatter the tranquillity of everyday *Dasein*, to perform for the community the role that anxiety performs for the individual. Anxiety brings *Dasein* back from its absorption in the world of everyday concerns by bringing it face to face with its finitude, by confronting it with its thrown Being-in-the-world. Once *mitsein* is fully recognized as a constitutive structure of *Dasein*, and once *Dasein*'s historizing is recognized as always a cohistorizing, it follows that the community of which *Dasein* is irreducibly a part stands in need of a similarly sharp reminder of *its* radical historical finitude, of the abyss-like nature of its ground.[30]

Politics then would be the irruption of being, disrupting the givenness of political relations. However, to what extent can we seamlessly map the language of anxiety and *dasein* into the political? I would agree with Simon Critchley's argument that you cannot simply transfer the language of the ontological into a political ontology. However, this is not to say that ontology is irrelevant to politics, but, rather, without metontology we must be careful of any simple relation or transposition. Villa seems to pose this ruptural quality of death for *dasein*, in the context of the community.

Villa suggests a 'shock-treatment' that would bring community out of its inauthenticity.[31] However, as I have already said, death cannot fulfil the same function in community as it did with *dasein*. For *dasein*, death is one's ownmost possibility and is thus constitutive of authentic *dasein*, the same is not the case for a community. While one's own death is the *only* futural event of which one can be certain, the death of a community is *not certain*. Therefore a community's own finitude is not its ownmost possibility (as it is with *dasein*). The very idea of a community dying is problematic. It presumes a certain (eternal) substance at the heart of community that could be extinguished, be this nation, religion, or civilization. This notion of community is the very obverse of what we are attempting to think. In terms of *dasein*, this thought would find some substance present at its core that is precisely the thinking of the subject. The death of a community is certainly not the futural event which would lead us towards an authentic *mitsein*. De Beistegui shows us this:

> But how can a community face its own death as its ownmost possibility without imposing a peculiar kind of closure upon its singularities? From the moment at which death is inscribed as the horizon that constitutes the community as such, a certain logic is under way: it is a logic of totalization and immanence, where the existing singularities are protected against a heroic-tragic understanding of their destiny. It is the logic of sacrifice, where the plurality of existences is absorbed into the immanence of the Same.[32]

Thus, while the notion of the interruption of the everyday is certainly useful. Villa's anxiety-based conception of this rupture is not satisfactory.

Villa's second sense of the politics – authority – of *Being and Time* is also unsatisfactory. Villa asks how would we think a rupture of the banalizing function of everydayness away from a simple mapping out of the existential analytic onto the community? She says:

> Such a reminder [of community's radical historicality and finitude] – presumably performed by authentic political speech and leadership – is necessary if the community is to be called back from its absorption in everyday life and politics, and made ready for a recommitment to its 'ownmost distinctive possibility,' a possibility opened at the founding of the community but long since covered over.[33]

Of what could such a 'reminder' consist? How would one remind a community that it is inauthentic? Villa clarifies this sense: 'The second role [in *Being and*

Time for politics] follows from the first. Simply calling the community back from its "lostness" to a sense of its finitude and, thus, to resoluteness is not enough. An authentic politics must do more.'[34] Villa positions Arendt alongside Heidegger and so *authority* emerges: 'the second role reserved for authentic politics and political speech: [is] to provide the *authority* needed to guide *dasein*'s choice, an authority that can be reconciled with the demands of resolve, an authority that is neither metaphysical nor traditional.'[35] The problem is of course that authority is that which makes resolve easier. It is traditionally the very function of the they; that which allows one to say 'it was not I, it was those others who required me to.' Authority is synonymous with superior orders, reason, nature, history, or dogma. Villa argues that Heidegger's answer emphasizes the role of an authentic political leader (capable of 'spiritual legislation') to 'enable citizens to "take over" their thrownness through the recognition of a shared destiny.'[36]

Villa argues that we need an authentic leader who will allow us, through his authority, to take on our own responsibility for our being. But we must be struck here by the ease at which Heidegger himself seemed to slide from the (essentially impossible) position of an authority that does not make things easier to the approval he expresses for the *Führer* in the Rectoral Address. Negri asserts that what is most to be despised in Heidegger are the moments when he is 'absolutely inimical to any determination of the strength of the multitude'.[37] There is not any simple equation here to fascism. It is not difficult to see that there are both proximities *and* distances: the authority, spiritual legislation, and general sense of 'authenticity' all seem very close to a certain fascism. However, at the same time, the Nazi sense of authority did not call people to the responsibility for their being, neither was their racial 'authenticity' in any way close to Heidegger's anti-biologism of *das Man*.[38] However, aside even from these, Villa's Heideggerian politics is hardly a radical reworking of the political in the same way that *Being and Time* reworks philosophy. One would wonder whether it is radical at all, seeing that it tends towards political forms already in existence or this impossible authority that does not authorize but only allows authentic decisiveness.

Let me return to Heidegger again, to close the direct confrontation with his work. Agamben correctly highlights that Heidegger 'was perhaps the last philosopher to believe in good faith that the place of the *polis* (the *polos* {pole} where the conflict between concealedness and unconcealedness, between the *animalitas* and the *humanitas* of man, reigns) was still practicable, and that it was still possible for men, for a people – holding themselves in that risky place – to find their own proper historical destiny.'[39] A significant moment in this is Heidegger's 1934 lecture course entitled *Logic as the Question Concerning the Essence of Language*. This was the first course he gave following his involvement as a functionary of the Nazi Party. The course had been billed as one on 'State and Science'. When Heidegger announced the subject change during the first lecture, a number of Nazi functionaries auditing the course expressed their disappointment and apparently did not continue to attend the class.[40] It presents a number of hugely important issues and can, in some ways, be viewed as Heidegger's engagement with political ontology. At the heart of the course is a sustained engagement with the *Volk* and the state. It is precisely this that I would like to use to reach the nub of the issue with Heidegger and community.

The early sections of the lecture course appear to repeat much of what has gone before in his *oeuvre*, although in quite distinct language. However, in §13, Heidegger makes a leap that hints at what is to come. He asks about the nature of the 'We', not as a simple collection (a numeric understanding, he says) but in terms of its selfhood. The question is 'Who are we ourselves?' Suddenly, Heidegger suggests a chain of signification:

> We, who we are now here [in the classroom], as we bluntly pronounce our present and local *Dasein*, are involved in the happening of education of a school, which ought to be the University of Academic Education. We subordinate ourselves to the demands of this education, prepare ourselves for vocations, whose practice is grounded in a knowledge characteristic of each . . . As we are fitted [*eingefügt*] in these demands of the University, we will the will of a State, which itself wills to be nothing else than the sovereign will of the government and the form of the government of a *Volk* over itself. We as *Dasein* submit ourselves [*fügen uns*] in a peculiar manner into the membership of the *Volk*, we stand in the being of the *Volk*, we are this *Volk* itself.[41]

Heidegger's method of taking ideas, turning them over and then rendering them crucial or problematic obscures the matter here. He seems to move away from the state too quickly for this brief flash to be significant. Nevertheless, the chain or circle of signification is clear in what he said. The subjection here is crucial. Away from all of the decisionism that we find elsewhere in the lecture course, Heidegger seems to grant a metaphysical stature to the state through its association with the *Volk*.

However, Heidegger moves beyond this idea quickly (although he does come back to it again) and suggests that 'the We . . . determines itself only in the decision. Now we see that the We is more than something that is merely nugatory: the We is no pushing together of persons into a mere sum, the We is a decision-like one. *How* the We is, respectively, is dependent upon our decision, assuming that we decide.'[42] He considers 'decision', which he places in terms of history. History is not the objective understanding of what happened, but rather *lore*. That is, it is what *lives* in history for the *dasein*. History in this sense is not simply for the present and the past, but also for the future. It is not history as an object, but rather being-historical: 'being-historical is nothing that one carries around with oneself like a hat; it is rather a deciding that is continually renewing between history and unhistory in which we stand.'[43] He argues that the *Volk*, at once, makes history but also is made by history: 'A *Volk* carries its history before itself in its willing and yet, on the other hand, is carried by history . . . the *Volk* enters into history, as it steps out of it.'[44] In this sense, it is constituted by the past, but also futural. Its

futurality opens the determinacy of the past. The past becomes not a closed determinate system generating pre-given answers, instead it provides the space from
which to leap out into the future. Thus, in typical mode, Heidegger gives us three
'assignments': 'Mandate – future; mission – beenness [past]; labour – present.'[45]
This threefold structure is the manner in which the *Volk* is temporal. Mandate and
mission are relatively straightforward in the sense of history that is not past or
present orientated, but rather future oriented.

In §28, seemingly from nowhere, Heidegger makes a turn back on himself.
Returning to §13's positing of the state:

> The State is the historical being of the Volk . . . The *Volk* is neither that
> spongy and jelly-like sentimentalism . . . nor is the State only the present shut
> down form of organisation, as it were, of a society. The State *is* only insofar
> and as long as the carrying out of the will of rule happens, which originates
> from mission and mandate and, conversely, becomes labour and work . . . All
> overcoming of the genuine and non-genuine tradition must [go] in the crucible
> of the critique of historical resoluteness. That applies last but not least to the
> title that shall characterize the formation of our historical being, of 'socialism'.
> It means no mere changing of the economic mentality; it does not mean a
> dreary egalitarianism and glorification of that which is inadequate. It does not
> mean the random pursuit of an aimless common welfare, but it means the
> care about the standards and the essential-jointure of our historical being and
> it wills, therefore, the hierarchy according to occupation and work, it wills the
> untouchable honour of every labour, it wills the unconditionality of service as
> the fundamental relationship with the inevitability of being.[46]

Heidegger's *Volk* is fundamentally implicated in fascism in an inescapable
fashion. We decide to be the *Volk* and in this decision we make an authentic leap.
In the labour of the state, we subject ourselves to the government which apparently 'itself wills to be nothing else than the sovereign will of the government and
the form of the government of a *Volk* over itself.' The *Volk* emerges from its spiritual mission into the form of the state. It is then the state that imposes itself on the
people in the name of being. With this, servitude to the state *becomes* authenticity.
Through this subjection, the same authority of the state is emphasized. The state
is sutured to authenticity, but what of those who decide against? Well, that would
be an inauthentic decision, surely. In other words, we have already gone too far
with Heidegger when we enter into his idea of the people. But what remains
without it?

In the left-Heideggerian literature, the attempt to rethink Heidegger's analytic
focuses upon the re-opening of the space of the political. It rejects the empty decisionism of the second half of *Being and Time* and the emphasis on authority/
authenticity, all of which is synthesized in the *Volk*. The *Führer* is the ultimate
expression of this utter failure of thought as Lacoue-Labarthe said. Fascism did
exactly what Heidegger warned of – among a great number of utter failures – it

made death present in the political community, mobilizing fear rather than anxiety. The death of the other became a proximate and present death. Fascism was the rule of the *everyday* (of *das Man*) as an *absolute authority*. It drew all together in an absolute unity under the state. It produced sacrificial others which were used in an attempt to cohere the unity of the *Volk*. It was, in Nancy's words, the 'grotesque or abject resurgence of an obsession with communion'.[47]

The *Volk* is to be rejected. It hermetically seals the human being from its own becoming. However, the question named by the *Volk* (in Heidegger at least) can be transposed to a number of other terms. It is not just 'people' or 'folk' but community, or being-together. It is the challenge to think togetherness against the subject. The traditional thinking, of which human rights is exemplary, begins with the 'one' (the individual, the subject, etc.) and then adds another and another. The challenge here is to think the two (a we, a ye or a them) before or at the same time as the one. That is, to think the (being-)with as equally originary to the (being-) there. There is no lonely monadic subject who 'discovers' others in the field of vision or touch. The *dasein* is with another in the very instant in which it is there.

However, increasingly in 'community' there are notes of the metaphysical: the many religious communities (the *umma*, the various Christian communions); the multiple national or 'racial' communities (*hinutva* and *hindu rashtra* or the Nazi use of Aryanism); or even the (quasi-)statist or economic communities (the European Community or various 'free trade communities'). Community increasingly becomes burdened and over-determined by the metaphysical. Of crucial importance then is the manner in which the metaphysical manifests itself. By asserting the (metaphysical) 'essence' of the community, it is possible to draw its border. In this 'community' is a process (even a technology) of inclusion/exclusion, rather than a fundamental being-together. This is what Heidegger's *Volk* leads to. When the logic of authenticity is transposed into the process of sublation under a state, it becomes the manner of determining the proper makeup of the people. Despite everything, Heidegger's thinking of *dasein* and its 'responsibility for the being that it itself is' becomes just another manner of determining the people of the state. With Schmitt then, the people is in the state of being-the-people, before the creation of a state.[48] It becomes the cause of the state and holds that constituent power to recreate the state that it itself already *is*. However, with this, the openness of being-with is already lost. From *mitsein* to the community of the *Volk*, we find the application of a border: the *delimitation* of who is proper to the community, who *belongs* within its confines and who *belongs properly* outside. This is the logic of the sovereign.[49] However, this is *precisely* the logic that must be challenged. Community is not necessarily that which puts itself to work in the generation of its own border. Rather there are two poles of being-together, what Nancy calls communion and community. This should be read as both a continuation of the concern expressed in this section and also as a fundamental break. The question remains that of being-together in late capitalist society. However, with the shift in theorist there is no pure authentic being-together, but rather a constant play of authenticity and inauthenticity.

The people, the political and community

The question of the *Volk* is one of how to gather a community of authenticity. At this stage it is worth beginning to reformulate the question of community. Iris Marion Young frames the problem:

> Racism, ethnic chauvinism and class devaluation, I suggest, grow partly from the desire for community . . . practically speaking, such mutual understanding can be approximated only within a homogenous group that defines itself by common attributes. Such common identification, however, entails reference also to those excluded. In the dynamics of racism and ethnic chauvinism in the United States today the positive identification of some groups is often achieved by first defining other groups as the other, the devalued, semi-human.[50]

Jean-Luc Nancy proposes two horizons of being-together or community: 'communion' and 'community'. Communion is the projection of a community conceived in terms of a unity. In its purest fashion, it demands that the 'Self' *joins* with the 'Other' in an expression of unification. This is a dream of *fusion* of individuals, and the projection of what he calls an 'immanentist' politics. Community, by the same token, is made up of difference. There is no unity of what is properly called 'community'. Nancy briefly sketches a classic temporality in the emergence of 'community': first, a pre-modern past that is entirely out of reach:

> *Gesellschaft* (society) . . . has taken the place of something for which we have no name or concept, something that issued at once from a much more extensive communication than that of a mere social bond (a communication with gods, the cosmos, animals, the dead, the unknown) *and* from much more piercing and dispersed segmentation of this same bond, often involving much harsher effects (solitude, rejection, admonition, helplessness) than what we expect from a communitarian minimum in the social bond.[51]

This is no long past utopia, neither is it a nasty and brutish time of one against all. It is neither violent nor peaceful anarchy; rather, we cannot name or conceive of it. As such we cannot return to it, it is utterly past and beyond us. All rhetorics of a return to this past ultimately are from within the logic of society, they are essentially projections of the now. What we *do* know about this past is that it is destroyed by 'society' – 'a disassociating association of forces, needs and signs'.[52] It is with society that Nancy's analysis really begins.

We are in the epoch of 'society' and from that we project the horizon of community. However, the ultimate projected 'end' of society is communion. Communion is more than mere unity, it is the end (*telos*) of *immanentism*. It forms the horizon of meaning of those metaphysical politics that take an essence at their heart. This essence is equally the soul, dignity, reason, production, or race. These metaphysical essences are the projected end of politics (that is, something to be worked towards, to be produced) but they are also a manner of measuring the present. The present is measured against the *telos* (end) and found to be wanting. Therefore, the present is worked on in order to produce the end:

> Nancy's constant resistance to 'essentialist' structures is, at least in part, a response to the paradoxical effects of the 'ends' they programme. The elevation of an eidetic predicate, supposed to define the generically 'human', projects a teleological horizon regulating the factical 'empiricity' subordinated to it. The paradox is that the end (*telos*) can only be the end (*finis*), the ideal-regulative positioning of this *telos* programming an infinite 'progress' towards the suppression of the separation ('essence'/'fact') upon which it nevertheless relies.[53]

The unification of all at the end, through the suppression of the difference between the real and the ideal, is the work of communion. The process is relatively straightforward: an essence of community is drawn down and metaphysically placed as the fundamental element of community (as above production, humanity, race, etc.). However, the key to this essence is that it is not actually manifested. It must be worked towards: a humanity fit to be called human, a working class fit to be called a working class, an Aryan fit to be called an Aryan must be *produced*. Thus, the essence is blindingly obvious in the now, it is all one sees around. However, it is also patently obvious that the essence is not manifested and so it must be worked for and produced. Thus, one sacrifices the difference between the now and the ideal and makes sacrifices within the now for the ideal. These sacrifices to the ideal, however, do not allow it to be created. Rather, because the world exceeds the ideal in each instance, it is this excess itself (the sheer multiplicity of difference) that is sacrificed in each instance. In truth, if these ends (*telos*, ideal) were ever to be reached, it would be an end (*finis*, death) to the community because the purification of the differences (from the essential/ideal) requires the destruction of difference, that is, the death of each singular being. This seems like a very bold statement but we will see that the work of communion is fundamentally the work of death.

There is no *dasein* without difference. Difference is the *sine qua non* of existence. Difference is destroyed in communion, by each adhering to the absolute essence. The 'immanentist' logic of communion is therefore the attempt to sacrifice difference(s):

> [A]ny community founded upon the supposedly universal substantiality of a 'common being' and projecting its own supra-particular unity . . . is first and foremost logically sacrificial, binding its particulars to the essential substantiality of a generality into who immanent *en-soi* they should, in principle, already have been absorbed. The 'transcendent' position of a 'common being' thus lays the logical foundation of which a certain figure of 'sacrifice' is the necessarily failing phenomenalism.[54]

Thus, sacrifice sacrifices difference.[55] Communion is, unsurprisingly, the final phase of sacrifice. However, communion is impossible, because there is no existence, no being, without its differentiation.

A clear instance of the logic of communion is Christian: God is transcendental only insofar as He suspends the point where each person, in death, joins with every other person (communion). Each time a Catholic 'takes communion' through the transubstantiated bread/body of Christ, he communes with others in the breaking of the bread/body. Of course, this is only a momentary and passing communion. Death then presents an absolute communion. Communion is thus originally the absolute immanence of one with the other in death through the absolute. The drive to this immanentism is a manner of responding to the harsh realities of the modern experience of the *loss* of the transcendental origin of sense, meaning and the world. God is dead and, in the face of this loss, theorists instead pose another absolute as the ground of community. The absolute, placed at the centre of a thought, leads to a structure that takes its absolute as a regulative and descriptive notion, as well as something to be aimed for in the future. Against the fleeing in the face of loss, Nancy asserts that there is another horizon. Only in the destruction or withdrawal of the immanence posed at the end of the transcendent ground is the possibility of community (of difference) opened. *Thus, with the death of God comes the possibility of a community that does not aim for communion.* Community is opened by being-abandoned. It is only because of this loss of the certainty of a metaphysical essence that the horizon of community is opened. We could not think this true sense of community before, it was unthinkable so long as communion remained the horizon of meaning. 'What . . . community has "lost" – the immanence and the intimacy of a communion – is lost only in the sense that such a "loss" is constitutive of "community" itself.'[56] Community, abandoned by the transcendental ground which would allow absolute immanence, is opened to being nothing but itself.

The critique of immanentism should then thread through much of political ontology. Nancy claims that humanism, the "Individual", or the "Subject", is 'immanentist', in that each obeys the logic of immanentism:

> This is to say that they [the individual, Subject and humanism] proposed an entity, community, or 'man', realizing its or his essence as work or as a work. The logic of immanence . . . is a logic of the same and of totalization which informs a whole series of concepts. The individual, for example . . . is an atomistic unit without relation, closed upon its own absoluteness. The concept of the Subject (the capital letter designating its characterization as a totality), is also informed by this logic of immanence; the eventual totalization of the subject of consciousness via the dialectic proposes no less a figure of closure and of the absolute. To this extent, communism and humanism remain profoundly equivalent and equally conditioned by the logic of immanence: community realizing its essence through the production of itself as work; 'man' realizing 'him'self through the production of his essence as Man.[57]

Humanism, the individual and the subject are all determined by the closing in on themselves, where each ultimately determines itself in an auto-nomy. The folding of these concepts on themselves implies a closure in and around their own essences. The 'subject' or the 'individual' is a closed totality, it has produced itself entirely and without remainder. It has become absolutely itself. The individual is 'by definition . . . the indivisible atom, a necessarily totally detached figure of immanence that is the ultimate for-itself. It is a figure of absolute certainty representing an absolute origin.'[58]

Communism subjugates community to a humanism and the essence of producing one's own essence as work and so tends towards communion as the ultimate horizon of meaning after the withering away of the state. This setting to work of essence in the generation of a communist community is:

> [p]recisely the immanence of man to man, or it is *man*, taken absolutely, considered as the immanent being par excellence, that constitutes the stumbling block of a thinking of community. A community presupposed as having to be one *of human beings* presupposes that it effect, or that it must effect, as such and integrally, its own essence, which is itself the accomplishment of the essence of humanness (into a *body* or under a *leader*). Consequently, economic ties, technological operations, and political fusion . . . represent or rather present, expose, and realize this essence necessarily in themselves.[59]

Nancy takes issue with the *human* or with *Man* of the thinking of community. He argues that it is the presupposition of the essence of "Humanity" or "Man" (which does not lie in existence, but rather in blood, work, reason, soul, etc.) subsequently effectuated, that leads to 'immanentism'. It is the setting to work of an essence of man that is, for Nancy, the generation of an immanence and it is this immanence that reaches its zenith in totalitarianism. The sublation of the death in the 'communist struggle' is a lie which perverts community. He says; 'generations of citizens and militants, of workers and servants of the State have imagined their death reabsorbed or sublated in a community, yet to come, that would attain immanence. But by now we have nothing more than the bitter consciousness of the increasing remoteness of such a community, be it the people, the nation, or the society of producers.'[60] By taking an absolute concept of man at its heart – which is either to be found out or produced – humanism ultimately aims for a communion in this absolute substance.

The model of communion, for Nancy, is the logic of humanism – 'the fully realized person of individualistic or communistic humanism is the dead person.'[61] Thus, Nancy's critique is simple: 'if [this dream of communion (or immanentism)] . . . were to come about, [it] would instantly suppress community, or communication, as such.'[62] Communication can only occur *between* existents, but there is not any 'between' in communion. Absolute immanence is impossible in life as existence is always the spacing out or dividing up of being.[63] 'Immanence, in other words, presupposes absolute closure and self-sufficiency. It denies relation.

Relation cuts into the logic of immanence at its limit, opening out at the limit of this closure a relation to something else. But in this opening out it submits all of the concepts maintained in the closure of immanentist thought to their potential ruin.'[64] Community is *not* a totality in which the people would share a common being: a common possession, a common body. Instead, community is the sharing of being-in-common, in fact community itself is the in-common.[65] There is no common property, but rather the very sharing of relations.[66] The in-operative community is to be distinguished from operative communities that set an essence to work[67] in the name of (comm)union, thus putting death to work in a sacrifice of difference from the ideal/*telos*. Communion is the final phase (the 'use') of sacrifice. In sacrifice, the victim's death is given (up) for the community.[68] In this is the dream that all will be (as) one. In fascism, communion is the dream of community of utter (abject) unity, literally fused under the leader, speaking through his mesmeric voice, mystically acting through his body, sacrificially unified in the absolute exposure to death (of which the Second World War is only the most literal manifestation of a destiny necessitated by the reification of death).

Fascism is of particular interest for Nancy because it is the purest example of the impossibility of a community of unity – communion. The Nazi regime did not just sacrifice 'others' in the abysmal reification and purification of the Aryan race. The final solution (that is the death of the Jew, the homosexual, the mentally or physically 'defective') is not the *end* of a purification of the Aryan (the final solution does not end with the last Jew, homosexual . . . etc.). Rather, genocide is the beginning of a sacrificial rite that ultimately ends with a 'total war', which is nothing other than a collective suicide. For instance, in Mao's Cultural Revolution, the sacrificial politics is ultimately a suicidal politics. No sacrifice ever unifies the community without remainder. Difference persists, therefore, the regime must continue to sacrifice. But these sacrifices do not stop. The process of othering is continuous, until ultimately everyone must be sacrificed. Only then, in death, is the dream of unity completed. Thus, communion is the work of death. Nazism's suicidal quest for immanence is not an exception, but is the purest expression of immanentism: 'the realization of the essence of man as work attains its purest expression in the production of death as work . . . The community supposed by the logic of immanence is a community of the dead which taken to its logical limit supposes the death of the entire community.'[69] The moment that the existent encloses on itself in the completion of its essence is the moment of death. The only time that the existent is an entirely enclosed entity, as the logic of the individual demands, is when it is sealed beneath the earth in its coffin. Until that time the existent is constantly exposed and open to the world. Instead of the immanentism of the individual, of the subject, or of humanism, Nancy proposes a different thinking of community, an inoperative community. That is, a community that unworks itself, that sets no end to itself that is made of singularities constantly exposed to each other in a plurality.

Nancy argues that the European history of community is a history of projected lost communities in response to 'the death of God'. However, as I have said, we have not lost community, there is no idyllic pre-social community to which we might get back. Community has not been 'crushed or lost, [instead it] is *what happens to us . . . in the wake of* society'.[70] This inversion is crucial; if community is futural and not to be returned to, then it is full of possibility.[71] Community holds within it the constituent *potentia*, the possibility of being otherwise and this is its *sine qua non*. It has not already happened in all its completeness. Instead, it is connected to the future with openness and possibility. In this, 'community' is transposed from a conservative concept to a radical one. As the horizon of communion (qua god, humanity, race, production) withdraws, we find ourselves in community with no beyond ourselves, no pre-given metaphysical certainty:

> Nothing, therefore, has been lost, and for this reason nothing is lost. We alone are lost, we upon whom the 'social bond' (relations, communication), our own invention, now descends heavily like the net of an economic, technical, political and cultural snare. Entangled in its meshes we have wrung for ourselves the phantasms of the lost community.[72]

We created the 'social bond' of society but it entangles us until we cannot escape our own creation. It is bound, and has bound us, to the subject as a mode of thinking and conceiving of the world. The death of god is not simply the loss of the transcendent source of the world, but also the loss of those metaphysical essences that would replace god with another shared common being. The loss of these common beings that would provide 'the immanence and intimacy of communion' *opens the possibility of community*.[73] Community is possible only because we are without an absolute.

Instead of communion as the ultimate horizon of community, Nancy proposes an 'inoperative community'. The term 'inoperative' is difficult, in French *désoeu-vrement* might be more literally translated as 'unworking',[74] 'unoccupancy'[75] or 'un-finishing'.[76] *La communauté désoeuvrée* is a community that is not-working, at a loose end and unemployed. It is distinguished from the conception of an 'operative' community: 'Community understood as a work or through its works would presuppose that the common being, as such, be objectifiable and produc-ible (in sites, persons, buildings, discourses, institutions, symbols: in short, in subjects).'[77] There is no common being, rather 'community takes place in what Blanchot has called the unworking [*désoeuvrement*]. Before or beyond the work, it is that which withdraws from the work, that which no longer has to do with production, nor with completion.'[78] Instead community is perpetually unworked by the sheer multiplicity of sense. Community 'unworks' or is 'unworking' itself (it deconstructs its own operativity). It is not a work, but rather something that is experienced ('the experience of finitude'). There is, of course, a connection here between an active 'worklessness' and Bataille's Kojèvean unemployed negativity of the dialectic in the end of history, as seen in Chapter 5. Inoperativity is, in fact, a radicalization of this philosophical 'unemployment'. In early Bataille, unemployed negativity occurs in the mediality of revolutionary heterogeneity (the dark night of the proletariat). However, inoperativity is fundamentally not the Bataillean work of sacrifice, rather it is the unworking of the grounds of the meta-physical. It is the exposure to the negativity of finitude, with all of the unworking implied in this. Community as an inoperativity is the experience of an active unworking, community is the auto-deconstruction of itself as unity. Yet this unworking cannot merely be restricted to community in unity, but rather extends outwards to deconstruct the givenness of the world.

It is sometimes said that by highlighting an ontological community, Nancy is, in fact, not proposing anything, that there is nothing which Nancy is *for*.[79] This is a misreading of the Nancean horizon. On one side, the community of unity as a politics must be resisted, community in itself resists this by always exceeding the possible unifying reductions. The significance of this critique cannot be under-stated. Nation and nationalism, ethnicity, class, culture, various religions, certain conceptions of the state and citizenship: all of these ideas turn on the very possi-bility of rendering the many as one. The community of unity is to be produced through sacrifice, but it is never enough to produce the unity without remainder. The sacrifice must continue, until finally it becomes a self-destructive and suicidal politics. Thus, there are fundamental acts that would negate, reject or override being-with.[80] Yet some commentators look to Nancy to provide immediate polit-ical 'solutions'. For instance, Willson, in passive voice, criticizes what she sees as the political implications of Nancy's thought:

> The imperative [for a Nancean politics] would seem to be to encourage social forms that allow greater expressions of community . . . What these forms are *not* is made very clear – they should not be a production, the making of a project, or the realization or production of a human essence. Such an approach evokes a withdrawal from the political arena and thus disregards the possi-bilities for realizing actual practical benefits or change. Yet practical action is precisely what Nancy sees as dangerous. To attempt to make something happen, to make something work, is to override or suppress the differences that exist into a totality. Such an orientation is open to the criticism of being politically disengaged and apathetic; of being so careful in description that the theory disempowers political direction or incentive. If community is always there, it risks negating the political and ethical value of community – reducing it to an inescapable part of life.[81]

However, the critique of immanentism in Nancy does not stop all action, it does not suspend any thought of justice in some 'apathetic' and 'disengaged' moment of postmodern irony or self-satisfied 'nihilistic' deconstruction. Willson has missed the crucial political element of Nancean ontology. Perhaps what she wishes for is some universal politics that could be applied to each and every situ-ation. If this *is* what she finds lacking (and I am not entirely certain that it is), Nancy is certainly not the place in which to look for it.[82] Rather, Nancy steers a course between the closed, timeless, absolute values of what he calls mythic thought and the nihilism of relativism.[83]

Nancy indirectly addresses this critique in the context of his argument for transformation of the sense of the world:

> Today anew it is precise to say that it is no longer a matter of interpreting the world, but of transforming it. It is no longer a matter of lending or giving the world one more sense, but of entering into this sense, into this gift of sense the world itself is. Karl Marx's concept of 'transformation' was still caught up ... in an interpretation, the interpretation of the world as the self-production of a Subject of history and of History as subject. Henceforth, 'to transform' should mean 'to change the sense of sense', that is, once again, to pass from having to being. Which means also that transformation is a *praxis*, not a *poiesis*, an action that effects the agent, not the work.[84]

It is a matter of transforming the world, but not in an immanentist manner: this would interpret the world and then in a gesture of closure, realize the interpretation through action. The immanentist project is ultimately that of closure of the world. However, the world is an unclosable multiplicity of sense. I will come back to this at the end of the next chapter. Work, action and production are problems when they squash 'difference' as such, not necessarily when they override differences. The problem of Wilson's mobilization of difference is that she appears to have reified it. This discourse too easily falls into the empty liberal 'respect all differences' platitudes. Nancy should be read neither as a communitarian nor universalist.

Nancy warns against the dangers of community when commenting on his interaction with Blanchot.[85] He says that the reason he moved away from 'community' towards the 'graceless expressions' of being-with and being-together is that the dangers of the term were encroaching on all sides: 'its invincibly full resonance – indeed a resonance bloated with substance and interiority – its quite inevitable Christian resonance (spiritual and brotherly community, communial community) or more broadly religious one (Jewish community, community of prayer, community of believers – *umma*), its usage to support the claims of supposed "ethnicities" could only put one on one's guard.'[86] He sees that we are constantly in motion, constantly changing. Where we essentialize differences (be they 'cultural', 'religious' or somehow more private and 'personal'), where we place them above the everyday interaction and challenge implicit in being then we have misunderstood difference.[87] In fact, paradoxically, this would already have succumbed to immanentism, by making difference static and closing the community or person in on itself. Willson takes concepts such as 'community' and transposes them simplistically into everyday pre-given communities of religion, nation, class, etc. But this betrays the insight by all too easily falling into an empty and given liberalism with its obscene supplement – capitalism. In these days of financial crisis, the failure of globalization is increasingly evident. The fundamental tension within globalization is between 'globe' and 'world' and it is to this tension to which I want to turn now. Ultimately, as we will see, it opens out onto a critique of technological thinking (qua capitalism), which is all around us in the over-determination of the political by the economic.

In this chapter, I have focused on the question of being-together, of the *Volk* and of community. Once the people is deconstructed, it becomes necessary to think of the being-together in the political on a different level. Thus, this chapter is a continuation of the last. In particular, the idea of the people in *statu nascendi* is rethought again from an ontological perspective. The significance of this cannot be understated for my project – it is from here that I can begin to think about constituent power *with* human rights. The being-together of the inoperative community is the first point of reference for my sense of a constituent power of another human rights. Nancy's ontology of being-together provides a radical challenge to the thought of the individual in human rights. However, as I will develop in the next chapter, it also provides a radical challenge to the statist meta-physics of sovereignty in which modern rights (despite their protestations other-wise) are utterly enmeshed. Thus, despite the fact that this chapter is probably unrecognizable from the perspective of human rights, I have begun to work towards a radically different thinking of human rights.

Chapter 8

On world: biopolitics, singularity and 'global' human rights

> It is the *horizons* themselves that must be challenged. The ultimate limit of community, or the limit that is formed by community, as such, traces an entirely different line. This is why, even as we establish that communism is no longer our unsurpassable horizon, we must also establish, just as forcefully, that a communist exigency or demand communicates with the gesture by means of which we must go farther than all possible horizons.
>
> Nancy, *The Inoperative Community*[1]

> Another life, another respiration, another weight, and another humanity is in the process of emerging ... A new departure for creation: *nothing*, which moves over to make a place or give occasion to *something*. Locations [*les lieux*] are de-localized and put to flight by a spacing that precedes them and only later will give rise [*donnera lieu*] to new places [*lieux nouveaux*]. Neither places, nor heavens, nor gods: for the moment it is a general dis-enclosure, more so than a burgeoning. Dis-enclosure: dismantling and disassembling of enclosed bowers, enclosures, fences. Deconstruction of property – that of man and that of the world.
>
> Nancy, *Dis-Enclosure*[2]

In Chapter 3, I argued that any return to human rights through constituent power would have to tackle its individualist and statist metaphysics. In Chapter 7, I began to suggest an alternative ontology to the traditional individualism. I put aside the crucial and potentially distinctive conjunction of human *being* and the juridical and political within human rights. But I must now return to this conjunction in order to further challenge the statist metaphysics and supplement it with a different thinking. The relation between human rights and sovereignty provides a starting point. The traditional international human rights law narrative poses a conflict between sovereignty represented by Article 2(7) of the UN Charter[3] and the supervisory mechanisms in the UN human rights declarations, covenants and treaties. However, this is only a conflict because some states do not submit to human rights regulation. When states do take on national and international human rights it is not difficult to see the manner in which they bind those principles into the ordinary functioning of the state. In fact, as I argued in Chapter 3, juridification forms the horizon of meaning of much of modern human rights. I now want to discuss the biopolitical nature of this move.

The idea of biopower[4] originates in Michel Foucault's work of the late 1970s and early 1980s, although it has been taken up by vast swathes of post-structural political philosophers.[5] In the first part of this chapter, I will briefly explain its development before engaging with an argument between Rancière and Agamben over the possibilities of human rights. In contrast to Agamben and Rancière's rendering of the resistant non-subject of human rights, I posit Nancy's consonant idea of singularity. Singularity frames the question of the subject of rights in a different fashion. It posits a figure of the human that could not easily be absorbed into the juridical logics of biopolitical sovereignty, precisely because it cannot be represented. However, the critique of biopolitics still stands, even with this radically different (non-)subject of human rights. Thus, I turn to the question of the political in Nancy, and the relation between the inoperative community (of the last chapter) and the political. This occurs in order to bring to light the crucial sovereign logic – enclosure. In its emphasis on the conjunction of life and power, biopower gets to the heart of modern politics but focuses in the wrong direction. Nancy reframes the problem as one of *ecotechnics*, that is, the technology of world formation. In globalization, we increasingly see the universalization of the global. Using the idea of *mondialisation* and the critique of globalization in Nancy, I argue that international human rights law once again demonstrates its failure to comprehend the creative potential of its own discourse. However, this time, instead of the introduction's simplistic positing of closure/opening or decision/demand, as though the legal form were itself the problem, I suggest that it is human rights' implication in capitalist forms that presents us with the problem.

Human rights, biopower and singularity

Foucault introduces the concept of biopower to name the new political technology that he sees emerging in the 17th century.[6] Biopower designates that which:

> [b]rought life and its mechanisms into the realm of explicit calculations and made knowledge-power an agent of transformation of human life. It is not that life has been totally integrated into techniques that govern and administer it; it constantly escapes them . . . But what might be called society's 'threshold of modernity' has been reached when the life of the species is wagered on its own political strategies. For Millennia, man remained what he was for Aristotle: a living animal with the additional capacity for a political existence; modern man is an animal whose politics places his existence as a living being in question.[7]

Power is increasingly concerned with, and legitimated by, its relation to a 'care' of the life of its population. It is no longer 'a matter of bringing death into play in the field of sovereignty, but of distributing the living in the domain of value and utility.'[8] By way of contrast, the population disciplines itself by interiorizing the concern with its life, welfare and security. Biopower builds on the earlier Foucauldian analysis of disciplinary power, which is the manner of generating bodies at once both docile and productive.

In *Discipline and Punish*, Foucault describes the shift in modes of punishment, from spectacular execution to banal incarceration. The reason for this shift, he tells us, is not an enlightenment concern for the suffering of others. Instead, he argues that 'an expanding capitalist system has a fundamental reliance on a social network that is completely calculable, dependable and efficient with regard to all aspects of the production of human labour power and the extraction of surplus value.'[9] Disciplinary power thus is concerned with producing 'docile bodies' through the operation of power-knowledge, that is, at least in part through the regulatory power of the norm. 'Disciplinary power rules in effect by structuring the parameters and limits of thought and practice, sanctioning and prescribing normal and/or deviant behaviours.'[10] McNay explains:

> Modern disciplinary society operates fundamentally through . . . strategies of normalization. The 'judges of normality', in the figures of the social worker, the teacher, the doctor, are everywhere assessing and diagnosing each individual according to a normalizing set of assumptions, or what Foucault calls the 'carceral network of power-knowledge.' Individuals are controlled through the power of the norm and this power is effective because it is relatively invisible. In modern society, the behaviour of individuals is regulated not through repression but through a set of standards and values associated with normality which are set into play by a network of ostensibly beneficent and scientific forms of knowledge.[11]

The population is analysed, it is measured, counted and then re-measured and re-counted. In the accretion of knowledge through the perpetual analysis and calculation of the population, biopolitics gathers its power. Biopower then denotes a 'life administration' that uses the norm of 'life' rather than the law's threat of death.[12]

With modernity and the power of the normal comes biopower: 'A normalizing society is the historical outcome of a *technology of power centered on life*.'[13] Human rights have always played a large role in biopower. At the end of the first volume of *The History of Sexuality*, Foucault explains that a newly emergent form of rights plays out a biopolitical function:

> It was life more than the law that became the issue of political struggles, even if the latter were formulated through affirmations concerning rights. The 'right' to life, to one's body, to health, to happiness, to the satisfaction of needs, and beyond all the oppressions or 'alientations,' the 'right' to rediscover what one is and all that one can be, this 'right' – which the classical juridical system was utterly incapable of comprehending – was the political

response to all these new procedures of power which did not derive, either, from the traditional right of sovereignty.[14]

Rights are deeply entwined with biopolitics and its disciplinary power. They demand that it is possible to resist sovereign power by identifying with rights and using them against the state. There are two logics here – sovereign power and biopower. However, Foucault argued that sovereign power, with its ultimate power over life or death, was long displaced by the disciplinary function of the normal and the subject's internalization of control. In this sense, sovereign power is obsolete. Instead, what we now call sovereignty is a mixture of biopolitics and traditional discourses of sovereignty. However, when human rights trace their lineage they do not see any break between traditional sovereignty and biopolitics. Only in the sense of pre-biopower sovereignty can human rights be seen in opposition to sovereign power. If Foucault is correct, then rights are no longer merely a resistance to state, they become crucial in performing, demonstrating and manifesting biopower as well. When one asserts one's rights against a state's incursion, one is at once resisting that state but also (re)performing the power of the state, and the subjectivity of its laws. For Foucault, human rights do not resist – they merely re-perform power.[15]

Biopower is frequently taken up in post-structuralist political theory.[16] However, perhaps the most important here is the debate between Agamben and Rancière concerning whether rights are recoverable after the biopolitical critique. While both agree that there may be something potentially recoverable – that there may be a subject capable of escaping the biopolitical trap – both ultimately focus on the question of the (admittedly de-subjectified) subject. Arendt's seminal chapter 'The Decline of the Nation State and the End of the Rights of Man',[17] which I dealt with in Chapter 3, forms the basis of the disagreement. In question is the subject of the rights of man. Arendt's essay deals with the dichotomy between man and citizen in the French Declaration of the Rights of Man and the Citizen. She demonstrates that rights belong on the most fundamental level to the citizen. There are no rights that accrue simply because one is man. 'If the destruction of civil rights also destroys human rights, this is because the latter are based on the former, and not the reverse . . . rights are not, or not primarily, "qualities" of individual subjects, they are *qualities that individuals grant each other*.'[18] The refugee or stateless person demonstrates this by remaining without 'the right to have rights' precisely at the moment when they most need that protection. Rancière summarizes Arendt's argument:

> [she] makes . . . [the Rights of Man] a quandary, which can be put as follows: either the rights of the citizen are the rights of man – but the rights of man are the rights of the unpoliticized person; they are the rights of those who have no rights, which amounts to nothing – or the rights of man are the rights of the citizen, the rights attached to the fact of being a citizen of such or such constitutional state. This means that they are the rights of those who have rights,

which amounts to a tautology. Either the rights of those who have no rights or the rights of those who have rights. Either a void of a tautology, and, in both cases, a deceptive trick.[19]

However, he is not happy with this, instead positing a third option: 'The Rights of Man are the rights of those who have not the rights that they have and have the rights that they have not.'[20] This is a much more radical formulation, and one which justifies his earlier assertion that the subject of the rights of man is the subject of politics as well.

Rancière highlights a double character of human rights, at once written and performed. In the first form, they become 'part of the configuration of the given. What is given is not only a situation of inequality. It is also an inscription, a form of visibility of equality.'[21] Human rights remain part of what Rancière else-where calls the distribution of the sensible or 'the police'. I discussed this in Chapter 6, but it is worth reminding ourselves that '[t]he police is not a social function but a symbolic constitution of the social. The essence of the police is neither repression nor even control over the living. Its essence is a certain manner of partitioning the sensible.'[22] It is the 'police' 'in the classical sense of the term, that is, prudent administration of interests of the governed by rational gover-nors.'[23] The everyday politics of the police order is a process of counting, of managing who and what counts and the manner in which they count.[24] Human rights as they are written in the UDHR, the Covenants and the multitude of other authoritative legal sources remain crucially part of the manner in which the 'who counts' is established.

However, according to Rancière, human rights have a second disposition:

> [T]he Rights of man are the rights of those who make something of that inscription, who decide not only to 'use' their rights but also to build such and such a case for the verification of the power of the inscription. The point is about what *confirmation* or *denial* means. *Man* and *citizen* do not designate collections of individuals. Man and citizen are political subjects. Political subjects are not definite collectivities. They are surplus names, names that set out a question or a dispute (*litige*) about who is included in their count. Correspondingly, *freedom* and *equality* are not predicates belonging to defi-nite subjects. Political predicates are open predicates: they open up a dispute about what they exactly entail and whom they concern in which cases.[25]

With this, Rancière re-opens Arendt's apparent closure of the subject of human rights. Not merely condemned to repeat the intentions or contradictions of the various texts, the 'part of no part' becomes the very subject of human rights. Discussing the Haitian Revolution, Nesbitt says that the 'signifier "general liberty" thus opened a gap or interval in that century, a gap inherent in the inade-quation between the slaves' political exclusion and the "universal" rights of man.'[26] This is what Rancière wants to suggest with his figuration of the subject of rights. Human rights name both a limitation, as I have discussed before, and a political subjectivization that goes beyond 'inclusion' within the UDHR:

> The Rights of Man are the rights of the demos, conceived as the generic name of the political subjects who enact – in specific scenes of dissensus – the paradoxical qualification of this supplement. This process disappears when you assign those rights to one and the same subject. There is no man of the Rights of Man, but there is no need for such a man. The strength of those rights lies in the back-and-forth movement between the first inscription of the right and the dissensual stage on which it is put to test.[27]

On its surface, this figuration remains fairly close to the liberal tradition of inclusion. Rancière has one more critical ace up his sleeve. He says that Olympe de Gouge's argument in *The Declaration of the Rights of Women and the Citizeness*, which was unrecognizable to the political discourse of the time, introduced or named a dissensus. 'A dissensus is not a conflict of interests, opinions or values; it is a division put in the "common sense": a dispute about what is given, about the frame within which we see something as given.' A dissensus is 'putting two worlds in one and the same world.'[28] It is to be contrasted with consensus which is:

> [m]uch more than the reasonable idea and practice of settling political conflicts by forms of negotiation and agreement . . . It means the attempt to get rid of politics by ousting the surplus subjects and replacing them with real partners, social groups, identity groups and so on. Correspondingly, conflicts are turned into problems that have to be sorted out by learned expertise and a negotiated adjustment of interests. Consensus means closing the spaces of dissensus by plugging the intervals and patching over the possible gaps between appearance and reality or law and fact . . . [In consensus] the political dissensus about the part-taking in the common of the community is boiled down to a distribution within which each part of the social body would obtain the best share it can obtain . . . To put it in other terms, *consensus* is the reduction of democracy to the way of life of society, to its *ethos* – meaning by this word both the abode of a group and its lifestyle.[29]

Rancière thus distinguishes what I have called the difference of human rights: at once consensus and dissensus, both struggle and pacification, decision and demand. What is extended in Rancière's dissensus is the political. Dissensus is the mode of politics (in Rancière's idiolect) or the political (in the Nancean language that I have used). However, this dissensus is not the disagreement of petty politics (or police ordering in Rancière), it resides on an ontological level.

This move towards the political subjectivization of the rights of man must be very carefully approached. For Agamben, Rancière's dissensus is potentially already caught up in the 'relation between sovereign power and bare life'.[30] The contestability of rights as political predicates does not grant a subjectivization already clear of biopolitics. Agamben takes up the Aristotelian distinction between *zoe* and *bios* (or between natural life and political existence). He suggests that there is no massive rift between sovereign power and biopower (as Foucault suggested through his historicization), but rather that 'the production of a biopolitical body is the original activity of sovereign power.'[31] The *homo sacer* is paradigmatic of the biopolitical body that sovereign power produces. This ancient Roman figure is defined by Pompeius Festus as:

> [T]he one whom the people have judged on account of a crime. It is not permitted to sacrifice this man, yet he who kills him will not be condemned for homicide . . . This is why it is customary for a bad or impure man to be called sacred.[32]

For Agamben, this reveals sovereignty's structuring of the exception.[33] 'In the exception, what is taken outside [excluded/*ex-capere*] (*zoe*) is not absolutely without relation to the inside, that is, to the rule (*bios*). On the contrary, what is excluded in the exception maintains itself in relation to the rule in the form of the rule's suspension.'[34] In biopower, 'inclusion' operates through the classical sovereign secular theology – that is, by producing an exception. Thus, the 'everyone' that is included by the state is constituted by an other – be they the inmates of Guantanamo Bay, the *Musselman* of the Holocaust, the illegal immigrant camps at Calais or the 'neomorts' on life support. These presences are included in the protections of the state *only by their exclusion*. They inhabit a zone of indistinction between *bios* and *zoe*. I discussed this rift in the context of the people in Chapter 6, where Agamben sets the structure to work in the difference between the common people and the people of sovereignty.

The crucial factor is that these figures (of the *homo sacer*) are declared exceptional and desubjectivized. For Rancière, rights are useful in a radical sense because they remain open to those who are not included in the distribution of the sensible. For Agamben, the excluded (the *homo sacer*) cannot be subjectivized through rights. However, beyond this desubjectivization of bare life, Whyte emphasizes that Agamben seems to see another emergent (non-subjectivized) 'subject':

> This subject would be without substantive identity, and would therefore be unable to be represented by a state, claim juridical rights, or form the basis for an exclusive community. Agamben's rejection of identity and his articulation of a non-juridical politics is premised on the view that any politics that presupposes a substantive subject leads to bloody forms of exclusion and to that capture of natural life that, he argues, is the originary act of sovereign power.[35]

With this, Whyte claims that Agamben goes beyond Rancière's 'part of no part' that opens the community to dissensus. The danger of the part of no part is that it easily becomes the object of liberation. This would be the liberal figuring of human rights that I discussed through Orend's telling of a human rights history in Chapter 2. For Agamben, it is the part of no part's status as the remnant of a process of inclusion that makes it interesting – it 'testifies to the wrong at the heart of every order of inclusion and, as the bearer of this absolute wrong, it cannot claim particular rights for itself. The remnant . . . "has a universal character by its universal suffering and claims no *particular right* because no particular wrong but wrong generally is perpetrated against it".'[36] The part of no part is thus significant in its remnance.

However, where is this desubjectivized subject? The danger of this figure in Agamben, as Whyte acknowledges, is that it 'depopulates the political stage of its actors.'[37] Thus, on one side is Rancière's apparently overly optimistic subjectivization of the part of no part with its potential collapse into liberal pre-figurings and on the other is Agamben's apparent pessimism of the desubjectivized anti-juridical subject. However, both would agree on the rejection of the already existent subject with its present properties, which the human rights discourse would simply discover/encounter and then protect. In their hands, the subject is either the 'part of no part' or the remnant. Either way, it remains included under sovereign power only in so far as it is excluded from that logic. The major difference emerges when this non-subject acts. Rancière's 'part of no part' demands equality thereby sowing dissensus, whereas Agamben seems reluctant to describe how the remnant acts, short of its withdrawal.

Between Rancière and Agamben is not so much an impasse, as a required decision about the possible utility of human rights, given the fact that they are determined by biopower. Both see a non-subjectified subject resisting the logic of biopower. This connects with my discussion of being-together in the last chapter and, in particular, with Nancy's concept of 'singularity'. Instead of the individual and community as distinct entities, with singularity the 'I' and the 'We' become inseparable. Crucially, '[s]ingularity refers to a subject's uniqueness that arises through the "we" but that cannot be captured, subsumed or understood in the "we".'[38] Singularity cannot be represented, it cannot be captured in the juridical logics of the subject. In this sense, it is very close to Agamben's desubjectified subject,[39] but different to Agamben's tendency toward 'figures whose lives border on death and whose extreme manifestations are the *Musselman* of the Nazi camps, and the neomort who survives merely by virtue of artificial respiratory technologies.'[40] With 'singularity', Nancy looks beyond these figures of destruction. Singularity is the point at which the attacks on statism and individualism collide.

In the *Sense of the World*, Nancy proposes three 'distinctive traits' of singularity.[41] The first trait is that singularity is each time *unique*. Singularity is unique without the absoluteness of the unique. To be absolutely unique would be to be unique in being unique. Rather, each singularity 'cannot *exist* through *consisting* by itself and in itself alone'.[42] The uniqueness of singularity is constituted by its very being-with-others. It is a differential uniqueness that is in a constant state of becoming. This interrupts any reduction to the individual. Singularity 'is not a matter of adding to a postulation of individuality or autonomy a certain number of relations and interdependencies, no matter what importance one may attach to such an addenda'.[43] The singular is always a play of the unique and the common, but this 'play' is itself different each time. Each singularity is different from the next, while maintaining the sharing of the in-common. Further, the singular is not the 'particular', which might be put in relation to a 'universal'.

The second trait is the curious *whatever*. Agamben explains us that the 'whatever' (*quodlibet*) of singularity should be understood as 'being such that it always matters', rather than 'being, it does not matter which'.[44] The difference between the two is crucial. Whatever singularity means that 'everyone is just as singular as every other one.'[45] However, this is not to be understood as a process of levelling down of one alike with the next, i.e. where difference itself is negated. This would be the logic of the individual in its universal reduction.[46] Rather, whatever singularity is such that in each case the singularity is shared. 'It amounts to considering that what is common to one and all, their communication with each other, is what singularizes them and consequently what shares them out and divides them up. What is commensurable in them is their incommensurability.'[47] Singularity is always open (always becoming). The whatever-ness of singularity is such that it always becomes, no matter what the content. 'The Whatever in question here relates to singularity not in its indifference with respect to a common property (to a concept, for example: being red, being French, being Muslim), but only in its being *such as it is*:'[48]

> There is relation as relation of *example*: every one, being born, dying, being-there, exemplifies singularity. Each proposes itself as *an* example, if you like, but it exposes this example, every time, as exemplary, in the sense of a remarkable model. That which is exemplary each time, that which sets an example, is singularity itself, insofar as it is never anything but *this* or *that* singularity, inimitable at the very heart of its being-whatever.[49]

Singularity is always this or that singularity, each time an example. Nancy suggests that curiosity is the manner of relating singularity with singularity. 'In order to have a relation with the example, one must be interested in it, one must be curious about what it exposes, about its sense as example ... It can open fear and desire, love and hate, pity or terror.'[50]

Finally, the third trait of singularity is that it is always *exposed*. As soon as it *is*, it is exposed. Nancean ontology is, at base, the assertion that we are exposed to the world/sense:

> The singular exposes every time that it is exposed, and that all of its sense resides therein. There is nothing to be expected from someone other than – exemplarity – its being-someone. Nothing more but also nothing less: every time, one can expect the act of self-exception, and this act, as act, is not a property that can be preserved, but an existence that exists.[51]

To be is to be exposed. There is no being that could be 'enclosed'. Exposure to the world is the *sine qua non* of existence. However, what is it to be 'exposed', what is exposed? Nancy says: 'if one wants to . . . [answer this in] the form of a sensible statement, [exposure] is something like: "I am well grounded in my existence".'[52] Nancy immediately clarifies that this 'ground' is not a foundation, rather it implies an 'attestation'. The exposure of singularity in each instance attests to existence.

Singularity in Nancy, as a rethinking of the 'human' or 'man', is an attack on the subject. That said, the logic of the singular should not be reduced to the 'person', 'human' or '*dasein*'. Singularity is a description of the exposition of being's being. As such, it is most useful in reconceiving of the 'human' or of 'man'. It is to be utterly distinguished from an individual, which is enclosed on itself. It engages with the world only through 'inter-subjectivity'. It obeys the logic of a totality, bouncing against other totalities. In the metaphysics of the individual subject there is nothing of what Nancy calls the inclination or the being-towards. '[O]ne cannot make the world with simple atoms. There has to be a *clinamen*. There has to be an inclination or an inclining from one toward the other, of one by the other, or from one to the other.'[53] The thought of the individual begins with the enclosed entity and once its subject is set out, be it as a possessive entity (Locke/Macpherson) or an imagining entity (Anderson), it is *added to the world*. Gradually the individual is inserted into its contexts and the degree to which these contexts then impact on the individual is of great fascination.

Singularity, by way of contrast, 'never takes place at the level of atoms, those identifiable if not identical identities; rather it takes place at the level of the clinamen, which is unidentifiable.'[54] Nancy's point is simply that as soon as one is, one is with. There can be no individual, there is no atom simply in itself; it must always already be inclined towards other atoms. 'It is a question of practicing singularities, that is, that which gives itself and shows itself only in the plural. The Latin *singuli* means "one by one", and is a word that exists only in the plural.'[55] Because we are with we are singular. Against the likes of Virno and Simondon,[56] there is to be no pre-individual that is constantly emerging into its individuation. Against Heidegger, there is no *dasein* that might emerge from the power of *das Man*, because each *dasein* is singular.[57] There is no in/authenticity of existence, rather each and every singularity is always already both singular and common.[58]

There is no process of singularization because there is nothing before singularity.[59] In fact, there is only *the nothing* before and after singularity. Being comes to presence from the nothing and then hurls itself inexorably towards its own end. Singularity appears, it is *born*. 'There is nothing *behind* singularity – but there is, outside and in it, the immaterial *and* material space that distributes it and shares it out as singularity . . . distributes and shares the confines of singularity . . . between it and itself.'[60] It is not a subject (to be distinguished from the object) and it is not an individual (with all the atomic misconceptions and contradictions of its implicit absolutism):

A singular being does not emerge or rise up against the background of a chaotic, undifferentiated identity of beings, or against the background of their unitary assumption, of that of a becoming, or that of a will. A singular being *appears*, as finitude itself: at the end (or at the beginning), with the contact of the skin (or the heart) of another singular being, at the confines of the *same* singularity that is, as such, always *other*, always shared, always exposed.[61]

Each being is a singular instance of being, of sense.

Singularity presents an opening onto a different thinking of human rights. Agamben, in one of his most interesting moments, asks what a politics of whatever singularity would be like. 'The novelty of the coming politics is that it will no longer be a struggle for the conquest or control of the State, but a struggle between the State and the non-State (humanity), an insurmountable disjunction between whatever singularity and the State organization.'[62] Where Agamben describes Tiananmen as the herald of this coming politics, we could equally look to the resistance in Greece over the last few years, which can be reduced neither to protest against the IMF nor to police brutality. Rather, a subject emerges in these events that 'has nothing to do with the simple affirmation of the social in opposition to the State ... Whatever singularities cannot form a *societas* because they do not possess any identity to vindicate nor any bond of belonging for which to seek recognition.'[63] The problem with these movements without representation or identity is that they cannot be accommodated within the state. With singularity, there is no different subject that could be opposed to the liberal subject (the representation of being-communist, being-fascist, being-capitalist, being-Muslim, being-Christian, being-liberal). Thus, singularity resists biopolitics.

World, globe and capital

While singularity, in its inability to be represented, resists the fundamental representation of needs and life that is crucial to biopolitics, it does not address the biopolitical critique directly. This is because it starts from a rejection of the subject, whereas biopolitics starts from the subject. Nancy both accepts and critiques biopolitics, arguing that while its insight is useful, the terms biopower and biopolitics are slightly wide of the mark. The term, he argues, is a misnomer and leads to a misrecognition of the problem itself. Crucially, the problem of biopolitics is better rendered in the term *ecotechnics*.[64] Nancy accepts the thrust of Foucault's rendering of 'biopolitics' in *History of Sexuality, Volume 1*.[65] However, he proposes that it is not the association of life (*bios*) and politics or power that is crucial. Instead he suggests that 'it is ... a destinal figure ('race' or 'the human worker') that comes to substitute for the classical figures of sovereignty.'[66] The 'destinal' figures of 'race' or 'the human worker' become realigned as 'natural life,' yet they no longer coincide with some form of simple 'life'. Rather:

[I]t is clear that so-called 'natural life', from its production to its conservation, its needs, and its representations, whether human, animal, vegetal or
viral, is henceforth inseparable from a set of conditions that are referred to as
'technological,' and which constitute what must rather be named *ecotech-
nology* where any kind of 'nature' develops for us (and by us).[67]

Ecotechnics is thus very similar to the biopolitics described by Hardt and Negri
in *Empire*. Following Deleuze, they argue that we have moved from disciplinary
society to a 'society of control'. 'Power is now exercised through machines
that directly organize the brains (in communication systems, information
networks, etc.) and bodies (in welfare systems, monitored activities, etc.)
toward a state of autonomous alienation from the sense of life and the desire
for creativity.'[68] The idea of a 'society of control' both intensifies and
generalizes the normalizing apparatus of discipline, but it also extends its
control beyond the sites that Foucault discussed (prison, clinic, asylum, etc.). In
society of control, biopower becomes crucial: 'Power can achieve an effective
command over the entire life of the population only when it becomes an integral,
vital function that every individual embraces and reactivates of his or her own
accord.'[69]

Through Deleuze, Hardt and Negri suggest that it is the technology-of-placing
that is distinctive about biopolitics. This is specifically what Nancy will suggest.
The term 'ecotechnics' emphasizes the technology (*technics*) of emplacement
(*eco*) rather than on life-politics or a power-through-life. Nancy argues that this
alteration allows us to see the essence of the problem which biopolitics only
alludes to: 'What *forms a world* today is exactly the conjunction of an unlimited
process of an eco-technological enframing *and* of a vanishing of an unlimited
possibilities of forms of life and/or of common ground.'[70] Biopolitics forms a
world that is becoming unworld (*immonde*). It names the process of the management of life, which is its reduction and limitation. However, this occurs through
the destruction of its 'world' (qua condition of possibility). Nancy himself says:
the ' "world" in these conditions, or "world-forming," is only the precise form of
this problem [of biopolitics].'[71]

If 'world-forming' is the problem, and not just biopower, then the question
becomes that of the worldhood of the world, of value and sense. Nancy distinguishes between two possibilities of what Kujundzic calls 'going global'.[72] On
one side is globalization, or the *glomicity* of the market – 'an enormous energy at
work that turns the world into the site of a circulation of goods, merchandise, the
work of *techne* and technicity, what Nancy calls *ecotechnie* (ecotechnics), and
into a universal equivalent (money).'[73] On the other is '*mondialisation*' that
does *not* allow itself to be translated without supplement. In fact, the difference
between these two terms is one of the best manners of showing the operation
of 'globalization' as a concept: while '*mondialisation* preserves something
untranslatable ... *globalization* has already translated everything in a global
idiom.'[74] *Mondialisation* must be translated in each instance, always maintaining

difference by its very untranslatability. In each case, it would imply a rejection of any universality of communication (through English). Globalization, on the contrary, is the (operation of the) same in each instance, in each language it attests to the translatability of each without remainder.

Raffoul and Pettigrew argue that in the two phenomena, there 'is nothing less than two possible destinies of our humanity, of our time':[75]

> On the one hand, there is the uniformity produced by a global economical and technological logic – Nancy specifies, 'a global injustice against the background of general equivalence' – leading toward the opposite of an inhabitable world, to 'the unworld' [*immonde*]. And, on the other hand, there is the possibility of an authentic *world-forming*, that is, of a making of the world and of making sense that Nancy will call . . . a 'creation' of the world. This creation of the world means, as he makes clear, 'immediately, without delay, re-opening each possible struggle for a world, that is, for what must form the contrary' of globality.[76]

Thus, the struggle of *mondialisation* is a resistance. Where globality is 'a totality to be grasped as a whole', an 'indistinct totality' . . . 'the worldly [or] world-forming calls to mind rather a "process in expansion".'[77]

World-forming is always within the world, immanently transforming the sense of sense. Globality, on the other hand, begins from the god–subject view of an outside. It takes this perspective and then fills the globe with the levelling down of everything until one is the same as the next. It is the operation of an empire that stands outside and enacts the world to its will:

> In the final analysis, what interests Nancy, in the distinction between world-forming and globalization, is that world-forming maintains a crucial reference to the world's horizon, as a space of human relations, as a space of meaning held in common, a space of significations or of possible significance. On the other hand, globalization is a process that indicates an 'enclosure in the indifferent spheres of a unitotality' that is perfectly accessible and transparent for a mastery without remainder.[78]

It is important to note that Nancy calls the world of capitalism, empire and globalization an *unworld* [*immonde*]. Globalization 'destroys' the world by reducing it, through the economic and technological logics of calculability, to a globe and its double, a *glomus*. The *glomus* is a ball of things that would be agglomerated: unconnected and unrelated things pushed together. In the *glomus*, 'we see the conjunction of an indefinite growth of techno-science, of a correlative exponential growth of populations, of a worsening of inequalities of all sorts within these populations – economic, biological and cultural.'[79] The unworld or *glomus*, 'in the end . . . takes place as if the world affected and permeated itself with a death drive that soon would have nothing else to destroy than the world itself.'[80] However, the *glomus* is always also the world, with its possibilities of creation and unworking. Žižek also connects global capitalism to this 'unworlding' of the world: 'although it is global, encompassing all worlds, it sustains a *stricto sensu* worldless ideological constellation depriving the great majority of the population of any meaningful "cognitive mapping".'[81]

Bataille argued that the hallmark of liberal society is the contract that establishes a *general equivalence* among men and things. Commensurability among elements of a contract is the key here. This is the reductive thought that Heidegger sees in technology and which is here called the *immonde* or unworld:[82]

> The becoming-world of the world does not mean what is usually called the 'uniformization' of everything and everyone . . . In many respects, world also differentiates itself, if it does not indeed shatter itself. The becoming-world of world means that 'world' is no longer an object, nor an idea, but the place existence is given to.[83]

Mondialisation is the becoming-world where we are abandoned to our existence. Where there is no divinity (pre-given truth) to order our meanings and sense, we are left to our world. In the last chapter, I showed how Nancy rejected immanentism in community, saying this would be a communion where every difference would be eliminated and where each, in death, would be (re) united with all else. This must be supplemented with the rejection of pure transcendence as well. There is no deity that could provide a foundation above the world. There is no metaphysical truth, no beyond the world. We are left with an immanence of the world. However, this is not the closed immanence of the representational notion of the world that would have an operative essence filling in the abandoned space of the transcendent. Rather this is the open trans-immanence of the world as that to which our existence is given. 'The world is an absolute, since it is no longer *relative* to another world. The sense of the world manifests this immanence, because the sense of the world is referred to a making-sense, which *is* the world as such: the world makes sense of itself by itself.'[84]

Globalization is the destruction of the singularity of the world, the making of an unworld. It is the reduction to a general equivalence of the market and, as such, it must be resisted. Raffoul and Pettigrew summarize Nancy's position:

> The sense of the world is not given *a priori*, and our coexistence in the world is not given either, nor is it able to rely on any substantial basis. Not able to rely on any given, the world can thus only rely on itself. That is to say, the world suddenly appears from nothing . . . from itself. The sense of the world, not given, is to create, because 'the withdrawal of any given thus forms the heart of a thinking of creation.' The world, resting on nothing, is to invent in an original *praxis* of meaning; 'meaning is always *praxis*', Nancy clarifies. It is never established as a given, it is never fulfilled or achieved; it is to be

made and enacted. Being itself, as it is always 'being without given', has the meaning of an act, of a making.[85]

The sense of the world, not given, is to create. This is the insight of Chapters 4, 5 and 6. However, at this point it is placed in the ontological rather than political register. There can be no law that would legitimate constituent power before the event. There is no pre-given sense of constituent power, but rather it is created *ex nihilo* in each instance, it is created with and from the *nothing*.

It is clear that here we are approaching Negri's position, of an open constituent power that is always creating. However, while this is entirely correct, I remain doubtful about Negri's ontology as there is no returning to the subject. There is no production producing the subject, rather there is creation that is not sublated. Thus, Negri's thrust is useful, but his philosophical position remains problematic. There is no transcendent, pre-given, sense or truth which could legitimate struggle (empire vs. multitude). Rather, in each case there is the sense of struggle in community against injustice. This struggle cannot be universal, except insofar as the struggle is shared by those who fight the same phenomenon. However, this 'solidarity' is immediately confronted with the fact that it is never the 'same phenomenon'. It would never take the same form, but would take on a singularity of its own. Each time, something new, each time, the creation *ex nihilo* of the world.

The creation *ex nihilo* does not propose a deity fashioning something from the outside, out of nothing.[86] This model of god-producer is secularized to the man-producer we see in Negri. Rather, for Nancy, there is an immanent creation *ex nihilo* that would in each instance be the 'making (sense) from *nothing given*',[87] a refusal to accept the 'given'[88] sense of the world. Instead of the given forms of life, creating from nothing, creation 'coming from nothing, and meaning, emerging from nothing, [which] allows the world to appear as a nothing-of-given and as without-reason.'[89] The world is without reason in that it *is*. It was not reasoned into existence, neither does it 'have reason'; rather, it is without cause ('neither efficient nor final').[90] In *The Inoperative Community*, Nancy proposes community as the sharing of being: the exposition of finitude *and* the sharing of the common (being). Singularity is unique each time, it is whatever-being and it is always exposed:

> For Nancy, this mutual exposure of the singularities is an undecidable tension from which the struggle for the creation of world must unfold. That struggle, in its singularity and the infinitely finite enactment of possible beginnings, is nothing less than, for Nancy, the condition and definition of justice.[91]

Thus we can see that in the question of the creation of the world we have moved from the question of community and the fundamental ontology of being-with to the question of the political and constituent power. 'To create the world means: immediately, without delay, re-opening each possible struggle for a world, that is for what must be the contrary of a global injustice against the background of general equivalence.'[92] Now, in this time of the crisis of capitalism, once more it is a matter of returning to and exceeding the past struggles for a world.[93]

The next chapter will break away from this philosophical questioning and look to the idea of 'right-ing' that I have posited throughout as the radical that has withdrawn from human rights. The radical is ultimately there in the potential of human rights, but it is over-determined by the biopolitical or ecotechnical destruction of world. 'Right-ing', as we will see, is creation from the nothing of manners and modes of being-together. It names the moment that human rights are utilized in an alegal fashion to draw together and resist the given 'sense of sense', or even the 'distribution of the sensible'. However, this creation of world itself acts on and (re)creates human rights. Without calcification or authority, human rights name a very different process; a demand, a gathering. Each time, singular; each time, common.

Chapter 9

On right-ing: constituent power and human rights

> To speak of 'meaning' and of 'truth' in the middle of military agitation, geo-political calculations, suffering, the grimaces of stupidity or else of lies is not 'idealistic': it is to get to the very nub of the thing.
>
> Nancy, *The Confronted Community*[1]

> [R]ights sought by a politically defined *group* are conferred upon depoliticized *individuals*; at the moment a particular 'we' succeeds in obtaining rights, it loses its 'we-ness' and dissolves into individuals.
>
> Brown, *States of Injury*[2]

In Chapter 1, I proposed that human rights draws together elements fundamental to both government and resistance, but that the immanent tension between these elements is never resolved. In that and the following chapters, I argued that the trace of the radical remains *even* when human rights become the *avant-garde* of biopolitical subordination, *even* when they open each of us up to the violence of the market. In this, human rights can at once hold the possibilities of an open resistance, but can also be a tool of empire or government: they are differential in essence. They can express an ideology of capitalistic–military–humanitarianism, which maintains minimal reform while largely continuing along the biopolitical or ecotechnic path to greater security, control and oppression through surveillance, exception and the camps.[3] Human rights and 'civil society' are often a shrouding morality for imperial power.[4] Yet there remains a fundamental *potentia* when a community gathers together to demand 'its rights'. This is not an attempt to prefigure the always heterogeneous expression of constituent power, but rather to attempt to reread this use of human rights, placing it at the heart of the corpus rather than on its periphery.[5] In this final chapter, I want to develop a sense of human rights as an event to be created each time rather than a property to be protected. I will use the term 'right-ing' to describe this. Following the chapters on constituent power, community and world, the question is now: how can the many dispersed shards of thought come together seamlessly in an alternative human rights? The answer is simple: they cannot. *There is not some sort of 'other' human rights that* we could oppose to the current practices. I am *not* suggesting another 'model' of human rights, but rather trying to trace a possibility of the discourse that is already distinctly within it. While the radical may have withdrawn from the narrative that human rights tells of itself, it remains as a trace.[6] What I have tried to do from a variety of starting points is to challenge the *necessity* of those conservative presuppositions about rights (liberal capitalism, individualism, globalism, statism and even law, narrowly conceived) that foreclose the possibilities immanent in the discourse. Through a retreat from the usual discussions about rights I have re-treated the discourse. I have circled around a human rights thought *with* constituent power, rather than against it.

The task of this chapter is to think about this differential human rights. To do this, I propose two parts to this concluding chapter. First, I want to look at two radical figurings of rights. I will begin with the erstwhile situationist Raoul Vaneigem's book, *A Declaration of the Rights of Human Beings*, which seeks to rewrite the canon. However, the text is an utter failure. Its utility here lies in demonstrating how *not* to rethink the radical in human rights. Despite its various interesting ideas, it remains attached to the *graphe-philia* so important to biopolitical regimes. Henri Lefebvre, by way of contrast, leads us along a different path with his figuring of 'the right to the city'. I argue that this gets directly to the heart of the difference of human rights. It is, at once, the banal suggestion of an individual right to have one's ownmost properties protected, *but also* a radical demand to unwork and rework both the world and the ones who take up the demand. In the second half of the chapter, by way of conclusion, I propose to sketch the theoretical basis of 'right-ing', emphasizing its collective, political and alegal dimensions. While I want to put these thoughts together temporarily, it should not be seen as an authoritative restatement of rights. I want to draw together a thinking of constituent power, a thought of the political *ensemble* of resistant action and a rendering of human rights that unworks its metaphysical predetermination. I must say, however, that this reconstruction is temporary and passing. The whole point is that this is not some sort of 'final' alternative model of human rights. Human rights are a complex ideology with a heterogeneous potential. They must be put together again and again. *There is neither model nor warranty, just the possibility of endless experimentation.* What is to be grasped, however, is the sense of a radical pole of this reconstruction – what I will call 'right-ing'.

Two radical notions of rights

The first radical attempt to rethink rights comes from ex-situationist Raoul Vaneigem. This is useful as it represents an interesting, if ultimately misplaced, approach to rights. In the influential text *The Revolution of Everyday Life*, he famously demanded that 'from now on the analysts are in the streets'.[7] In 2003 a translation of his *A Declaration of the Rights of Human Beings: On the Sovereignty of Life as Surpassing the Rights of Man* was published.[8] The back cover of this text suggests that his aim is to do nothing less than create anew the various declarations of rights as 'we can no longer make do with the liberties derived from free exchange, while the free circulation of capital is establishing a tyranny that reduces humankind and the earth to a commodity.' The starting points appear extremely useful in rethinking the pole of a radical human rights, particularly his link between human rights and mercantile freedoms that replay 'the dictatorship of exchange value'.[9] The suggestion throughout the text is that the state is part of the fundamental problem of current human rights discourse (although his suggestion of a 'sovereignty of life' already suggests a problematic response to this). Equally, it connects both with the question of technology in globalization/*mondialisation*, and the emphasis on use value in Lefebvre's right to the city as we will see in a moment. In other words, it would seem to cohere well with the themes of this work.

Vaneigem's book is an interesting mix of highly dubious and potentially incisive engagements with rights. Take his second article: every human being has the right to life.[10] While the 'possession' of a right, especially a right of 'life' is problematic, the first subsection attempts to clarify: 'Life is not given but a movement, a coming into being over which everyone has the means to exert an influence by the strength and awareness of what he or she possesses that is most alive.'[11] While the possession of a right to life is subverted, we instead find the human posed as the problematic subject that possesses 'the will to live'. At times Vaneigem mixes apposite critique with a very strange naiveté. In Article 3(1), it is asserted that no one has to comply with an order, kneel before an authority, bow before any self-styled superior, to show any respect, etc.[12] It is not difficult to see the drive for a sort of very basic anarchistic sense of 'freedom', but surely this sort of political writing is at once far too idealistic and also far too liberal in its outlook. It seems to suggest some sort of decaffeinated subject (as Žižek would say), wrapped in cotton wool and protected from the violence of everyday life. The very interaction of one with another involves levels of 'violence' – and I mean that in the broad sense that would incorporate symbolic and linguistic violence alongside the physical. There is the suggestion of an isolated monad at play in his own imagining. In many instances he seems to strike an anti-capitalist note; the (albeit simplistic) rejection of rights as mercantile freedoms, the rejection of the levelling down of everything in exchange value, the rejection of the association of time with money.[13] However, as the writers at *Not Bored* point out: 'Vaneigem thinks [that it is capitalism that] is powering the "gradual" "transition" to a fully and truly human society.'[14] They observe that his ideology at times seems close to neo-liberalism as proposed by 'any number of "progressive" politicians and "green capitalists". There is a *very* good reason that, in its review of this book, *Le Monde* said that "all opponents of globalization should carry it in their luggage": this book will help make sure that the "anti-globalization" movement never becomes an *anti-capitalist* movement.'[15] However, this is not the reason why I argue that Vaneigem's conception of rights should be dismissed.

To begin with, it seems to have no affective element. One crucial aspect of human rights is their ability to insert themselves into political struggles. However, it is difficult to imagine people at the barricades shouting: 'All human beings have the right to take delight in themselves, in others and in the world',[16] 'Every human being has the right to vanquish terror and tame fear'[17] or 'Every human being has the right to replace state governments with a world federation of small local collectives in which the quality of the individuals guarantees the humanity of societies.'[18] This is no manifesto. Its meanings are often opaque, its explanations are far from the life that it claims to attach to. More significantly, perhaps, it is a declaration and the history of this form is overwhelmingly statist. This directly conflicts with Vaneigem's anti-statist aims and explications. His statism manifests itself deep in the very fibre of the text that claims to undertake the writing of life. As such, Vaneigem's text both grasps and misses what is most essential to human rights as they stand: they are deeply bound to the human, in an attempt to exhaustively *write his nature*. Vaneigem falls into this trap, by declaring the sovereignty of life he seems to be far more attached to the *graphe-philia* that lies at the heart of postmodern regulatory and governmentality regimes. Each mode of the human is written – from the freedom to dress as one wants to, the right to make mistakes, the right to speak, to be idle, to create, to have a personal sense of beauty. What we get from this exercise is not a radical sense of human rights distinguished in their anti-capitalism from the 'mercantile freedoms', presumably including the UDHR. Rather, we get just another rendering of the human which ultimately can be easily accommodated within the liberal–capitalist tradition. What the text begins by promising, but never quite achieves, is a sense of the human as the creative–destructive being, that is open in its essence. Certain rights reach towards this, for example; 'the right to become human'[19] and 'the right to create and to self-creation'.[20] Yet, the placing of these within the framework of rights strips the openness of the creation and places them in a chain of limitation. Creation is not the defining feature, rather the right is. Thus, 'the right' as a mode of political action is not challenged in its hegemony. Only by placing right as creation can we get to this challenge.

Vaneigem's own words come back to haunt him: 'If anyone says or writes that practical reason must henceforth be based on the rights of the individual and the individual alone, he invalidates his own proposition if he doesn't incite his audience to make this statement true for themselves.'[21] While he may incite, this has fallen on deaf ears. This is not because people are somehow not ready for it, but rather because the *hyper-graphe* of the text is not comfortable on the streets. 'The great collective illusions . . . have given way to the thousands of pre-packed ideologies sold by consumer society like so many portable brain-scrambling machines. Will it need as much blood again to show that a hundred thousand pinpricks kill as surely as a couple of blows with a club.'[22] Vaneigem's rights become just another one of those ideologies, the political equivalent of a pre-packed ready meal. In his words, it is just another pinprick, as likely to kill any radical hope for rights as the clubbing that such politics gets from neo-liberalism and neoconservativism.

Against Vaneigem's recent rights, it is useful to instantiate the radical possibility of 'right-ing' through Lefebvre's idea of the 'right to the city'. This crucially renders the city as an *oeuvre*, that is, 'a work in which all its citizens participate.'[23] For Lefebvre:

> Cities were necessarily *public* – and therefore places of social interaction and exchange with people who were necessarily different. Publicity demands heterogeneity and the space of the city . . . assured a thick fabric of heterogeneity, one in which encounters with difference were guaranteed. But for the encounter with difference to *inhabit* the city . . . had always to be struggled for . . . Out of this struggle the city as a work – as an *oeuvre*, as a collective if not singular project – emerges, and new modes of living, new modes of inhabiting, are invented.[24]

For Mitchell, however, the problem is that even this *oeuvre* is alienated. The city is not simply created and to be created anew, rather the creation has been expropriated by a 'dominant class'. Mitchell explains that 'more and more the spaces of the modern city are being produced *for* us rather than *by* us. People, Lefebvre argued, have a right to more; they have the right to the *oeuvre*.'[25]

The crucial aspect, however, of this association of 'right' and 'city' is that, unlike Vaneigem, the right itself does not remain the same. The right to the city (qua *oeuvre*) radically refigures 'right' making it differ from itself. If the city is constantly being made, then the right itself takes on the fundamental instability of its object. Merrifield explains that this 'isn't any pseudo right, Lefebvre assures us, no simple visiting right, a tourist trip down memory lane, gawking at a gentrified old town; neither is it enjoying for the day a city you've been displaced from.'[26] Instead, the 'right to the city manifests itself as a superior form of rights: right to freedom, to individualization in socialization, to habitat and to inhabit. The right to the *oeuvre*, to participation and *appropriation* (clearly distinct from the right to property), are implied in the right to the city.'[27] The 'superiority' of the right to the city must not be misunderstood: it is not merely superior in some quasi-naturalistic or theological sense of a higher law; neither is it similar to the assertion that you sometimes see in the jaded debate about socioeconomic versus civil and political rights, that one or other set of rights is superior for whatever reason. Rather, the right to the city is superior in the sense that it clarifies the contradictions of rights, revealing the struggle that lies at their heart. In fact, it alters the priority of traditional rights struggle. Ordinarily, as I have continually circled, one appeals to the state or more specifically the judiciary in order to vindicate one's rights. The right to the city, however, proposes something that the state cannot protect. There is no property around which the triplet property–protection–prestruction can take hold and effect an exclusion of others through the force of law. The right to the city is a 'demand and cry' for the centrality of making-with-others, the material struggle of the *oeuvre* itself. Importantly for this work, Lefebvre's idea of this right demonstrates the radical pole of human rights that I underlined in the Introduction.

There is a second element here. The right to the city immediately places rights in a historical and spatial (a spatio-historical or a historico-spatial) sense. The traditional rights struggle is placed between the state and the individual, perhaps gathered together with others, but essentially alone. However, because the city is understood as making-together and a making-of-the-together, it starts from the always already of community and city. The right to the city asserts the historically situated nature of the struggle. Against the traditional ahistorical tendency of rights, the right to the city begins from the fact that the city is an accumulation of injustice. The city is always already alienated and alienating. Thus, the right to the city proposes, in a radical sense, beginning from spatio-historical injustice. The spatial cannot be decoupled from the historical. Lefebvre argued that: 'To change life means to change space as well . . . The transformation of social relations . . . means a transformation of socio-spatial relations, a production of a new, liberatory space.'[28] In the production of space, we produce ourselves. There is no efficient cause here. Crucially, the city demonstrates the difference of what is planned from what is produced. The right to the city, therefore, begins from a position of instability, an instability of 'right', of 'city' and of 'subject'. In this sense, Tushnet's critiques of instability and indeterminacy become important *positive* aspects of rights.[29] The radical in rights is recoverable *precisely because* they do not somehow have a final determinate content, because they do not have a stable meaning over time. All the exercises in stabilization (from declaration and convention to (quasi-)judicial decision and authoritative interpretation) cannot hide the real possibility of rights.

Elden explains that, for Lefebvre, the right to the city is a call from the periphery for centrality. However, this is not a simple distinction between the excluded and included. His notion of time is crucial. Lefebvre sees history 'as a succession of static periods, times of stagnation and relative balance, separated by creative bursts and revolutions – the 'events'. But these [the situation and event] cannot be separated, because each lies as a germ in the heart of the other.'[30] It is in this sense that the cry of the 'right to the city' takes shape. It should not be reduced to juridical rights as Mitchell seems to do at times (I will return to this later). Rather, it is the right to 'reclaim' the being-together of the city.[31]

The radical sense of the right to the city can be further understood through an *analogy* with his idea of the 'right of autogestion'. Autogestion, in its simplest sense, means self-production. As Elden explains, it was a tactic floated by the Eurocommunists in the seventies whereby factories would be run by the workers. The crucial aspect of a 'right of autogestion', whether we are convinced by its content or not, is that the right folds into its object. It is the *right* itself that becomes self-forming, it is digested by the autogestion, emerging at once utterly different and uncannily similar to other conceptions of rights. The radical in rights is retraced, rendering the right itself in the process of creation as it acts out, creates or performs its own object. Like the right to the city, 'autogestion is not something established but is itself the "site and stake of struggle."'[32] While I should not abstract 'right-ing' from what is called for within each particular moment, it is perhaps instructive now to formulate it: right-ing is a demand or cry that is not established but projects the site and stake of struggle. Of course, such a formulation comes with the caveat that this is not some sort of universal determination of right-ing as such (as though such a thing could exist). Crucially, for Lefebvre, autogestion did not provide a 'magic formula' to solve all of society's ills. He criticized:

> [c]ertain Yugoslavs [who] committed the error of seeing in autogestion a system, and therefore a model, that could be established juridically and that could function without clashes and contradictions, in a sort of social and political harmony. Instead, autogestion reveals contradictions in the State, because it is the very trigger of those contradictions ... Autogestion must continually be enacted. The same is true of democracy which is never a 'condition' but a fight.[33]

To clarify, I am not proposing the right to autogestion, rather, I want to suggest that it is useful to understand the manner in which the right to the city is a 'superior' right. A critique of the right to autogestion would include the observations that as a political intervention autogestion is at once a little too situated in Fordism (therefore lacking political purchase in post-Fordist economic conditions), a little too close to the humanist rendering of the subject and, taken out of context, even a little similar to David Cameron's 'Big Society'. The sense in which autogestion relies on an *auto* and/or self would have to be examined in further depth, along with its sense of creation or production. At the same time, the practices of Lefebvre's autogestion would need to be compared to managerial theories, such as the so-called 'distributed leadership' idea which seeks to 'do away with the manager' while maintaining the alienation of the workers. While Lefebvre does indeed clarify some of these issues, this is not the place for such a discussion.[34]

Returning to the right to the city, when Lefebvre is taken up, the radical refashioning of rights itself comes into question. Don Mitchell's influential *The Right to the City*[35] demonstrates a tendency towards the withdrawal of the radical and a recovering of juridical stability, highlighted in Chapters 2 and 3. Interestingly, however, this is not the usual withdrawal of all radical political possibilities that we find in the UN Covenants. Rather, with Mitchell we find a slipping back into statist and even individualistic forms while maintaining quite a radical position on social and political questions. I want to suggest that the problem here is with his conception of rights. He begins by asking: 'Just how do "rights" and "rights talk" do what I claim they do?'[36] Immediately, he caricaturizes Foucault, Derrida and others, saying that it is inaccurate to say that 'discourses' produce things (his rendering of 'discourse', however, is risible).[37] Instead, he picks out the relational sense of rights (they 'are social relations and hence a means of organizing the actual social content of justice')[38] and attempts to place that against the critique of indeterminacy of language.[39] He says that rights have real force, they 'establish an important *ideal* against which the behaviour of the state, capital, and other

powerful actors must be measured – and held accountable. They provide an institutionalized framework, no matter how incomplete, within which the goals of
social struggle can not only be organised but also attained.'[40] By eliding the
Foucauldian disciplinary power of rights, Mitchell can make it a matter of 'us'
and 'them'; the poor and excluded fighting for what the rights 'actually mean' and
the state misappropriating them. This misses the crucial aspect of rights – there is
no such thing as a law that can 'grant freedom'[41] – freedom can only be 'performed'
(for want of a better word).[42] The rejection of the indeterminacy thesis and the
insights of post-structuralism leads Mitchell down the blind alley of reducing
disciplinary power and the state to police power.

Mitchell's slip from a radical conception of the city (as *oeuvre*) to a more traditional rendering of rights is quite clear:

> The right to the city implies the right to the uses of city spaces, the right to
> *inhabit*. In turn, and highly germane to the current American city, where we
> are reduced to arguing over whether one has the right to publicly urinate if he
> or she is homeless, the right to inhabit implies a *right* to housing: a place to
> sleep, a place to urinate and defecate without asking someone else's permis-
> sion, a place to relax, a place from which to venture forth. Simply guaran-
> teeing the right to housing may not be sufficient to guaranteeing a right to the
> city, but it is a necessary step toward guaranteeing that right.[43]

In other words, one can conceive of the right to the city in terms of a gradual
process of enshrining its protection. In this view, the city as *oeuvre* loses its
almost ontological stature and, instead, becomes a metonym for social, economic
and political rights. With this, Lefebvre's assertion that the right to the city is a
'superior form' of rights gets reduced to a categorical superiority – it stands for
all the other rights as a super-category.[44]

Crucially, both 'radical' and 'reformist' poles (this is heuristic; I am not
proposing such a crude dichotomy) are *proper* to the right to the city. Both are
'authentic' renderings of the right, there is no authoritative statement of its
content. In other words, this is a differential right. The danger of an authoritative
restatement is calcification, as I argued in Chapter 3. Along with the authoritative
juridical statement that Mitchell seems to desire, those capable of (re)creating and
(re)fashioning the right would become limited to a judiciary or legislature. The
creative sense of being-together withdraws and instead a regulative order enters.
Mitchell sees rights as a unitary concept which can *accommodate* radical politics.
However, it is necessary to understand the tension between the human rights of
the constituted order and the radical right to the city. Human rights become
radical only when they are *appropriated*. In other words, it is not a matter of
placing the right to the city within the current rights discourse (this would be his
suggestion of a 'right to pee in public' or sleep on the street). Rather it is a matter
of recharging the discourse with the possibilities of right-ing. It is not a matter
of fitting radical demands into the traditional form, but of re-forming and

reappropriating rights through the radical demand. With this appropriation the difference of human rights emerges once more: neither constituted order nor constituent power, but *both*.

The point of this chapter is not to highlight an 'other' right that is somehow 'more human rights than human rights'. The point is not that the 'right to the city' in Lefebvre's hands gives us *the* radical human right, but that its radical potential lies in most if not all human rights. The 'spirit'[45] of the right to the city is there within the heterogeneity of human rights itself. Freedom of speech or association, for instance, when reappropriated against the statism and individualism of the traditional discourse can be just as radical as the right to the city. The radical lies within human rights, at once constantly revealing itself and at the same time withdrawing. In this double movement the difference of human rights occurs. To rethink or re-treat the radical or political pole of rights is an attempt to circle the aspect of rights that is a process of creation rather than a plea to authority for limitation. The right to the city is the best example that I can find of such a right-ing. This is so because the assertion of the particular right is understood as an event that attempts to challenge the historic relation by creating for itself the space of interaction; it is always already collective; it is faced towards others rather than the state; it does not seek its own abstraction but instead attempts to manifest the political of a right-ing community; and, finally, it does not demand its own universalization, it could not be used as a metric of 'development' or 'civilization' or enforced through invasion.

Right-ing and the sovereignty of human rights?

To end this book, let me restate the problem by describing human rights as they currently stand. Traditionally, human rights are opposed to constituent power as opposite poles of the liberal democratic settlement. Democracy, placed within a liberal symbolic framework, draws together the process of representation and election with the limitation of law and rights. With human rights, the idea remains that a people (*demos*) is limited by a rule which lies beyond their power (*kratos*), but this rule comes from the very existence of each of the people's constituent parts (each and every 'human'). The 'human' stands for a limitation or restriction of the state, of the people and of other people. Even the empowerment implicit in human rights discourse is framed within a certain structuring. This structuring places sovereignty at the end (*telos*) of the discourse. It seeks to change the practice of the state, altering the law, the function of the police or the army. Whether the state itself is the agent of violation or is merely failing to protect the individual from others, human rights becomes a framework in which a 'peaceful' ordering is possible. To do this the discourse interweaves metaphysical positions about sovereignty with the essence of the human:[46] (S)he eats, sleeps under shelter, talks and associates with others, moves around, must be free of torture. The human of this norm is a bare entity of mere function. Life may be full of others, of identities, of discourses, of power, joy, taste and sense; however, the human is stripped of these particularities and rendered as an empty shell. As this empty shell, it stands for each and every particular individual and with this its *majesty* grows. Majesty here is an important term, as it is the point at which human rights inserts into traditional sovereignty:

> Humanity is a newly conceptualized form of social integration, going beyond that of other bonds in the shape of tribal regional or national loyalties. It does this not only as an abstraction but as a reality, given legal form in various international organizations as well as actual form as a result of present day globalization. Stretched to the limits, the concept is an ongoing development, offering 'humanity' a new type of sovereignty.[47]

It is precisely the 'greatness' or 'dignity' of the idea that traditional accounts use to defend the discourse, setting it metaphysically above the conflict of the political. It is not surprising that 'dignity' is a crucial term for the discourse's self-legitimation. The UDHR explains that: 'recognition of the inherent dignity and of the equal and inalienable rights of all members of the human family is the foundation of freedom, justice and peace in the world.' With this association human rights are rendered with the transcendent majesty of sovereignty. The majesty of the human towers over the power of any people. Thus, with this trope of sovereignty in place, the traditional dichotomy is established; the people versus human rights.[48]

I have argued implicitly throughout this work that it is this structuring of human rights through sovereignty and as sovereign that is problematic. It is time to draw this out now, making it explicit in closing. As I explained in Chapter 3, traditional human rights are statist and individualistic. This framework establishes a juridical metaphysics at the heart of human rights. This comes through in the attempt to establish a 'new sovereignty' of humanity, as Mazlish would have it. The logic of sovereignty demands a metaphysical point above the world from which to cleave the 'inhuman' from humanity. This posited 'beyond' is theological in origin, what Heidegger called the onto-theological. However, as Heidegger said '[t]he minute the question concerning the essence counts as settled, a door is opened to unessence.'[49] The juridical attempt to fix the properties of the human, finds an underlying reason or a fixed systemic understanding of being. But this entirely misunderstands being. This metaphysical view sees 'is' merely in terms of presence. Thus, by introducing time as being, Heidegger revealed that being is a constant coming to presence, being is constantly arriving. What the metaphysical systems miss, especially the natural law from which human rights emerge, is the change at the heart of what *is*.

In an attempt to escape this I have posed a distinction between constituent and constituted power. It is fair to point out that in the traditional usages constituent power was generally a secularized theology. However, I argued that traditionally the constituent moment was only ever constructed for and by the constituted power. Constituted order looks to constituent power for the authority and legitimacy of its sovereign assertions. It is utilized as the 'beyond' of the constituted order that can transcend and legitimate its existence. This view mistakes the constituent, only seeing it through whatever constituted order may or may not follow. Rather, I suggested that it must be understood in its essence as creation *ex nihilo*. As I suggested in Chapter 8, Nancy explains that this is not the traditional figuration of an efficient cause generating the universe from nothing (the Christian take on creation). Rather this is the idea of creation from *the nothing*. This creation is, of course, situated within discourse. 'There is no starting point', as Althusser reminds us. The creation emerges from the nothing, in a confluence of discourses.

'Right-ing' is the term that Douzinas uses to describe the radical aspect of human rights. It is time now to begin to set out what right-ing describes and draws together in this work. This is not a normative prescription, but rather an attempt to highlight an aspect of human rights that is unthought, an approach to political action which remains all too often hidden. Nancy explains that the task is:

> [n]ot to weigh out as best as one can equal amounts of submission and revolt, and always end halfway between reform and accommodation, but to *make* the world into the place, never still, always perpetually re-opened, of its own contradiction, which is what prevents us from ever knowing in advance *what* is to be done, but imposes upon us the task of never making anything that is not a world.[50]

It is a matter of invention of a world. This is the meaning of the 'constituent', which is removed from any dialectic of the constituent–constituted and away from the Negrean sense of the human producing his essence as work. This is the ineluctability of invention of the world *without model or warranty*. This is the opening of human rights to the process of right-ing within them.

However, it remains too abstract at this, so let me hazard a little more in the way of material observation. Right-ing cannot be undertaken by governments, it cannot be found in the decisions of this or that international authority. These authorities, by their nature (*as* authorities) attempt to speak *for* the human, squaring one norm with another. Stemming from singularity, which is unrepresentable, right-ing cannot be expressed *for* anyone. Rather right-ing occurs when a group gathers around the saying of a demand. This group is inoperative in the sense that there is no natural or ineluctable property that could bind them. It is not inoperative in Wilson's sense that it must do nothing. The demand challenges the state of the situation. In the current 'distribution of the sensible' this might tend towards some aspect of anti-capitalism, because in our neo-liberal post-political age the economic tends to entirely over-determine other discourses. However, it may stem from any of the heterogeneous axes of oppression. Finally, the saying of the demand will tend towards the creation of worlds. This does not mean that the demand must be fitted into an old or new worldview, that a protestor must have a 'plan for afterwards'. In fact, precisely the opposite. As I argued in the last chapter and throughout, it entails the attempt to create new ways of being together that would resist the logics of security and biopolitics.

It may be objected that without normative content, there can be no guarantee of 'right-ing': it could be claimed by neo-fascists, racists or reactionary civil society movements. In recent years we have seen a number of conservative movements that seem to follow the 'bottom-up' model of human rights; the anti-Aristide politics of Haiti in the run up to his 2004 overthrow,[51] the anti-Chavez groups in the run up to the 2002 coup or, more recently, the anti-government protests of 2008 in Thailand. In each instance, conservative forces gathered together around a model of 'human rights' that are used to determine the discourse through the privatized media channels. Some might suggest that these movements could fit into this bottom-up notion of right-ing, precisely because it fails to take a normative political position. Yet it is a little more complex than this. To be right-ing, these parties and groups would have to demand thought and disrupt the sensible. However, I am not convinced that they do. The anti-Aristide and anti-Chavez politics certainly were the embodiment of an expansive Americanism. They are empire in the clothes of the multitude. They merely feed off the already-given of geopolitical imaginaries, which is the foremost tool in the armoury of empire. Thus, they do not 'disrupt the sensible'. The flipside of this is that other racist or neo-fascist groups might claim to disrupt the sensible, which they claim is expressed in multiculturalism – I am thinking particularly about the English Defence League (EDL), which apparently has a lesbian, gay, bisexual and transgender division.[52] Yet these groups usually determine their identity as a group by enclosing themselves around an ethnic, sexual or racial identity (or a mixture of each) that is violently policed. With the EDL, this is through a rabid Islamophobia. As such, these groups make the community itself operative and perform the sacrificial logic of sovereignty that I looked at in Chapters 7 and 8. Theirs is not a right-ing by any stretch of the imagination.

The assertion of constituent power as the starting point for a politics of 'human rights' would be very different from the current universalist (or communitarian) legalism. The rejection of the logic of sovereignty is crucial, but this could never be an absolute turning away. There could be no pure anti-sovereign logic. By its nature this would set sovereignty in process either in its negative imprint or by setting its *anti*-sovereignty as a sovereign concept. Thus, the question must be how could right-ing be instantiated in such a way as to perform a turning away from the logic of sovereignty. It goes without saying that it could not begin with the state's power of legitimate violence or majesty of decision or the conceptualization of the individual and state. Perhaps not quite as obviously, it could not begin with the international as a sphere distinct from the state. The international is the space in which national regimes seek the camaraderie and legitimation of other like-minded entities. In fact, the very idea of starting from an already author-ized point would be questioned. Right-ing could not authorize anyone at all, it would not empower or legitimate action. Rather, it describes a call to political creation, a call to think being together in the world. Resistance happens. It is not necessary for human rights to legitimate it for to occur.

The key, I suspect, to this different thinking of right-ing is that human rights should not be thought through the traditional property/protection/prestruction lens, which I described in Chapter 3, but rather as an enactment or performance. Human rights, stripped of the self-satisfied globalizing universal answer of a pre-given right, becomes a name for something quite different. Douzinas, introduces the term in the course of a description of a non-metaphysical humanism:

> A non-metaphysical humanism would not treat people as synthetic entities for which the prosthetic operation of fragmentary rights satisfies discon-nected wants. Community would not be constructed by the following of the past or obedience to tradition but by the exposure to the other person, whose trace creates self . . . [I]t would reverse the arrogance of subjectivity and assign rights, if at all, because, as humans, we have been destined to be near Being and to care for the human as well as the other entities in which Being discloses itself. Some human rights may be consistent with non-metaphysical humanism. But the overall form of the social bond would change from rights and principles to being-in-common, to the public recognition and protection of the becoming-human with others, a dynamic process which resists all attempts to hold humanity to an essence decided by the representatives of power. *To coin a term, this would be a process of 'righting' and not a series of rights and, like writing, it would open Being to the new and unknown as a condition of its humanity.*[53]

Right-ing is the opening of human rights by constituent power, a confluence of the two discourses. It is a figuration of the (already withdrawn) radical in rights.

Douzinas gives the example of the 'Spanish soldiers [who] met the advancing Napoleonic armies, shouting "Down with freedom!" It is not difficult to imagine', he says 'people meeting the "peacekeepers" of the New Times with cries of "Down with human rights!".'[54] This is not merely an anecdote detailing the infi-nite reversibility of human rights, rather, the cries of the soldiers and the new imperial subjects perform the *differential structure of human rights*. The Spanish soldiers or the imagined conquered peoples of the New Times, perform *the differ-ence* between politics and the political. They reject the 'freedom' or 'human rights' of the conquering power and, in so doing, they shatter the distribution of the sensible. Those aspects that we consider universal goods are differed from themselves, the Spanish soldiers perform the truly *free* act by decrying imperial 'freedom'. In the same way, that the imagined 'Down with human rights!' chant challenges the givenness of human rights to justify an imperial invasion, this distribution of the sensible is challenged with the most intimate aspect of human rights – the oppressed voice demanding and rupturing the given.

Right-ing is a process of creation, an exercise of constituent power, a process of being-with which struggles for the in-common rather than merely reducing it to the bland monotony of everyday politics. It is a creative praxis. By placing the resistance that human rights name as that which is proper to the spirit of human rights we begin to see their sense. This is not the endless transformation of desire into right, which is intrinsic to the liberal–capitalist system.[55] That is, the evacuation of sense from right-ing. It levels down all rights claims to the point at which my right to freedom from torture is on the same level as my right to free-range eggs and organic milk. Rather, the always arriving sense of human rights means that human rights are ontologically open to the becoming of being (the to-come). The transformation of the sense of sense, from having to being, is precisely what is needed in human rights. The starting point of the possessive individual is set aside through the being-with of community in which we discover our ownmost *potentia.* Together, we are exposed to the potentiality of world creation. This is not the Negrean position of the (ontologically) productive multitude, but rather it is the Nancean plural singularities with their necessity of creating *ex nihilo.* I propose a right-ing that stands (each time singularly) against: the 'denudement of sense and value [which] marks the withdrawal of the world';[56] against the unworlding of the world; against the human rights which turn into the moral cover for neo-imperial warfare and domination; against 'the withdrawal of sense [that] has made human rights infinitely reversible'. The radical heart of human rights still beats. It once sought protection against the power of the state, but now seeks to resist the biopolitical domination or the Nancean soft totalitarianism of the 'economic-socio-techno-cultural complex' – ecotechnics. Right-ing is always a singular politics, the transformation of the sense of the world.

The Nancean 'transformation of the sense of sense' or 'world-creation' is what distinguishes right-ing. It displaces the juridical metaphysics of sovereignty and instead proposes no transcendent solution, no model that might come with guarantees from the experts of its definite success. The constituent in rights provides no warranty. Right-ing is an expression of an open constituent *potentia*, a bottom-up thought of human rights. It is a politics of singularity that demands thinking in each instance. Right-ing is the demand for the impossible, which forces a revaluation of the possible. Like the Lefebvrean 'right to the city', it draws its 'force from the suffering of the past and the injustices of the present and act[s parasitically] . . . on the body of rights, consuming the host and projecting a future out of a rather bland legal history.'[57] It shifts the emphasis in rights from the fetishistic focus on already given legal and quasi-legal texts. Beyond the alleged safety of human rights enshrined in covenants, it seeks to emphasize their constituent generation of the sense of the world:

> Invention is always without model and without warranty. But indeed that implies facing up to turmoil, anxiety, even disarray. Where certainties come apart, there too gathers the strength that no certainty can match.[58]

Notes

Chapter I Democracy, radical politics and a differential human rights

1 Fitzpatrick correctly suggests that there 'is a convenient poverty to occidental conceptions of resistance in social and legal thought. The very etymology is compliant: *re*
   back and *sistere* to stand, hence *resistere*, to stand back, to withstand. The impover-
   ished conceptions of resistance tend to reflect the etymology. Resistance stands back in
   a position apart, a position from which it tends to affirm the integrity of what is resisted,
   a position from where it elevates what is resisted while itself becoming diminished and
   parasitic. So we find that even with finely observed and sympathetic accounts, the
   monumental solidity of what is resisted confronts a resistance rendered as local or
   quotidian, reactive or dependent, interstitial or evanescent' (P. Fitzpatrick, 'Introduction'
   in *Law as Resistance* (Ashgate, Aldershot, 2008): 1).
2 Evans sees this difference, although as can be seen I would frame it very differently:
   'The political discourse on human rights therefore seems to offer two possible views of
   the role of power. The first suggests "power to the people" in that it offers the oppressed,
   the excluded and the victims of tyrannical government an opportunity to gain the
   "moral high ground" in the struggle for emancipation and freedom. The second sees
   human rights as "power over people", expressed in exclusionary practices that deny the
   full participation of those who fail to support the interests of the dominant group. Thus,
   the conception of human rights often supports competing conceptions that give focus
   to deeply rooted political struggles. Put another way, the formal, institutionalized and
   legal practices of human rights reflect and sustain the interests of a dominant group in
   the existing order, while informal, privately motivated and, on occasion, extra-legal
   action reflects the interest of an alternative order' (T. Evans, *The Politics of Human
   Rights* (Pluto Press, London, 2001): 18).
3 A good example of this privileging is Pearlman's argument that human rights, because
   they begin from dignity and protection, properly belong to law: 'if respect for human
   dignity conditions the juridical conception of human rights and if one seeks to guarantee this respect in such a way as to surpass what is merely desirable by establishing an
   effective political protection of that respect, then we must admit as a corollary to this
   foundational condition the existence of a legal system with the power of constraint.
   Within this system, respect for human rights imposes an obligation to respect the
   human person both upon every human being – concerning himself as well as other
   human beings – and upon all authorities charged with protecting these rights. If such an
   obligation is not placed upon the authorities themselves, they run the risk of becoming
   tyrannical and arbitrary under the very pretext of protecting human rights. In order to
   avoid such an arbitrary state of affairs, it becomes necessary to limit the powers of

every authority charged with protecting the respect owed to the dignity of persons, and for this it is necessary to presuppose a State of Law (*Rechtsstaat*) and the independence of judiciary power. For this reason, a doctrine of human rights which would be anything other than a simple moral or religious ideal requires a State of Law: the two are correlative notions' (C. Pearlman, 'The Safeguarding and Foundation of Human Rights', 1.1 *Law and Philosophy* (1982):119–120).

4   While it approaches the point I am trying to make here, I would not subscribe to Gearty's unitary sense of the history of human rights. He suggests that in a few generations in the enlightenment 'the language of human rights mutated from a radical voice into an intensely reactionary one' (C. Gearty, *Can Human Rights Survive* (Cambridge University Press, Cambridge, 2006): 77). Certainly, the hegemonic voices of human rights in those eras were more reactionary than radical, but there remained those who used the general discourse to democratically challenge the state of the situation. I will deal more with this in the next chapter.

5   C. Mouffe, *The Democratic Paradox* (Verso, London, 2009): 2.

6   Ibid: 5.

7   This is against the many and varied theories that see democracy as a shorthand for liberal democracy. Brettschneider, for instance claims a hegemony for this: 'It is settled judgment, so much so that it is simply assumed in almost all of the literature of democratic theory, that no regime can properly be regarded as democratic without the rule of law' (C. Brettschneider, *Democratic Rights: The Substance of Self-Government* (Princeton University Press, Princeton (NJ), 2007): 38). Or, in a more reasoned manner, 'Democracy assures participation, whereas rights protect dignity. However, dignity can hardly exist without participation – and true democracy is not really possible without the recognition and protection of individual dignity. Democracy and human rights are interdependent' (W. Osiatynski, *Human Rights and their Limits* (Cambridge University Press, Cambridge, 2009): 72).

8   Evans, *The Politics of Human Rights*: 55.

9   Here, I would suggest Peter Fitzpatrick 'Terminal Legality: Human Rights and Critical Being', in P. Fitzpatrick and P. Tuitt (eds) *Critical Beings: Law, Nation and the Global Subject* (Ashgate, Aldershot, 2004):119.

10 'Proper' here is used in the Heideggerian sense. *Eigentlich* in *Being and Time* was originally translated as 'authentic'. However, as Derrida and others have pointed out, it is better rendered as proper. It suggests that something accords to its own being. However, this should be read alongside Derrida's deconstruction of authenticity or the proper. Beings play between the proper and the improper, there is no purity. I will use proper in this manner throughout the book.

11 I will not spend much time on this, but these three terms have very different senses. Oscillation suggests a rhythmic movement, perhaps even mechanical. It is the end of a process. Vibration, by way of contrast, is far less controlled. It is a byproduct of another process and perhaps suggests greater speed. Trembling, as may be familiar to readers of Jean-Luc Nancy, is again very different. It suggests the enormity of either pole and the significance of how to put them together. Human rights are differential, but there is no pure pole. Rather, in each instance they are put together differently. I do not think this can be reduced to strategy, but that could be one way of understanding what I mean.

12 I. James, 'On Interrupted Myth', 9.4 *Journal for Cultural Research* (2005): 336.

13 An excellent example of this is Obama's recent discussion with Hu Jintao. There he suggested 'that countries prospered when they respected basic human rights'. Thus, human rights and the economy become the tool of necessity – you must have human rights, just as you must have the market, because that leads to prosperity' available at http://www.guardian.co.uk/world/2011/jan/19/barack-obama-hu-jintao-welcome (accessed 23/01/2011).

14 Ibid: 336.
15 This difference between politics and the political plays a similar role to ontological difference in Heidegger. See O. Marchart, *Post-foundational Political Thought: Political Difference in Nancy, Lefort, Badiou and Laclau* (Edinburgh University Press, Edinburgh, 2007).

Chapter 2 Challenging human rights histories

1 'The clergy and professional philanthropists have always collaborated with the army in this bloody exploitation. The colonial machinery that extracts the last penny from natural advantages hammers away with the joyful regularity of a pole ax. The white man preaches, doses, vaccinates, assassinates and (from himself) receives absolution. With his psalms, his speeches, his guarantees of liberty, equality and fraternity, he seeks to drown the noise of his machine guns' (A. Breton, et al., *Murderous Humanitarianism* (S. Beckett trans.) available at http://racetraitor.org/murderoushumanitarianism.html (accessed 19/08/10).
2 Moyn calls a church history that which reads itself back into history in a reverse teleology, seeing martyrs and visionaries, see Paul Lauren Gordon *The Evolution of International Human Rights: Visions Seen* (University of Pennsylvania Press, Pittsburgh, 2003) for a very clear example of this. See Moyn, available at http://www.youtube.com/watch?v=oqtFJZB27M8 (accessed 04/01/11). See also S. Moyn, *The Last Utopia: Human Rights in History* (Harvard University Press, Cambridge (MA), 2010).
3 For this periodization, see E. Hobsbawm, *The Age of Revolution: Europe 1789–1848* (Vintage Books, New York, 1996), *The Age of Capital, 1848–1875* (Vintage Books, New York, 1996) and *The Age of Empire, 1875–1914* (Vintage Books, London, 1989).
4 Just taking one instance of this (and there are so many): Mahoney's index of his history section is instructive: 'Ancient Classical World. The World of the Bible. The Medieval World. Renaissance and Reformation Thought. Hobbes and Rousseau. Revolution in England. American Independence. French Declaration of the Rights of Man. English Resistance to Human Rights. German Developments: Kant and Marx' (J. Mahoney, *The Challenge of Human Rights: Origin, Development and Significance* (Blackwell, Oxford, 2007).
5 B. Orend, *Human Rights: Concept and Context* (Broadview Press, Peterborough, ON, 2002): 197.
6 Ibid: 198.
7 See Moyn's first chapter for a useful rendering of the differences between pre- and post-Second World War ideas of rights (Moyn, *The Last Utopia*). I will come back to this when I look at the third strategy.
8 Bates repeats this misunderstanding, suggesting that *Magna Carta* 'had little to do with the rights of the common man, and much to do with securing rights for powerful barons against an overbearing king of England' (E. Bates, 'History' in D. Moeckli, S. Shah and S. Sivakumaran (eds) *International Human Rights Law* (Oxford University Press, Oxford, 2010): 19).
9 P. Linebaugh, *The Magna Carta Manifesto, Liberties and Commons for All* (University of California Press, Berkeley, 2008): 31.
10 Chapter 47: 'All forests that have been made such in our time shall forthwith be disafforested; and a similar course shall be followed with regard to river-banks that have been placed "in defence" by us in our time.' And chapter 48 reads: 'All evil customs connected with forests and warrens, foresters and warreners, sheriffs and their officers, river-banks and their wardens, shall immediately be inquired into in each county by twelve sworn knights of the same county chosen by the honest men of the same county, and shall, within forty days of the said inquest, be utterly abolished, so as never to be

restored, provided always that we previously have intimation thereof, or our justiciar, if we should not be in England.'

11 Linebaugh, *The Magna Carta Manifesto*: 31.
12 Ibid: 7.
13 To her great credit, Ishay attempts to include some of these in her *History of Human Rights* (M. Ishay, *The History of Human Rights: From Ancient Times to the Globalization Era* (University of California Press, Berkeley, 2008)).
14 Winstanley is a perfect example. He is generally excluded from the histories, but even when he is included like in Belden Fields' *Rethinking Human Rights for the New Millennium* (Palgrave, New York, 2003) he can be rendered of lesser importance: 'Although Winstanley was an articulate advocate of the Digger position, he was not a philosopher. The first philosopher . . . [was Hobbes]' (ibid: 10). Winstanley is brought within the tradition but rendered not as important as the usual suspects – Hobbes, Locke, Rousseau, etc.
15 Capt. Johnson, *A General History of the Pyrates* (Dover Edition, New York, 1999). See the stories concerning Capt. Misson.
16 See, for instance, Shuler's *Calling Out for Liberty*, which just looks at the Stono Slave revolt (J. Shuler, *Calling Out for Liberty, The Stono Slave Rebellion and the Universal Struggle for Human Rights* (University Press of Mississippi, Missouri, 2009)).
17 See M. Engler, 'Toward the 'Rights of the Poor': Human Rights and Liberation Theology', 28.3 *Journal of Religious Studies* (2000): 339, for a contemporary discussion of this through the ideas of liberation theology, particularly its use of the rights of the poor.
18 For instance, Locke's ideas on poverty (J. Locke, 'An Essay on the Poor Law' in J. Locke, *Locke: Political Essays* (Cambridge University Press, Cambridge, 1997): 183) or colonialism are distinctively of his time (J. Locke, *Second Treatise on Government* (Cambridge University Press, Cambridge, 1963): 16, briefly discussed in A. Pagden, 'Human Rights, Natural Rights and Europe's Imperial Legacy', 31.2 *Political Theory* (2003): 183). These ideas are understood to be merely unfortunate contradictions or errors, they can be elided, but the ideas relevant to now are understood as of the utmost importance.
19 To some extent, Perry defends this by his inexorable connection of human rights to a religious morality (M. J. Perry, *Human Rights: Religion, Law, Courts* (Cambridge University Press, Cambridge, 2007)). I think Paul Lauren Gordon's *The Evolution of International Human Rights* remains on the border between these teleologies, at times asserting a metaphysical teleological approach, but at other times seeing that they are social constructs. He says: 'Among all these great visions, perhaps none have had a more profound impact than those of international human rights. Thoughtful and insightful visionaries in many different times and places have seen in their mind's eye a world in which all people might enjoy certain basic and inherent rights simply by virtue of being human beings. They have viewed these rights or fundamental claims by persons to obtain just treatment as stemming from nature itself and thus inherited by all men, women and children on earth as members born into the same human family' (ibid: 1). He constantly hints that the visionaries were getting at something essential or fundamental about being human (see, for instance, ibid: 2), while simultaneously suggesting that they are not essentialist and have been constructed historically, a view that Perry has difficulty with.
20 Ibid: 90.
21 M. Haas, *International Human Rights: A Comprehensive Introduction* (Routledge, Abingdon, 2008).
22 Ibid: 56–57. See also Kälin and Künzli's rendering of the social conflict of the 19th century. They tell us that 'efforts to protect the working population led to recognition in the Versailles peace treaty . . . of the fact that world peace 'can be established

only if it is based upon social justice' (W. Kälin and J. Künzli, *The Law of International Human Rights Protection* (Oxford University Press, Oxford, 2009): 12). While their text looks specifically at the question of protection, the reversal of this struggle (Versailles struggles to protect working people rather than working people struggling into the international arena) is typical of the process of the withdrawal of the radical in human rights. It must constantly focus on how international law protects potential victims, rather than how those victims are active and change the world.

23 Haas, *International Human Rights*: 56–57.

24 Palumbo does something similar. In his history, he only discusses US labour history. And then only the National Labour Union, the Knights of Labour and the American Federation of Labor. In this, he highlights the initial failure due to the apparent weakness of organizing of skilled and unskilled labour. Then he says: 'It was not until the formation of the American Federation of Labor under Samuel Gompers in 1886 that a strong union was formed in the US. Gompers avoided politics and utopian ideals and concentrated on practical issues of higher wages and better working conditions. The AFL contained only skilled workers who had some bargaining power' (M. Palumbo, *Human Rights: Meaning and History* (Robert E Krieger Publishing, Miami, 1982): 55. In this rendering, human rights are associated with the 'successful trade union struggle' that disassociated itself from politics and utopian ideals, in order to do business and settle disputes with the powers that be.

25 D. Mitchell, *The Right to the City: Social Justice and the Fight for Public Space* (Guilford Press, New York, 2003), as discussed in Chapter 9.

26 Engler, 'Toward the 'Rights of the Poor'.

27 Significantly, Haiti is perhaps the reason that the British never destroyed the French Revolution: 'The losses suffered by the British in Saint Domingue weakened them in their war against revolutionary France: Sir John Fortescue, a British military historian, observed that the secret of Britain's failure to crush the French Revolution "may be said to lie in the fatal words [Toussaint L'Ouverture]" ' in A. J. Williams-Myers, 'Slavery, Rebellion and Revolution in the Americas: A Historiographical Scenario on the Theses of Genovese and Others', 26.4 *Journal of Black Studies* (1996): 396).

28 For the purpose of this brief history, I do not want to engage with the politics of naming, which it goes without saying are crucial to such renderings of racial politics. The terms 'white' 'black' and even 'mulatto' are used because they are the terms that circulated at the time and because they are the terms the historical discourse utilizes.

29 F. W. Knight, 'The Haitian Revolution', 105.1 *American Historical Review* (2000): 12.

30 I say 'continental French' in order to distinguish those who arrived specifically to fight the war on St. Domingue after 1791, from those who arrived beforehand and can be folded into one of the factions. It must be said, of course, that the *grand blancs, petits blancs* and *gens du couleur* were generally all French to begin with. Equally, at many stages the slaves asserted their French citizenship.

31 Ibid: 112.

32 The revolt's leaders asked for little more than their freedom and a prohibition on punishment. For this, they would promise to return the slaves to servitude. However, the *grand blancs*, certain of their upper hand, refused outright.

33 'Letter to the General Assembly from Biassou, Jean François and Toussaint Louverture', in N. Nesbitt, *Toussaint L'Ouverture, The Haitian Revolution* (Verso, London, 2008): 6.

34 C. Fick, *The Making of Haiti: The Saint Domingue Revolution from Below* (University of Tennessee Press, Memphis, 1990): 75.

35 Apparently, he spelled his name Toussaint Louverture, without the apostrophe after the L, as it has sometimes been rendered since. I will only use the alternative French rendering of his name when I am quoting directly from a source that uses it.

36 Curtin mentions the connection with the American ex-colonies in the 1780s that may also have 'had its part in showing the slaves of Saint-Domingue that some slaves were

being freed, and increased their own desire for freedom' (P. D. Curtin, 'The Declaration of the Rights of Man in Saint-Domingue, 1788–1791', 30 *Hispanic American Historical Review* (1950): 160, citing D. Lescallier, *Reflections sur le sort des noirs dans nos colonies* (Paris, 1789): 8.

37 What Guardiola-Rivera highlights as a strategy of over-identification (O. Guardiola-Rivera, *Being Against The World* (Birkbeck Law Press, London, 2008)).

38 Fick points to marronage as the most obvious mode of resistance. She also suggests that infanticide and suicide were also modes of striking against the system that made one's very body the object of ownership (ibid).

39 In L. Dubois, *Avengers of the New World, The Story of the Haitian Revolution* (Belknap Press of Harvard University Press, Cambridge (MA), 2004): 102–103.

40 S. N. Grovogue, 'No More, No Less: What Slaves Thought about Their Humanity', in G. K. Bhambra and R. Shiliam, *Silencing Human Rights: Critical Engagements with a Contested Project* (Palgrave, New York, 2009): 55. Equally, Curtin makes a similar point, although it is highly problematic in its tendency to reduce the level at which the slaves would have engaged with the declaration of the rights of man: 'With them the Declaration of Rights did not take the form of sophisticated natural rights philosophy as it spread by word of mouth from one plantation to another. The slaves did not have the intellectual background to understand it at that level. It was merely a new instalment of an old idea, but it had one important new twist. It was not important that the slaves thought that they had a natural right to be free. They heard the French say, "All men should be free." Even the colonists talked this way' (Curtin, *The Declaration of the Rights of Man in Saint-Domingue*: 175). The slaves wove the words of the French into their own traditions.

41 Unlike in the *métropole*, in the colonies there was precisely a direct conflict between Art. I ('Men are born and remain free and equal in their rights. Social distinctions may be based on common utility') and Art. XVII ('Property being an inviolable and sacred right, no one may be deprived of it except for an obvious requirement of public necessity, certified by law, and then on condition of a just compensation in advance'). However, the common understanding that slaves were to be excluded from the rights of man can be very clearly seen when we read that 'in the debates of the colonists Article XVII was not important until after 1791' (Curtin, *The Declaration of the Rights of Man in Saint-Domingue*: 161). Everyone knew there was no conflict between these two because the slaves were not subjects of the rights of man and therefore the fact that they were maintained in subjugation presented no major conflict.

42 Grovogue, 'What Slaves Thought about Their Humanity': 55.

43 M. R. Trouillot, *Silencing the Past: Power and the Production of History* (Beacon Press, Boston (MA), 1995): 73, 82, 89.

44 For accounts of the former, see Chapter 4 of Dubois, *Avengers of the New World*. For instance, regarding the latter, see the account by Gros, 'In the Camps of the Insurgents' (1791), in L. Dubois and J. D. Gorrigus, *Slave Revolution in the Caribbean 1789–1804: A Brief History with Documents* (Bedford/St Martins, New York, 2006).

45 These style of rumours were not uncommon. In 1789 there was a slave revolt on Martinique as a result of an equivalent rumour. Equally, the provincial assembly on St. Domingue started stealing the ministerial mail because they thought that Governor Peynier was hiding the orders of convocation for the estates general (Fick, *The Making of Haiti*: 78).

46 Ibid: 92.

47 Dubois, *Avengers of the New World*: 107.

48 Ibid: 107.

49 Thornton says that: 'It is generally true that African states were ruled by kings, or at least by executive figures who could be called kings, but this may not be a particularly helpful statement. African states possessed a bewildering variety of constitutions: mon-

archs might be hereditary or elected, and they might exercise direct and fairly untrammeled power or be seriously checked by a variety of other institutions. Kongo was no exception. Although it was always ruled by a king, his powers and the basis for his authority were never static or fixed' (J. K. Thornton, ' "I am the Subject of the King of Congo": African Political Ideology and the Haitian Revolution', 4.2 *Journal of World History* (1993): 187).

50 Dubois, *Avengers of the New World*: 108–109, quoting Thornton, 'I am the Subject of the King of Congo': 186.
51 For a theoretical engagement with this, see Guardiola-Rivera, *Being Against the World*.
52 Nesbitt, *Toussaint L'Ouverture*: xlv.
53 Grovogue, 'What Slaves Thought about Their Humanity': 56.
54 Nesbitt, *Toussaint L'Ouverture*: 21.
55 T. Evans, 'Universal Human Rights: "As Much Round and Round as Ever Onward" ', 7.4 *International Journal of Human Rights* (2003): 159, quoting M. Mutua, *Human Rights: A Political and Cultural Critique* (University of Pennsylvanian Press, Pittsburgh, 2002): 53.
56 Take for instance Michael Palumbo's *Human Rights*. In his section on slavery, he skips straight from a description of that vile system into the English legal cases and then the middle-class abolition movement. Alongside this apparently banal absence, we should note that when detailing abolition in the West Indies (1833) he describes how the proposed 'long term apprenticeships for the free slaves' did not work. 'The system quickly broke down since once they had tasted freedom the West Indian blacks would no longer accept *de facto* slavery' (ibid: 44). The slaves only free themselves because the English had allowed them to taste their freedom. This culinary metaphor is clear in positioning the western liberatory subjects and slave objects. The slaves were freed by their own action in the end, but only as a result of the taste of the liberty of the great English juridical tradition. The many and various slave rebellions in the West Indies remain unmentioned.
57 It is worth noting that he is not alone in this, commentators such as Tomuschat and Krasner among others have also pointed to abolition as an important moment in the genesis of human rights. C. Tomuschat, *Human Rights: Between Idealism and Realism* (Oxford University Press, Oxford, 2003): 13–14); S. D. Krasner, *Sovereignty: Organised Hypocrisy* (Princeton University Press, Princeton (NJ), 1999): 105.
58 Lauren Gordon, *The Evolution of International Human Rights*: 38.
59 Ibid: 38, my emphasis. Lauren Gordon's seemingly innocuous description: 'thoughtful' is highly significant. One wonders if he is consciously delimiting the likes of John Clarkson from his less thoughtful or at least educated sailor/informants or indeed the slaves (see M. Rediker, 'Thomas Clarkson and History from Below', 8 *Naked Punch* (2006): 19). The inhumanity of the slave is often traditionally premised on their 'lack' of written language: 'In this sense, reason and literacy were closely, even inseparably linked. Organized warfare was the litmus test of a civilization's capacity in all these respects' (M. J. Rodríguez-Salgado, 'How Oppression thrives where Truth is not allowed a Voice: The Spanish Polemic about American Indians', in G. K. Bhambra and R. Shiliam, *Silencing Human Rights: Critical Engagements with a Contested Project* (Palgrave, London, 2009): 20). It is also worthwhile noting the ex-slave Equinano's anti-slavery political treatise is important because the author constitutes himself as a thinking subject for the English audience precisely through the political treatise. As such in a sense he *makes himself human* – by performing the *cogito* he proves the *sum* of his *humanitas*.
60 Lauren Gordon, *The Evolution of International Human Rights*: 38.
61 Mutua, *Human Rights*: 201.
62 Ibid: 202.
63 'The 'good' state controls its demonic proclivities by cleansing itself with, and internalizing, human rights. The 'evil' state, however, expresses itself through an illiberal,

anti-democratic, or other authoritarian culture. The redemption or salvation of the state is solely dependent on its submission to human rights norms (ibid: 203).

64 Mutua suggests that the state is an empty vessel or receptacle into which the political cultures that underlie it find their expression. While it is certainly the case that the state did not just pop up, fully formed with a reason and nature of its own, and that it remains fundamentally constructed and constructible, it is also necessary to see that states do have a logic of their own. Kafka's writings here are of the utmost importance. To some extent, states discipline any attempt to alter their internal logic.

65 Bottici helpfully defines 'imaginal': 'English language provides us with a helpful and clear indication in this sense: "imaginal", from Latin *imaginalis*, denotes what is made of images (*imagines*). As such, it can be both the product of an individual faculty and of a social context, as well as the result of a complex, yet-to-be-determined interaction between the two. As such, the concept differs from that of "imaginative", which, as its etymology points out (*imaginatus*), is a synonym of "imagined" and denotes therefore either the quality of a person endowed with the individual faculty of imagination or an action of imagining that has already taken place. In sum, while "imaginative" is the result of the work of imagination, the "imaginal" is what makes it possible in the first place' (C. Bottici, 'Imagining Human Rights: Utopia or Ideology', 21.2 *Law and Critique* (2010): 114). Later she says that 'The concept of imaginal therefore comes before the distinction between "real" and "fictitious", because the latter only makes sense within a specific form of the imaginal. The definition of what is real is not an a priori of human understanding, but something that depends on the imaginal itself and that has therefore continuously been changing over the centuries. (ibid: 115).

66 See C. Douzinas, *Human Rights and Empire* (Routledge, London, 2007).

67 I. Wall, 'On Pain and the Sense of Human Rights', 29 *Australian Feminist Law Journal* (2008): 53. available at http://papers.ssrn.com/sol3/papers.cfm?abstract_id=1431898 (accessed 20/01/11).

68 *Universal Declaration of Human Rights* Preamble (my emphasis) available at http://www.un.org/Overview/rights.html (accessed 09/04/07).

69 This can be associated with Žižek's assertion '[t]he ideological constellation that characterizes our epoch of worldwide triumph of liberal democracy [is] the universalization of the notion of the victim' (S. Žižek, *The Metastases of Enjoyment* (Verso, London, 2005): 213) or compared to the understandings and rhetorics of suffering in Christianity or Rousseau's oeuvre as discussed in Fernando Escalante Gonzalbo's *In the Eyes of God – A Study on the Culture of Suffering* (University of Texas Press, Austin, 2006).

70 Mutua, *Human Rights*: 204.

71 'It is not to put fire-arms nor any other weapon of offence into the hands of the Negro subjects of Great Britain. It is not to produce in their situation any local change. Where they are, there they would remain. The abolition which we propose is not the abolition of legal restraints. Let laws as strict, or stricter than those of our own Country, restrain the commission of crime. What then is the abolition of Slavery. It is the abolition of the use of the cart-whip, – it is the abolition of the use of the brand-mark. It is the abolition of the separation of families. It is the abolition of putting up women and children to sale, – it is the abolition of the decrease of the negro race in our colonies, – the abolition of cruelty in the dark corners of the British Empire. It is to give wages to all who work, but to let the idle starve. It is the abolition of despotism, – of injustice, – of that unlimited power, which in those islands is given to man over man: while it is to punish every injury done by the Negro to his master, it is to punish as severely every injury done by the master to the Negro. It is the institution of marriage – the gift of religious instruction. It is to afford to its objects the opportunity of walking conformably to the dictates of religion. It is not to supply to the Negroes the power of committing acts of violence, but it is to take away from them the inducement.' This is taken from the pamphlet

entitled 'Thoughts on the prompt abolition of British Slavery' (1829) which cites 'The Second Report of the Female Sheffield Anti-slavery Association' (1827). The pamphlet is to be found in the University of Manchester's Wilson Anti-slavery Collection.

72 It is interesting to place the works of the overwhelmingly middle class pamphleteers and parliamentarians, alongside the militant anti-slavery labourers and artisans (see C. J. Robinson, 'Capitalism, Slavery and Bourgeois Historiography', 23 *History Workshop* (1987): 131). Equally, for a further multiplication of the subjects of anti-slavery, see M. Rediker, 'Thomas Clarkson and History from Below' (ibid), who argues that sailors were fundamental to Clarkson's narrative, by providing early evidence of the terrors of the slave trade through the threats and violence of their masters.

73 E. Williams, *Capitalism and Slavery* (University of North Carolina Press, Chapel Hill, 1944): 178.

74 See, for instance, R. Anstey, *The Atlantic Slave Trade and British Abolition* (Gregg Revivals/Macmillan, Basingstoke, 1993). However, whether abolition seriously impacted on the profits made from the slave trade can be questioned. For the continued involvement of Britain in the slave trade, see M. Sherwood, 'Britain, the Slave Trade and Slavery, 1808–1843', 46 *Race Class* (2004): 54.

75 A. M. Rees, 'Pitt and the Achievement of Abolition', 39.3 *Journal of Negro History* (1954): 167, at 169. Rees is summarizing Williams' momentous work, *Capitalism and Slavery*.

76 Rees (ibid), for instance, attacks Williams' rendering of Pitt's motives. He suggests that Pitt's motives were much less Machiavellian and, instead, based on a variety of character traits. However, I am not entirely sure that this multiplication of reasons negates Williams' argument. Williams argued that 'Politics and morals in the abstract make no sense. We find the British statesmen and publicists defending slavery today, abusing slavery tomorrow, defending slavery the day after. Today they are imperialist, the next day anti-imperialist, and equally pro-imperialist a generation after. And always with the same vehemence. The defense or attack is always on the high moral or political plane' (Williams, *Capitalism and Slavery*: 211). Where Rees looks to the multiple character traits of Pitt, Williams suggests that the broader geopolitical and economic trends were fundamentally at play. 'The capitalists had first encouraged West Indian slavery and then helped to destroy it. When British capitalism depended on the West Indies, they ignored slavery or defended it. When British capitalism found the West Indian monopoly a nuisance, they destroyed West Indian slavery as the first step in the destruction of West Indian monopoly' (ibid: 169).

77 A. Smith, *An Inquiry into the Nature and Causes of the Wealth of Nations*, Chapter II, 9 available at http://oll.libertyfund.org/?option=com_staticxt&staticfile=show.php%3Ftitle=220&chapter=111899&layout=html&Itemid=27 (accessed 12/12/09). There is an investigation of this view in *The Injurious Effects of Slave Labour: an impartial appeal to the reason, justice and patriotism of the people of Illinois on the injurious effects of slave labour* (1824, available in the Wilson Anti-Slavery Collection). There the author details a number of experiments carried out in colonies with the productivity of slaves and freemen.

78 Trouillot, *Silencing the Past*: 81.

79 E. Bloch, *Natural Law and Human Dignity* (MIT Press, Cambridge (MA), 1987): preface, xxix.

Chapter 3 The withdrawal of the radical in human rights

1 R. Vaneigem, *The Revolution in Everyday Life* (Practical Paradise Publications, London, 1975): 8.

2 For further reading, I suggest a number of excellent engagements with Heidegger that might give those interested a greater insight into the oeuvre. See M. de Beistegui,

Heidegger and the Political, Dystopias (Routledge, London, 1997), W. Blattner, *Heidegger's Being and Time: A Readers Guide* (Continuum, New York, 2006), J. D. Caputo, *Demythologizing Heidegger* (Indiana University Press, Bloomington (IN), 1993), H. L. Dreyfus, *Being-in-the-World, A Commentary on Heidegger's Being and Time, Division I* (MIT Press, Cambridge (MA), 1991), G. Harman, *Heidegger Explained: From Phenomenon to Thing* (Open Court Publishing, Chicago (IL), 2007), S. Mulhall, *Heidegger and Being and Time* (Routledge, London, 2005), J. Young, *Heidegger, Philosophy, Nazism* (University of Cambridge Press, Cambridge, 1997) or in the context of human rights and law more generally, see O. Ben-Dor, *Thinking About Law, In Silence with Heidegger* (Hart Publishing, Oxford, 2007), C. Douzinas, *The End of Human Rights* (Hart Publishing, Oxford, 2000).

3 J.-L. Nancy and P. Lacoue-Labarthe, *Retreating the Political* (Routledge, London, 1997).

4 J. Locke, *Second Treatise on Government* (Cambridge University Press, Cambridge, 1963): §27.

5 Ibid: §123.

6 It is the foundation for his assertion that 'though the things of nature are given in common, yet man, *by being master of himself,* and *proprietor of his own person,* and the actions or labour of it, had still in himself the great foundation of property; and that, which made up the great part of what he applied to the support or comfort of his being, when invention and arts had improved the conveniences of life, was perfectly his own, and did not belong in common to others' (ibid: §44). The two axioms are: Man is master of himself (the willing subject of enlightenment); *and* proprietor of his own person (the possessive individual).

7 Ibid: §124.

8 Skinner tells us that 'the right to revolution' is only formulated in the sense that we know it by the Monarchomachs (Q. Skinner, *The Foundations of Modern Political Thought, Vol. 2* (Cambridge University Press, Cambridge, 1978)). These Huguenot constitutionalists were in a precarious position as a religious minority in Catherine's France. Constantly under threat of religious repression, they developed a form of constitutionalism that legitimated revolution as a right. Under certain conditions, the lesser magistrates leading the people were entitled *by right* to overthrow the king. Skinner tells us that it was the precariousness of the Huguenots' minority position that lead them to seek a constitutionalist position that might allow them to draw support from the majority, the moderate Catholics, who resented the concentration of power in the hands of the monarch by the Absolutists. Crucially, the Monarchomachs move beyond the traditional Calvinist and, indeed, fundamentally theological question, by distinguishing between the *foedicus* (the duty of all to uphold the laws of God) and the *pactum*, which is the agreement between the people and its monarch. The form of the theological is replicated while the grounds of the agreement are shifted from the transcendent to the immanent. Instead of a directly theological justification of revolution, we find the beginnings of a constitutionalist revolutionary ideology. Skinner says: 'As Beza declares "wherever law and equity [have] prevailed", no nation has ever "created nor accepted kings except upon definite conditions". It is this contention that leads the [Huguenots] to speak of a second and purely political contract [*pactum*], one that takes the form, in Beza's words, of a 'mutual oath between the king and the people' (ibid: 331). It is taken up after 1580 in the Netherlands as a justification for the resistance to Spanish rule. Buchannan, in Scotland, ultimately takes up and develops further the idea. His singular addition is the emphasis on the people as the subject of this right.

9 Locke, *Second Treatise*, §220.

10 Ibid: §221.

11 P. Kain, *Marx and Modern Political Theory; from Hobbes to Contemporary Feminism* (Rowman & Littlefield, Lanham (MD), 1993).

12 J. Locke, 'Considerations of the Consequences of Lowering of the Interest and Raising the Value of Money', in J. Locke, *Locke: Political Essays* (Cambridge University Press, Cambridge, 1997), quoted and discussed in Kain, *Marx and Modern Political Theory*: 55–56.

13 C. B. MacPherson, *The Political Theory of Possessive Individualism: Hobbes to Locke* (Oxford University Press, Oxford, 1962): 224.

14 Kain, *Marx and Modern Political Theory*: 56.

15 Macpherson, *Possessive Individualism*: 224.

16 T. Corns, A. Hughes and D. Loewenstein (eds), *The Complete Works of Gerrard Winstanley* (Oxford University Press, Oxford, 2010).

17 Halfway through *Justice Accused*, Robert Cover points out: 'I have spoken so far of a domesticated natural law: a tame, legalistic reflection of the driving impulse of the American revolution. But the domesticated and wild creatures [of revolutionary America] both trace their ancestry honestly, to the pre-Revolutionary [same] sources. The coexistence of the two rather different offspring uneasily persisted, for they served different functions. The same man could appreciate the limits to which natural law must be subject in the formulation of rules of decision by the judiciary while holding the identical substantive doctrines sufficient basis for acts of revolution' (R. Cover, *Justice Accused* (Yale University Press, New Haven (CT), 1975): 105).

18 M. Foucault, *Society Must Be Defended* (Picador, London, 2003): 73.

19 Ibid.

20 See L. Hunt, *Inventing Human Rights – A History* (Norton & Co., New York, 2007).

21 Derrida says of the attempt to define philosophy: 'Philosophy has always insisted upon this: thinking its other. Its other: that which limits it, and from which it derives its essence, its definition, its production' (Derrida, 'Tympan', in J. Derrida, *Margins of Philosophy* (Harvester Press, Brighton, 1982): x).

22 J.-L. Nancy and P. Lacoue-Labarthe, *Retreating the Political*: 5.

23 Preamble, Universal Declaration of Human Rights, available at http://www.un.org/Overview/rights.html (accessed 09/04/07).

24 1793 Dec, Section XXXV.

25 As regards the indeterminacy thesis, Douzinas says: 'Human rights are the one area in which the realist and critical legal claims have been almost universally confirmed' (C. Douzinas, *Human Rights and Empire* (Routledge, London, 2007): 188). In support of this claim, he suggests further readings: D. Kennedy, *A Critique of Adjudication* (Harvard University Press, Cambridge (MA), 1977): 304–309, M. Koskenniemi, 'The Effects of Rights on Political Culture', in P. Alston, *The European Union and Human Rights* (Oxford University Press, Oxford, 1999): 99–116, D. Kennedy, 'The International Human Rights Law Movement, Part of the Problem?' 3 *European Human Rights Law Journal* (2001): 245–267.

26 Shaw sets out a number of these possibilities: 'The principle of self-determination provides that the people of the colonially defined territorial unit in question may freely determine their own political status. Such determination may result in independence, integration with a neighbouring state, free association with an independent state or any other political status freely decided upon by the people concerned' (M. Shaw, *International Law* (Cambridge University Press, 2008, 6th edn): 257).

27 E. Christodoulidis, 'Against Substitution: The Constitutional thinking of Dissensus', in *Paradox of Constitutionalism* (M. Loughlin and N. Walker (eds) (Oxford University Press, 2007): 207.

28 Shaw explains the conservative view that under international law, the 'self' of self-determination 'must be determined within the accepted colonial territorial framework [i.e. under the principle of *uti possidetis*, the freezing of colonial borders, except by mutual consent]. Attempts to broaden this have not been successful and the UN has always strenuously opposed any attempt at the partial or total disruption of national

unity and territorial integrity of a country. The UN has based its policy on the proposition that 'the territory of a colony or other non-self-governing territory has under the
[UN] Charter a status separate and distinct from the territory of the state administering
it' and that such status was to exist until the people of that territory had exercised the
right to self-determination' (Shaw, *International Law*: 256).

29 Smith defines a nation as a 'named unit of population with common ancestry myths and
shared historical memories, elements of shared culture, a link with a historic territory,
and some measure of solidarity, at least among the elites' (A. D. Smith, 'Nations and
History', in M. Guibernau and J. Hutchinson (eds) *Understanding Nationalism* (Polity
Press, London, 2001): 19).

30 Daes relatively uncontroversially asserts that 'whether a group constitutes a 'people'
for the purposes of self-determination depends, in my view, on the extent to which the
group making a claim shares ethnic, linguistic, religious or cultural bonds, although the
absence or weakness of one of these bonds or elements need not invalidate the claim.
The extent to which members within the group perceive the groups identity as distinct
from the identities of other groups should be evaluated according to a subjective standard' (E.-I. Daes, 'The Right of Indigenous Peoples to Self-Determination in the
Contemporary World Order', in D. Clark and R. Williamson, *Self-Determination,
International Perspectives* (Macmillan, Basingstoke, 1996).

31 B. Bowring, *The Degradation of International Law* (Glasshouse Press, Abingdon,
2008).

32 Ibid: 129. In this chapter, having engaged with Badiou's utter rejection of human rights
(as symptomatic of a deeper malaise) in *Ethics*, Bowring makes a very questionable
equation between Badiou's idea of the event and the involvement of rights in (the
French and Russian) revolutions. He says his account of a 'real' human rights (qua
definition and content of human struggles) 'is already strongly implied in Badiou's
thought' (ibid: 129).

33 This is a crucial point but I want to make sure it is fully clarified: first, by 'modern
human rights law', I am not dismissing human rights as such, that much is, it is to be
hoped, clear thus far. I argue instead that for a variety of reasons, assertions of human
rights fold all too easily and too readily into their modern limited legal figurations.
Within the discourse of international human rights law, there remain only traces of the
constituent. Second, those familiar with Nancy and Lacoue-Labarthe's work, as noted
briefly in the Introduction, will see that this withdrawal of the radical, leads me to
retreat from the discourse in order to re-treat the discourse itself. This re-treatment
entails attempting to rediscover the radical potential of human rights – the difference
that is most proper to them.

34 C. Pearlman, 'The Safeguarding and Foundation of Human Rights', 1.1 *Law and
Philosophy* (1982).

35 H. Arendt, *The Origins of Totalitarianism* (Harvest Books, New York, 1973). While
Moyn is entirely correct to point out that there is a clear distinction to be drawn between
the state building of the French Declaration and the international outlook of the UDHR,
the statism of the earlier document is only intensified and universalized in the UDHR
(S. Moyn, *The Last Utopia: Human Rights in History* (Harvard University Press,
Cambridge (MA), 2010).

36 G. Agamben, *Means without End: Notes on Politics* (University of Minnesota Press,
Minneapolis, 2000): 21.

37 Arendt, *The Origins of Totalitarianism*: 279.

38 S. Parekh, 'Resisting 'Dull and Torpid' Assent: Returning to the Debate over the
Foundations of Human Rights', 29 *Human Rights Quarterly* (2007): 757.

39 See Douzinas, *The End of Human Rights* or P. Linebaugh and M. Rediker, *The Many
Headed Hydra: The Hidden History of the Revolutionary Atlantic* (Verso, London,
2002).

40 M. Engler, 'Towards the "Rights of the Poor": Human Rights in Liberation Theology', 28.3 *Journal of Religious Ethics* (2000): 345.

41 M. Heidegger, 'Letter on Humanism', in *Basic Writings, From Being and Time to the Task of Thinking* (Harper & Row, London, 1977): 200.

42 Ibid: 202.

43 However, this should not be simply distinguished from what is 'becoming'. Being is the process of coming to presence, but I will come back to this temporality shortly.

44 Nancy explains, ' "metaphysics" . . . denotes the representation of being [*être*] as beings [*étant*] and as beings present [*étant présent*]. In doing so, metaphysics sets a founding, earranting presence beyond the world (viz., the Idea, *Summum Ens*, the Subject, the Will). This setup stabilizes beings, enclosing them in their own beingness [*étantité*]' (J.-L. Nancy, *Dis-enclosure, The Deconstrction of Christianity* (Fordham University Press, New York, 2008): 6).

45 As a formulation of this, Feenberg suggests that 'being appears in producing itself'. A. Feenberg, *Heidegger and Marcuse: The Catastrophe and Redemption of History* (New York, Routledge, 2005): 50.

46 Even Bowring, who claims to look to the material relations that rights define and give content to, ultimately ends with the juridical protection and vindication of rights (Bowring, *The Degradation of International Law*).

47 It is certainly the case that people need to sleep, eat, talk, etc. However, this does not get at the fundamental problem.

48 Douzinas, *Human Rights and Empire*.

49 M. Heidegger, *Logic as the Question Concerning the Essence of Language* (State University of New York Press, New York, 2009): 19.

50 W. Hamacher, 'The Right not to Use Rights: Human Rights and the Structure of Judgments', in H. de Vries and L. E. Sullivan, *Political Theologies; Public Religions in a Post-Secular World* (Fordham University Press, New York, 2006): 671, at 679–680. Hamacher interestingly continues: 'The right to one's own person secures freedom only as a property, which stands in competition with other properties and turns the *status iuridicus* into a permanent condition of civil war, injuring all freedoms. The basic rights that are supposed to be the essential rights of man are national and international rights of civil war. Because they determine man in his *humanitas* as man-against-other-men and furthermore as man-against-man-himself, they are structurally . . . not human rights but rather the rights of objects: nonhuman institutions not only of reciprocal limitation but also of reciprocal elimination. Right is right-against-right, and therefore, *ex definitone*, unjust. It is a category not of humanity but rather of self-reification and self-destruction' (ibid).

51 Heidegger, *Logic*: 34.

52 Ibid: 34.

53 K. Axelos, *Alienation, Praxis, and Techne in the Thought of Karl Marx* (University of Texas Press, Austin, 1976): 12.

54 However, Heidegger suggests that (phenomenologically) encountered 'facts' are *meaningfully* (hermeneutically) experienced. The world cannot be disassociated from the hermeneutic within which we experience it. As he puts it late in his oeuvre – language is the house of being. Thus, to describe the world, we are already interpreting it. There is no pure experience of the world, no pure description. There-ness *is* the experience of being and meaning.

55 M.Heidegger, *Being and Time* (Robinson E. Macquarrie trans.) (Blackwell, Oxford, 1962): 155.

56 '[E]xistence *is* only in being partitioned and shared . . . [and] *we* are what it divides and parcels out' (J.-L. Nancy, 'Of Being-in-Common', in The Miami Theory Collective (eds), *Community at Loose Ends* (University of Minnesota Press, Minneapolis, 1991): 5).

57 M. King, *A Guide to Heidegger's Being and Time* (State University of New York, New York, 2001): 76.

58 I will maintain Heidegger's capitalization of *das Man* in order to distinguish it from man.

59 Dreyfus sees that Heidegger's problem with authenticity lies in the analytic's relation to the in-common. *Das Man* is a question of conformity with norms of behaviour and modes of life. Thus for instance 'averageness is the tendency to conform our behaviour to a norm, even if that norm is frequently violated' (Dreyfus, *Being-in-the-World*: 153). The norm is the average or givenness of the world into which we have always already fallen. Dreyfus divides the in-common in two: the good in-common that constitutes or socializes *dasein*; and the bad in-common of levelling-down and dispersal of responsibility for being. Harman summarizes, 'solicitude [*Fürsorge*] can be either harmful or helpful. The harmful kind leaps in and relieves the other *dasein* of its responsibility, and thereby secretly dominates the other. But the other kind of solicitude leaps ahead and restores the other *dasein's* care to it in authentic form for the first time' (Harman, *Heidegger Explained*: 66).

60 Heidegger, *Being and Time*: 164.

61 Heidegger says: 'In utilizing public means of transport and in making use of information services such as the newspaper, every Other is like the next. This Being-with-one-another dissolves one's own *dasein* completely into the kind of Being of 'the Others', in such a way, indeed, that the Others, as distinguishable and explicit, vanish more and more. In this inconspicuousness and unascertainability, the real dictatorship of the 'they' is unfolded' (ibid: 164).

62 Ibid: 165.

63 Ibid: 165. Interestingly, this description of publicness would include the more recent phenomena of the market. Particularly, the process whereby the correctness of a decision is given by the reaction of the markets. Not because of any engagement or thought regarding the actual decision itself, but because the market reacts in a certain way.

64 Ibid: 377.

65 Heidegger says he is not making any claim about an after-life, or about the existence of a deity, but that death presents the end of one's being-there.

66 Heidegger, 'Letter on Humanism': 205, That is, it is not based in and around the liberal subject.

67 To stand-out is the direct translation of the Greek ek-stasis, from which ek-sistence is rendered.

68 Caputo, *Demythologizing Heidegger*: 47.

69 In *Being and Time* the term prestruction is dropped; Heidegger, however, continues to criticize this manner of being-towards, which does not understand the futurality of the future. Protecting against death is a temporal extension of the they. It levels down the to-come and makes it fundamentally 'safe'. I have written elsewhere on this subject, arguing that human rights inscribes a relation between the political and suffering. This relation is twofold: it facilitates the radical aspect of human rights' struggle against domination, but at the same time seems to reduce the human rights horizon to the short-term philantropism of humanitarianism. This is because pain disrupts the all-encompassing security provided by the will. 'Pain's appearance means the emergence of something which escapes Will's total control and planning. In and through pain, the will is brought face to face with the insufficiency of its own plans and designs' (P. Emad, 'Heidegger on Pain: Focusing on a Recurring Theme in his Thought', 36.6, *Zeitschrift für Philosophische Forschung* (1982): 354). Thus human rights at once announce a relation between the political and pain, but at the same time they attempt to flee from it. This can be seen in Bryan Turner's analysis of vulnerability and human rights (B. Turner, *Vulnerability and Human Rights* (Pennsylvania State University Press, Old Main, 2006)). For further discussion of this, see I. Wall, 'On Pain and the Sense of Human Rights', 29 *Australian Feminist Law Journal* (2009): 53.

70 It is very clear that this triplet is constantly backward looking. Thus, unlike the triplets of Heidegger's work, which are temporally oriented towards a future, human rights increasingly become a conservative doctrine, in the traditional notion at least. In this triplet, the present is privileged most clearly by the increasing consonance of human rights and security, or rather the increasing reading of human rights *as* security.

71 Douzinas, *Human Rights and Empire*: 55. More than this forgetting, as Brown shows us, there is a paradox here. She says 'rights sought by a politically defined *group* are conferred upon depoliticized *individuals*; at the moment a particular "we" succeeds in obtaining rights, it loses its "we-ness" and dissolves into individuals' (W. Brown, *States of Injury: Power and Freedom in Late Modernity* (Princeton University Press, Princeton (NJ), 1995); 98.

Chapter 4 The authority of change: Sieyès and Kant

1 Georges Burdeau, *Traité de Sciences Politique*, Vol. 4 (Paris Librairie générale de droit et de jurisprudence, Paris, 1983): 171), cited in A. Negri, *Insurgencies* (University of Minnesota Press, Minneapolis, 1999): 1.

2 M. Loughlin, *The Idea of Public Law* (Oxford University Press, Oxford 2004): 99. For a further examination of this relation see M. Loughlin and N. Walker (eds), *Paradox of Constitutionalism* (Oxford University Press, Oxford, 2007).

3 Sieyès says: 'All public powers without distinction are an emanation of the general will, *all come from the People, that is to say, the Nation. These two terms ought to be synonymous*' (quoted in M. Forsyth, *Reason and Revolution, The Political thought of the Abbé Sieyès* (Holmes & Meier Publishers, New York, 1987)): 75, my emphasis.

4 C. Schmitt, *Constitutional Theory* (Duke University Press, Durham (NC), 2008): 127.

5 Forsyth, *Reason and Revolution*: 6.9

6 E.-J. Sieyès, *Political Writings* (M. Sonenscher (ed.)) (Hackett Publishing Co., Indianapolis (IN), 2003): 12.

7 M. Foucault, *Society Must Be Defended* (Picador, London, 2003): 218.

8 Ibid: 219. Negri points out that Sieyès is the first to insert Labour into the question of constituent power, although he does so in an essentially conservative manner (Negri, *Insurgenies*: 213).

9 Foucault, *Society Must be Defended*: 219–220.

10 Ibid: 220.

11 The Third Estate are the commoners, distinguished from the First (clergy) and Second (nobles) Estates in the French Estates General.

12 Ibid: 221.

13 Forsyth *Reason and Revolution*: 70.

14 Foucault, *Society Must be Defended*: 221–222.

15 Cited in Foucault, ibid: 238.

16 Forsyth, *Reason and Revolution*: 70. It is worth remembering that 'What is the Third Estate?' along with Sieyès other revolutionary texts are essentially primary political texts that are deeply involved in the emerging crisis. His 'Views on the Means of Execution' (1788) proposed that in the Estates General they should sweep away the distinctions and vote as one nation. It was not until it became clear that the nobles were going to hold fast to their own traditional privileges and refuse to co-operate with the 'work of national regeneration', that the Abbé put his weight behind the Third Estate.

17 Quoted in Forsyth, ibid: 81.

18 Ibid: 81.

19 Negri, *Insurgencies*.

20 E. Christodoulidis, 'Against Substitution, The Constitutional thinking of Dissensus', in M. Loughlin and N. Walker (eds), *Paradox of Constitutionalism* (Oxford University Press, Oxford, 2007), Negri, *Insurgencies*.

21 M. Boscagli (trans.) in Negri, *Insurgencies*: ff1 Ch1: 337.
22 A. Negri, quoted in J. Frank, 'The Abyss of Democracy: Antonio Negri's Democratic Theory', 4.1 *Theory & Event* (2000).
23 Negri is particularly interested in distinguishing himself from the constitutional thought of Rudolf Smend, which sees constituent power as immanent to the constitution – the constitution for Smend is 'the dynamic principle of the State's becoming' (Negri, *Insurgencies*: 7).
24 Contra Schmitt, Negri affirms that 'One of the gravest errors of political theorists is considering constituent power a pure political act separate from existing social being, mere irrational creativity, the obscure point of some violent expression of power. Carl Schmitt, along with all the fascist and reactionary thinkers of the 19th and 20th centuries, always tried to exorcize constituent power this way, with a shiver of fear. Constituent power, however, is something completely different. It is a decision that emerges out of the ontological and social process of productive labour; it is an institutional form that develops a common content; it is a deployment of force that defends the historical progression of emancipation and liberation; it is, in short, an act of love' (M. Hardt and A. Negri, *Multitude, War and Democracy in the Age of Empire* (Penguin, New York, 2004): 351).
25 H. Arendt, 'What is Authority', in *Between Past and Future: Eight Exercises in Political Thought* (Viking Press, New York, 1968): 120.
26 Schmitt, *Constitutional Theory*, ff1, 459.
27 Arendt, 'What is Authority': 123.
28 Ibid: 124.
29 Schmitt, *Constitutional Theory*, ff1, 458–459.
30 Ibid: 459.
31 Janus is traditionally associated with doors. Yet this two-faced deity is something of an enigma; his origins were lost even to the Romans. Certainly, the basis of the opening of the doors of his temple in the forum during war and the closing of them during peace has excited quite an amount of debate among classicists. It is quite fitting then that we do not know the origin of this god of origins.
32 Reflection 8051; Ak. XIX 594–595, cited in L. Beck, 'Kant and the Right of Revolution', *Journal of the History of Ideas* (1971): 412.
33 An account of this rumour can be found in G. P. Gooch, *Germany and the French Revolution* (Longmans, Green and Co., London, 1920): 276–277, and is repeated in Beck 'Kant and the Right to Revolution': 411.
34 C. Korsgaard, 'Taking the Law into our Own Hands; Kant on the Right to Revolution', in A. Reath, B. Herman and C. Korsgaard (eds), *Reclaiming the History of Ethics, Essays for John Rawls* (Cambridge University Press, Cambridge, 1997): 300.
35 Kant, 'Principles of Politics': 50; 'Werke', VI: 383.
36 Kant, *The Metaphysical principles of Justice* (Macmillan, New York, 1965): 318, cited in E. Christodoulidis, 'The Aporia of Sovereignty: On the Representation of The People in Constitutional Discourse', 12.1 *King's College Law Journal* (2001): 112, emphasis in original.
37 Ibid: 111.
38 Ibid: 112.
39 This interregnum of anarchy is one reason why Kant and, indeed, Burke reject revolution. See S. Axinn, 'Kant, Authority and the French Revolution', 32.3 *Journal of the History of Ideas* (1971): 427.
40 M. Foucault, 'The Art of Telling the Truth', in *Politics, Philosophy, Culture: Interviews and Other Writings* (Routledge, London, 1988): 90.
41 Ibid: 91.
42 Kant, para VI of second dissertation of 'The conflict of the Faculties', quoted in Foucault, ibid: 91.

43 Ibid: 92.
44 Kant, cited in Foucault, ibid: 92.
45 Ibid: 93.
46 Ibid: 94.
47 Ibid: 94.
48 Ibid: 95.
49 B. Arditi, *Politics on the Edges of Liberalism; Difference, Populism, Revolution, Agitation* (Edinburgh University Press, Edinburgh, 2008): 121.
50 Ibid: 121.
51 Beck 'Kant and the Right to Revolution': 420.
52 S. Kouvelakis, *Philosophy and Revolution: From Kant to Marx* (Verso, London, 2003): 22–23.
53 Korsgaard, 'Taking the Law into Our Own Hands': 313.
54 Kant, 'The Metaphysics of Morals': 162, quoted in Kouvelakis, *Philosophy and Revolution*: 21.
55 Kouvelakis, *Philosophy and Revolution*: 22–23.
56 I have looked at only two here, but the attempt to legitimate overthrow runs through western political theory and theology for centuries: St Augustin's *City of God*, Aquinas's *On Princely Government*, Machiavelli's *Discourses on the First Ten Books of Livy*, all contain debates around the legitimacy of revolt. This is even without mentioning the Huegenots, Locke, Rousseau, Paine, Hegel, Marx, etc.

Chapter 5 An open constituent power: Sorel, Benjamin and Bataille

1 J.-L. Nancy, 'The Compearance: From the Existence of Communism to the Community of Existence', 20.3 *Political Theory* (1992): 371, 375.
2 In the next chapter, we will begin to think critically about the people, introducing Derrida and Rancière among others, in order to deconstruct the people as a solid unity of everyone countable under the state. These two chapters, thus, must be read together.
3 There are indeed proto-fascist elements of the theory and Sorel himself did at times (albeit for very short periods) associate with conservative royalists and other rightists.
4 We do not deny that Sorel was crucial in the emergence of certain strands of fascism. Laclau describes Sorel's disciple Edouard Berth's combination of nationalism and syndicalism, which sought 'the complete expulsion of the kingdom of gold and . . . the triumph of heroic values over ignoble bourgeois materialism in which the present day Europe is suffocating' (E. Laclau and C. Mouffe, *Hegemony and Socialist Strategy* (Verso, London, 2001): 41). However, Laclau goes on to defend Sorel's thought, arguing that it does not necessarily end in fascism, first citing Gramsci who was indebted to Sorel, and then arguing that this teleological view 'analytically unfounded, because . . . [it] assumes that the transition from class to nation was necessarily determined by the very structure of Sorel's thought, whereas the latter's most specific and original moment was precisely the indeterminate, non-a priori character of the mythically constituted subjects. Furthermore, this indeterminacy is not a weakness of the theory, for it affirms that social reality itself is indeterminate (*mélange*) and that any unification turns on the recomposing practices of a *bloc*' (ibid: 41).
5 T. Goldhammer, *The Headless Republic* (Cornell University Press, Ithaca (NY), 2005): 113.
6 R. Luxemburg, *The Mass Strike: The Political Party & The Trade Unions* (Merlin Press, London, 1928): 27.
7 Of interest here is Tudor's notion of myth, which Canovan takes up in her discussion of the people and to which we will come back in the next chapter. Tudor highlights three aspects of myth: 'A political myth as he understands it has dramatic form; it

concerns a political collectivity of some kind; and it has a practical point. As the collective story of a state, a nation, or some other political group it is neither pure fiction nor straightforward history, but it is invoked because it makes sense of political experience' (M. Canovan, *The People* (Polity Press, Cambridge, 2005): 124).

8 Laclau and Mouffe, *Hegemony and Socialist Strategy*: 40.

9 Goldhammer, *The Headless Republic*: 113.

10 Hegel defines sublation (*Aufhaben*): ' *"To sublate"* has a twofold meaning in the language: on the one hand it means to preserve, to maintain, and equally it also means to cause to cease, to put an end to. Even "to preserve" includes a negative elements, namely, that something is removed from its influences, in order to preserve it. Thus what is sublated is at the same time preserved; it has only lost its immediacy but is not on that account annihilated' Hegel, *The Science of Logic*: Book I. Sublation is the negation involved in the dialectic process.

11 J.-L. Nancy, *The Inoperative Community* (University of Minnesota Press, Minneapolis, 1991): 13.

12 Goldhammer, *The Headless Republic*: 18.

13 I. Berlin, 'Georges Sorel', *Times Literary Supplement*, 31/12/1971: 1621.

14 G. Sorel, *Reflections on Violence* (George Allen & Unwin, London, 1916): 195.

15 Force comes in two forms: scattered violence 'which resembles the struggle for life', and organized force of the state. These are separated from 'violence properly called' (ibid: 196–197). This distinction is drawn on the grounds of a relation to authority: '*force* aims at authority, endeavouring to bring about an automatic obedience', whereas *violence* 'would smash that authority' (ibid: 200–201).

16 Goldhammer, *The Headless Republic*: 29. Interestingly, while Sorel appears to have received little information about the Russian revolution, he seemed very enthusiastic about what he heard. He seems to have eschewed the idea that this was another Jacobinism. Nevertheless, throughout his work he rejected violence exercised by the state because he associated it with the Terror after the French Revolution.

17 Ibid: 147.

18 Summarized by B. Arditi, *Politics on the Edges of Liberalism; Difference, Populism, Revolution, Agitation* (Edinburgh University Press, Edinburgh, 2008): 128.

19 S. B. Plate, *Walter Benjamin, Religion and Aesthetics* (Routledge, London, 2005): 28.

20 W. Benjamin, 'Critique of Violence', in *Reflections* (Schoken Books, New York, 1978): 279.

21 See Hamacher for the translation of 'positing': W. Hamacher, 'Afformative, Strike, Benjamin's "Critique of Violence" ', in A. Benjamin and P. Osborne, *Destruction & Experience* (Clinamen Press, Manchester, 2000): 108.

22 Ibid: 108–109.

23 Ibid: 109.

24 Benjamin, 'Critique of Violence': 286.

25 Ibid: 286.

26 Benjamin says: 'Police violence is . . . is law-making, for its characteristic function is not the promulgation of laws but the assertion of legal claims for any decree, and law-preserving, because it is at the disposal of these ends. The assertion that the ends of police violence are always identical or even connected to those of general law is entirely untrue. Rather the "law" of the police really marks the point at which the state, whether from impotence or because of the immanent connections within any legal system, can no longer guarantee through the legal system the empirical ends that it desires at any price to attain. [We will see a connection later with Bataille's critique of liberalism use of imperative abjection in this assertion.] Therefore, the police intervene "for security reasons" in countless cases where no clear legal situation exists, when they are not merely, without the slightest relation to legal ends, accompanying the

citizen as a brutal encumbrance through a life regulated by ordinances, or simply supervising him. Unlike law, which acknowledges in the "decision" determined by place and time a metaphysical category that gives it a claim to critical evaluation, a consideration of the police institution encounters nothing essential at all. Its power is formless, like its nowhere tangible, all pervasive, ghostly presence in the life of civilized states' (ibid: 286–287).

27 See G. Agamben, *State of Exception* (University of Chicago Press, Chicago, 2006): 54, in *Constitutional Theory*, which Agamben argues has already incorporated Benjamin's notion of pure violence in the decision on the state of exception, Schmitt retains constituent power (*die verfassungsgebende Gewalt*), which is literally constituent violence, but translated by Seitzer as constitution-making power. This translation gives the exact sense of constituent power that Benjamin critiques.

28 Hamacher, 'Afformative, Strike': 113.

29 Ibid: ff2, 125.

30 Ibid: 113.

31 Ibid: 116.

32 I will come back to the question of singularity in Chapter 8, through Jean-Luc Nancy and biopolitics.

33 Benjamin, 'Critique of Violence': 292.

34 G. Sorel, *Reflections of Violence*: 250, cited in Benjamin, ibid: 291.

35 Benjamin, 'Critique of Violence': 295, my emphasis.

36 Ibid: 297.

37 Niobe's hubris in comparing her childbearing to Leto's (Niobe gave birth to 12 children, where Leto, goddess of fertility, had only two) results in Leto sending her two children, Apollo and Artemis, to kill all Niobe's children. Devastated by their death, Niobe weeps for days until she turns to stone, which still continues to weep. In the myth of Niobe is the very logic of the law-making violence, the triplet: force–subject–guilt. Because Niobe challenges the uncertain realm of fate, she brings law to light. However, the 'violence [of Apollo and Artemis] *establishes* a law far more than it punishes for the infringement of one already existing' (Benjamin, 'Critique of Violence': 294, my emphasis). The story shows law as not actually destructive but rather bringing a guilt to bear in the most violent of manners (here the police is again the clearest example of mythic violence): 'Although it brings a cruel death to Niobe's children, it stops short of the life of their mother, whom it leaves behind, more guilty than before through the death of the children, both as an eternally mute bearer of guilt and as a boundary stone on the frontier between men and gods' (ibid: 295).

38 Ibid: 297, my emphasis.

39 J. Butler, 'Benjamin's Critique of Violence', in *Political Theologies* (L. Sullivan and H. de Vries (eds)) (Fordham University Press, New York, 2006): 211.

40 Plate, *Walter Benjamin, Religion and Aesthetics*: 33.

41 Hamacher, 'Afformative, Strike': 117.

42 S. Critchley, 'Violent Thoughts about Slavoj Žižek', *Naked Punch Supplement 1*: 1.

43 Benjamin, 'Critique of Violence': 298.

44 Butler, 'Walter Benjamin's Critique of Violence': 212.

45 Benjamin, 'Critique of Violence': 300.

46 Hamacher, 'Afformative, Strike': 122–123.

47 See F. Fanon, *Black Skin, White Masks* (Pluto Press, London, 1967) and F. Fanon, *The Wretched of the Earth* (Penguin, London, 2001).

48 P. Klossowski, quoted in *The College of Sociology (1937–39)* (D. Hollier (ed.) (University of Minnesota Press, Minneapolis, 1988): 219), cited in M. Weingrad, 'The College of Sociology and the Institute of Social Research', 84 *New German Critique* (2001): 131.

49 Goldhammer, *The Headless Republic*: 12.

50 Ibid: 153.
51 Bataille, in *Acéphale*, cited in Goldhammer, ibid: 155, my emphasis.
52 M. Richman, 'Reviewed: Georges Bataille in *"La Critique Sociale"* ', 14.3/4 *South Central Review*: 28.
53 Goldhammer, *The Headless Republic*: 160.
54 It 'offers them a visceral reminder that their humanity is thoroughly intertwined with what humans reject as radically other, namely death or not-being. Thus the antidote to reification in the modern age consists not in regenerative morality or reconstructed wholeness but rather in a confrontation with what Bataille calls the accursed share' (ibid: 162).
55 Goldhammer, *The Headless Republic*: 162.
56 Foucault, *Society Must be Defended*: 259–260.
57 This excess is something I have looked at in the last chapter; in the next, I will return to it through Rancière and in Chapter 8, through Agamben and biopolitics.
58 See G. Bataille, 'The Notion of Expenditure', in *Visions of Excess* (A. Stoekl (ed.)) (Minnesota University Press, Minneapolis, 1985): 116.
59 Goldhammer, *The Headless Republic*: 168.
60 Ibid: 169.
61 G. Bataille, 'The Psychological Structure of Fascism', in *Visions of Excess* (A. Stoekl (ed.)) (Minnesota University Press, Minneapolis, 1985): 139.
62 Goldhammer, *The Headless Republic*: 169.
63 A. Stoekl, 'Introduction' in Bataille, *Visions of Excess*: xvii.
64 Goldhammer, *The Headless Republic*: 173.
65 D. Hollier, *Against Architecture: The Writings of Georges Bataille* (MIT Press, London, 1989): 126.
66 Goldhammer, *The Headless Republic*: 191.
67 B. Noys, *Georges Bataille, A Critical Introduction* (Pluto Press, London, 2000): 22.

Chapter 6 Differing the people: Derrida and Rancière

1 J.-L. Nancy, 'On Finitude and Sovereignty' partially available at http://www.critical-legalthinking.com/?p=128.
2 C. Schmitt, *Constitutional Theory* (Duke University Press, Durham (NC), 2008): 128.
3 Ibid: 166.
4 H. Lindahl, 'Constituent Power and Reflexive Identity: Towards an Ontology of Collective Selfhood', in *Paradox of Constitutionalism* (M. Loughlin and N. Walker (eds)) (Oxford University Press, Oxford, 2007): 13.
5 Ibid: 13.
6 Schmitt, *Constitutional* Theory: 131.
7 Ibid: 131.
8 H. Kelsen, *Allgemeine Staatslehre* [1925] (Vienna: Österreichische Staatsdruckerei, 1993): 154–155, cited in Lindahl, 'Constituent Power and Reflexive Identity': 11.
9 Lindahl, 'Constituent Power and Reflexive Identity': 11.
10 Ibid: 9.
11 P. Virno, *A Grammar of the Multitude* (Semiotext(e), Los Angeles, 2004): 21.
12 Ibid: 22.
13 T. Hobbes, *De Cive*: Chapter XII, Section VIII.
14 Hobbes, *De Cive*: Chapter XII, Section VIII.
15 Virno, *A Grammar of the Multitude*: 23.
16 A. Negri, *Insurgencies* (University of Minnesota Press, Minneapolis, 1999): 26.
17 Ibid: 26.
18 Ibid: 26.

19 M. Hardt and A. Negri, *Empire* (Harvard University Press, Cambridge (MA), 2001): 103.

20 Virno, *Grammar of the Multitude*, p42.

21 Ibid: 42.

22 E. Laclau, *On Populist Reason* (Verso, London, 2005): 224.

23 I must say that Lindahl has published widely on the question of constituent power, however, at this moment it is useful to simply focus on the text: 'Constituent Power and Reflexive Identity'. For different readings of constituent power, some of which will be addressed later in this chapter, see H. Lindahl, 'The Opening: Alegality and Political Agonism', in A. Schaap, *Law and Political Agonism* (Aldershot: Ashgate, 2009); H. Lindahl, 'Dialectic and Revolution: Confronting Kelsen and Gadamer on Legal Interpretation', in 24.3 *Cardozo Law Review* (2003): 769; H. Lindahl, 'Collective Self-Legislation as an *Actus Impurus*: A response to Heidegger's Critique of European Nihilism', in 3 *Continental Philosophy Review* (2008): 323; and H. Lindahl, 'A-legality: Postnationalism and the Question of Legal Boundaries', in 73.1 *Modern Law Review* (2010): 30.

24 Lindahl, 'Constituent Power and Reflexive Identity': 19.

25 Ibid: 20.

26 Ibid: 20.

27 Ibid: 18.

28 Ibid: 18.

29 Ibid: 18.

30 The problem of the people is enunciated by Canovan: 'How ... could the people who are the source of legitimate authority actually exercise that ultimate sanction?' (M. Canovan, *The People* (Polity Press, Cambridge, 2005): 6). The point is precisely that so long as the people is understood as everyone under the state, it cannot possibly exercise the ultimate sanction on the government, either because there will always be a minority which is for the government, or because the unity of the people is given by their subjection to the state that they originate.

31 Lindahl, 'Constituent Power and Reflexive Identity': 20.

32 For further discussion on 'disagreement' see J. Rancière, *Dis-agreement – Politics and Philosophy* (University of Minnesota Press, Minneapolis, 1999); for 'dissensus', see E. Christodoulidis, 'Against Substitution, The Constitutional thinking of Dissensus', in *Paradox of Constitutionalism* (M. Loughlin and N. Walker (eds)) (Oxford University Press, Oxford, 2007); or, for 'antagonism', see E. Laclau and C. Mouffe, *Hegemony and Socialist Strategy* (Verso, London, 2001).

33 It has been suggested to me that a more important point here is that the constituent remains constituent *even after* a new constituted order emerges. Ultimately, I think, to do this justice, it would require a whole different text – certainly with more to do with Deleuze than this work. The point is that when a constituted order emerges the potentiality of the constituent is not exhausted. It is not 'one or the other', constituent power or constituted order. The potential of the constituent moment is heterogeneous, and this potential remains even after an order is (re)established. We just have to look to Shay's Rebellion and the many like it to see this in action.

34 W. Hamacher and D. E. Wellbery, 'Editor's Introduction', in G. Agamben, *Potentialities* (Stanford University Press, Palo Alto (CA), 1999): 11.

35 Ibid: 16, citing Aristotle's Metaphysics (1050 b 10).

36 J.-L. Nancy, '*Nous Autres*', in J.-L. Nancy, *The Ground of the Image* (Fordham University Press, New York, 2005): 103.

37 Ibid: 103.

38 Derrida is here playing with the phonic similarity in French between ontology and hauntology, which sound almost identical. In this way, he implies his earlier work on *différance*.

39 J. Derrida, *Spectres of Marx* (Routledge, London, 1994): 3, quoting Shakespeare, *Hamlet*, Act I, scene v.

40 Ibid: 25.

41 Ibid: 23.

42 Ibid: 77.

43 Ibid: 11.

44 Ibid: 99.

45 Derrida, *Spectres of Marx*: 39

46 H. Lindahl, 'The Opening: Alegality and Political Agonism': 59.

47 As I said earlier, Schmitt says that the greatest weakness of the people is that 'their expressions of will are easily mistaken, misinterpreted, or falsified'. Schmitt, *Constitutional Theory*: 131

48 Lindahl, 'The Opening: Alegality and Political Agonism': 60.

49 Ibid: 60.

50 J. Derrida, 'Declarations of Independence', 15 *New Political Science* (1986): 8.

51 Ibid: 8.

52 Ibid: 8.

53 Ibid: 10.

54 Ibid: 10.

55 Ibid: 10, my emphasis.

56 Hobbes, *De Cive*: Ch XII section VIII.

57 G. Agamben, *Means Without End: Notes on Politics* (University of Minnesota Press, Minneapolis, 2000): 30.

58 Ibid: 31.

59 Ibid: 32.

60 Ibid: 33.

61 N. Hewlett, *Badiou, Balibar, Rancière – Rethinking Emancipation* (Continuum, New York, 2007): 101.

62 J. Rancière, *Le Mésentente* (Galilee, Paris, 1995): 169; (J. Rancière trans.), *Dis-agreement – Politics and Philosophy* (University of Minnesota Press, Minneapolis, 1999), cited in N. Hewlett, *Rethinking Emancipation*: 101.

63 J. Rancière, 'Ten Theses on Politics' available at http://abahlali.org/node/3434 (accessed 08/05/08): 6–7.

64 E. Balibar, *We the People of Europe, Reflections on Transnational Citizenship* (University of Princeton Press, Princeton (NJ), 2004): 72.

65 Rancière, 'Ten Theses on Politics': 5–6.

66 On this, Hewlett asserts that here Rancière comes close to his old teacher, Althusser, and his conception of an ideological state apparatus.

67 S. Sayers, 'Review of The Politics of Aesthetics', *Culture Machine*, http://scm-rime. tees.ac.uk/Reviews/rev54.htm (accessed 08/05/08).

68 Badiou equates Rancière's jargon of the police with his sense of the 'state of the situation' (A. Badiou, *Metapolitics* (Verso, London, 2005): 116).

69 In his early work, *The Nights of Labor*, Rancière selects subjects of his historical study by their shared reaction to injustice. He frames this injustice as such: 'What they found intolerable was not exactly poverty, the low wages, the uncomfortable housing, or the ever-present spectre of hunger. It was something more basic; the anguish of time shot everyday working up wood or iron, sewing clothe, or stitching footwear, for no other purpose than to maintain indefinitely the forces of servitude with those of domination; the humiliating absurdity of having to go out begging, day after day, for this labour in which one's life was lost' (J. Rancière, *The Nights of Labor – The Workers Dream in 19th Century France* (Temple University Press, Philadelphia, 1989): vii).

70 Rancière, *Dis-agreement*: 8–9, 11–12, cited in Balibar, *We the People of Europe*: 73.

71 Badiou describes Rancière's process of politics emerging: 'Politics exists . . . because the whole of the community does not count a given collective as one of its parts. The whole counts this collective as nothing. No sooner does this nothing express itself, which it can do only by declaring itself to be whole, than politics exists. In this sense the "we are nothing, let us be everything" of *the Internationale* sums up every politics (of emancipation or equality)' (Badiou, *Metapolitics*: 115)

72 Hewlett, *Rethinking Emancipation*: 107.

73 S. Žižek, 'The Lesson of Rancière', in J. Rancière, *The Politics of Aesthetics* (Continuum, London, 2004): 70.

74 Rancière, 'Ten Theses on Politics': 6.

75 Rancière, 'Ten Theses on Politics': 6.

76 G. Rockhill, 'Translator's Introduction', in Rancière, *Dis-agreements*: 3.

Chapter 7 On being-together: beyond the subject of human rights

1 N. Fraser, 'The French Derrideans, Politicizing Deconstruction or Deconstructing the Political?', 33 *New German Critique* (1984): 141.

2 M. Heidegger, *Basic Writings, From Being and Time to the Task of Thinking* (Harper & Row, London, 1977): 187.

3 If we discount the question of fascism, for now, there have been essentially two approaches to the political in Heidegger. The first, and perhaps most prevalent, comes from his writing on technology. I will deal with this in a mediated fashion in the next chapter, especially focusing the problem of 'the world' and modernity (qua capital). However, the second and more difficult strand of questioning stems from the importance of sociality, historicity and authentic being-with in *Being and Time* (M. Heidegger, *Being and Time* (Robinson E. Macquarrie trans.) (Blackwell, Oxford, 1962)). This strand is made all the more difficult because Heidegger implicitly seems to exclude political questions from this analytic. Unlike the engagement with technology that tends to lend itself to an analysis of alienation, his work on authenticity and sociality seem to withdraw from the political, or worse, seem to lead us down the blind alley of nationalistic and even fascist thought. The question for what remains of this chapter therefore, is can we begin to recover a (radical democratic) political insight from Heidegger's early work. There has been much recent work on this and I particularly want to draw on some of the more interesting recent engagements. See S. Elden, *Speaking against Number* (Edinburgh University Press, Edinburgh, 2006), M. de Beistegui, *Heidegger and the Political* (Routledge, London, 1997), G. Fried, *Heidegger's Polemos: From Being to Politics* (Yale University Press, New Haven (CT), 2000), F. Schalow, *The Incarnality of Being: The Earth, Animals and the Body in Heidegger's Thought* (SUNY, New York, 2006). Equally, there have been a number of secondary collections and monographs on Heidegger's relation to other more political thinkers, D. R. Villa, *Arendt and Heidegger, The Fate of the Political* (Princeton University Press, Princeton (NJ), 1996), A. Feenberg, *Heidegger and Marcuse* (Routledge, London, 2005), A. Milchman and A. Rosenberg (eds) *Foucault and Heidegger: Critical Encounters* (University of Minnesota Press, Minneapolis, 2003).

4 Arendt, cited in Villa, *Arendt and Heidegger*: 215.

5 The political in *Being and Time* is traditionally associated with the 'anti-public rhetoric' (of §27 and §38), in which 'publicness' is associated with fallenness, inauthenticity and the they. Habermas sees this and says that the promise of *Being and Time* is broken by defining authenticity in opposition to 'the nefarious sphere of everydayness'. He says 'the "they" now serves as a foil before which a Kirkegaardian existence, radically isolated in the face of death . . . can now be identified as the "who" of *Dasein*'

(J. Habermas, *The Philosophical Discourse of Modernity: Twelve Lectures* (Polity Press, Cambridge, 1987): 150).

6 J. Ortega y Gasset, *The Revolt of the Masses* (W. W. Norton, New York, 1994).

7 Nazism's purposeful racial misunderstanding of Heidegger's thought excreted the Jews and gypsies, communists and homosexuals into the camps. They were the sacrifice of everydayness that was to cleanse the populace. This is the absolute horror of the they; when attached to the judicial or administrative system of authentics it is the figure that allows the creation of the camps. It is the law of the sovereign that presents *zoe*. This is the importance of the they, it is the figure to be excluded to bring us to an authentic understanding of our *dasein*. However, in this very structuring is a complete misunderstanding, which Heidegger was at least partially responsible for. The key to this is in the externalization of the they: 'It is not me that is inauthentic, but them, at the hands of "they".' The irony is, of course, that this dispersal of responsibility for one's own existence (this blaming them) is precisely the nature of the they. In the they, *dasein* places the responsibility for the suspense of the authentic understanding of its own death, and its responsibility for its own being.

8 M. Gelven, *A Commentary on Heidegger's Being and Time* (Harper Torchbooks, New York, 1970): 212.

9 Heidegger, *Being and Time*: 435.

10 Heidegger says: 'Our fates have already been guided in advance, in our being-with-one-another in the same world and in our resoluteness for definite possibilities' (*Being and Time*: 384).

11 De Beistegui, *Heidegger and the Political*: 16.

12 Ibid: 19.

13 Ibid: 19.

14 M. Heidegger, *Logic as the Question Concerning the Essence of Language* (W. T. Gregory and Y. Unna trans.) (SUNY, New York, 2009): 16.

15 See §28 and, in particular, the shocking conclusion that 'socialism', of which he presumably is talking about both the right (or national) and left variants, 'means no mere changing of the economic mentality; it does not mean a dreary egalitarianism and glorification of that which is inadequate. It does not mean the random pursuit of an aimless common welfare, but it means the care about the standards and the essential-jointure of our historical being and *it wills, therefore, the hierarchy according to occupation and work*, it wills the untouchable honour of every labour, it wills the unconditionality of service as the fundamental relationship with the inevitability of being' (Heidegger, *Logic*: 137, my emphasis).

16 M. Heidegger, *Introduction to Metaphysics* (Yale University Press, New Haven (NJ), 2000): 40.

17 Ibid: 4.0.

18 Elden, *Speaking against Number*: 139–140, citing Heidegger's *Beiträge*.

19 Quoted in Elden, *Speaking against Number*, in Heidegger *GA 9* (*Pathmarks* in translation): 308–309.

20 '*Ge-* denotes a bringing together, therefore *Gemäße* is a bringing together of measure, or a bringing things to the same measure ... *Schalten* is to direct, govern or rule; *Schaltung* is connection or wiring. Because *Gleich* means same or identical, this implies making similar, a forced conformity, an ordering around a prescribed norm' (ibid: 145).

21 Ibid: 145.

22 Heidegger, *Introduction to Metaphysics*: 162.

23 M. Heidegger, *Parmenidies* (Indiana University Press, Bloomington, 1998).

24 G. Fried, *Heidegger's Polemos: From Being to Politics* (Yale University Press, New Haven (CT), 2000): 141.

25 Ibid: 141.

26 Villa, *Arendt and Heidegger*: 212.

27 Heidegger, *Being and Time*: 224.

28 G. Harman, *Tool-Being: Heidegger and the Metaphysics of Objects* (Open Court Publishing, Chicago (IL), 2002): 68.

29 Harman, *Heidegger Explained*: 53.

30 Villa, *Arendt and Heidegger*: 215–216.

31 We are very suspicious of any suggestion of a 'shock doctrine', which, as Naomi Klein argues, is connected to the neo-conservative ideology and psychology. N. Klein, *The Shock Doctrine; The Rise of Disaster Capitalism* (Penguin, London, 2008).

32 De Beistegui, *Heidegger and the Political*: 18.

33 Villa, *Arendt and Heidegger*: 216.

34 Ibid: 216.

35 Ibid: 216.

36 Ibid: 218, quoting Heidegger, *Being and Time*: 436, and *Philosophical and Political Writings* (Continuum, New York, 2003): 6.

37 Negri, *Insurgencies*: 317.

38 There are many accounts of Heidegger's understanding of race and his racism, but for a recent interesting and balanced account, see R. Bernasconi, 'Race and Earth in Heidegger's Thinking during the late 1930s', 48.1 *The Southern Journal of Philosophy* (2010): 49.

39 G. Agamben, *The Open; Man and Animal* (Stanford University Press, Palo Alto (CA) 2004): 75.

40 Heidegger's notes for this course appeared lost; however, SUNY has recently translated the course, put together from student's notes, under the title: M. Heidegger, *Logic as the Question Concerning the Essence of Language* (W. T. Gregory and Y. Unna trans.) (State University of New York, New York, 2009).

41 Heidegger, *Logic*: 49–50.

42 Ibid: 52.

43 Ibid: 94.

44 Ibid: 72.

45 Ibid: 127.

46 Ibid: 136–137.

47 J.-L. Nancy, *The Inoperative Community* (University of Minnesota Press, Minneapolis, 1991): 17.

48 See C. Schmitt, *Constitutional Theory* (Duke University Press, Durham (NC), 2008).

49 This gathering can be tied neatly to the encircling or enfencing that is the prerequisite of sovereignty. See Chapter 2 of W. Brown, *Walled States, Waning Sovereignty* (MIT Press, Cambridge (MA), 2010). This will be the focus of the next two chapters in various manners.

50 Iris Marion Young, quoted in D. Harvey, 'Contested Cities: Social Process and Spatial Form', in R. T. Legatus and F. Stout, *The City Reader* (Routledge, Abingdon, 2007): 230.

51 Nancy, *The Inoperative Community*: 11.

52 Ibid: 11.

53 N. C. Levett, *Finitude, Singularity, Community: An Introduction to the Thought of Jean-Luc Nancy* (unpublished PhD thesis, University of Sussex, 2002): 112–113.

54 Ibid: 117.

55 R. Girard, *Violence and the Sacred* (Continuum, London, 2005).

56 Nancy, *The Inoperative Community*: 12.

57 P. Ffrench, *After Bataille, Sacrifice, Exposure, Community* (LEGENDA, London, 2007): 138.

58 A. Luszczynska, 'The Opposite of the Concentration Camp, Nancy's View on Community' 5.3 *New Centennial Review* (2005): 169.

59 Nancy, *The Inoperative Community*: 2–3.
60 Ibid: 13.
61 Ibid: 13.
62 Ibid: 12.
63 For Nancy, *différance* is the materiality of existence; see J.-L. Nancy, *The Sense of the World* (University of Minnesota Press, Minneapolis, 1997).
64 Ffrench, *After Bataille*: 139.
65 As Esposito says: 'The truth is that these conceptions are united by the ignored assumption that community is a "property" belonging to the subjects that join them together [*accomuna*]: an attribute, a definition, a predicate that qualifies them as belonging to the same totality [*insieme*], or as a "substance" that is produced by their union. In each case community is conceived of as a quality that is added to their nature as subjects, making them *also* subjects of community' (R. Esposito, *Communitas: The Origin and Destiny of Community* (Stanford University Press, Palo Alto (CA), 2010): 2.
66 J.-L. Nancy, 'Love and Community, Roundtable Discussion at the EGS' http://www.egs .edu/faculty/nancy/nancy-roundtable-discussion2001.html (accessed 02/01/2009): 2.
67 The linguistic connection here is obvious between work and operative (L.L. *opperativus*), 'inoperative' equally is politically connected even with the then current *opperismo* movement in Italy.
68 This is done for a variety of possible reasons, such as Girard's hypothesis that the sacrificial victim is the scapegoat who ends a spate of violent mimesis (Girard, *The Scapegoat*). The destruction of the violence between parties which stemmed from difference is through the transference of the violence onto a martyr who takes on the violence and dies with/for it.
69 Ffrench, *After Bataille*: 139.
70 Nancy, *The Inoperative Community*: 11.
71 We might attribute to the very term community with all of its baggage the differing readings of the *Inoperative Community*, which led one German publication to call it a fascist text and another to claim for it the return of communism (J.-L. Nancy, 'The Confronted Community', in 6.1 *Postcolonial Studies* (2003): 23).
72 Nancy, *The Inoperative Community*: 11–12.
73 Ibid: 12.
74 This is Pierre Joris', the translator of Blanchot's *The Unavowable Community*, translation of *désoeuvrement*, suggested to him by Christopher Fynsk. P. Joris, 'Translator's Preface', in M. Blanchot, *The Unavowable Community* (Station Hill Press, New York, 1988): xxiii.
75 Nancy, 'The Confronted Community': 30.
76 P. Kamuf, 'On the Limit', in Miami Theory Collective, *Community at Loose Ends* (University of Minnesota Press, Minneapolis, 1991): 13.
77 Nancy, *The Inoperative Community*: 31.
78 Ibid: 31.
79 M. Willson, *Technically Together – Rethinking Community within Techno-society* (Peter Lang, New York, 2006).
80 In *Eulogy for the Mêlée*, Nancy rails against the rape of Bosnian women (during the wars over the break-up of Yugoslavia), which sought to destroy the women themselves and their 'race' by forcing them to beget 'bastards'. This was 'rape in order to show that in every possible way there do not have to be relations between communities. Rape is the zero act; it is the negation of sex itself, the negation of all relation, the negation of the child, the negation of the woman. It is the pure affirmation of the rapist in whom a 'pure identity' (a "racial" identity . . .) finds nothing better than the submission to the ignoble mimicry of what it denies: relation and being together' (J.-L. Nancy, *Being Singular Plural* (Stanford University Press, Palo Alto (CA), 2000): 155). In a sense, Nancy demands a fidelity to being-with, a fidelity to our together-ness and hence a

rejection of those actions that negate relation. More than a rejection, a struggle against those acts and thoughts that conceal or negate the possibilities of our being-with. Nancy demands a constant interrogation of the together, no matter what the relation.

81 Willson, *Technically Together*: 154–155.

82 For instance, Nancy says that we must not view the question of 'the sense of the world?' 'as a problem to be solved nor as a discovery to be made. If viewed in this way, it would be pitiably laughable or dangerously paranoid to propose a book titled *The Sense of the World*, in a gesture that was supposed to mean "here is the solution" ' (Nancy, *The Sense of the World*: 8).

83 J. S. Librett, 'Translator's Foreword, Between Nihilism and Myth: Value, Aesthetics and Politics', in Nancy, *The Sense of the World*: vii.

84 Ibid: 8–9.

85 *The Inoperative Community* was taken up by Blanchot, who responded with *The Unavowable Community*.

86 Nancy, 'The Confronted Community': 31. Elsewhere, he says 'community does not consist in the transcendence (nor in the transcendental) of a being supposedly immanent to community. It consists on the contrary in the immanence of a "transcendence" – that of finite existence as such, which is to say, of its "exposition". Exposition, precisely, is not a "being" that one can "sup-pose" (like a sub-stance) to be in community. Community is presuppositionless: this is why it is haunted by such ambiguous ideas as foundation and sovereignty, which are at once ideas of what would be completely suppositionless and ideas of what would always be presupposed. But community cannot be presupposed. It is only exposed' (Nancy, *The Inoperative Community*, Preface: xxix).

87 James argues that 'in untying the inter-related questions of decision and judgment from established criteria or universal norms Nancy does not aim to endorse any form of arbitrariness or relativism, nor to promote decisions made for or in the name of this or that particularly *against* the notion of the universal' (I. James, 'On Interrupted Myth', in 9.4 *Journal for Cultural Research*: 345). I would adopt this position and add to it the damning critique of Laclau, Mouffe and Žižek, which argues that cultural relativism replaces the absolutism of universals with the absolutism of culture, the 'essentialism of society with the essentialism of the dialects' (B. Arditi, *Politics on the Edges of Liberalism; Difference, Populism, Revolution, Agitation* (Edinburgh University Press, Edinburgh, 2008): 31). It is ultimately a question for cultural purity, what Visker calls 'cultural condoms' (quoted in Arditi, ibid: 32).

Chapter 8 On world: biopolitics, singularity and 'global' human rights

1 J.-L. Nancy, *The Inoperative Community* (University of Minnesota Press, Minneapolis, 1991): 9.

2 J.-L. Nancy, *Dis-enclosure, The Deconstruction of Christianity* (Fordham University Press, New York, 2008): 160–161.

3 'Nothing contained in the present Charter shall authorize the United Nations to intervene in matters which are essentially within the domestic jurisdiction of any state or shall require the Members to submit such matters to settlement under the present Charter; but this principle shall not prejudice the application of enforcement measures under Chapter VII.'

4 It has been variously suggested to me that I should distinguish between biopower and biopolitics. Following one suggestion in particular, I will take biopolitics as the instrumentalization of the broader mechanisms of biopower. This seems a little more in line with Hardt and Negri's reading of biopower/ politics than Foucault or Agamben, but I would like to mark that my usage should not be taken as signifying greater political possibility in biopolitics.

5   Hardt and Negri suggest three strands of contemporary analysis of biopower. Ewald and Esposito utilize a very limited version of biopower, focusing on the actuarial administration of life. The second stream is Agamben's, to which I will return shortly. The third is artificially constructed around a sense of 'a certain autonomy conceded to biopolitical subjectivity' in Chomsky, Simondon, Steigler and Sloterdijk (M. Hardt and A. Negri, *Commonwealth* (Harvard University Press, Cambridge (MA), 2009): 57–58). Hardt and Negri's reading of biopower – through Deleuze – would presumably provide a fourth strand.

6   There have been a variety of really excellent introductions to Foucault, in general, and biopower more specifically. See, for instance (and in no particular order), B. Golder and P. Fitzpatrick, *Foucault's Law* (Routledge, London, 2009), M. Hardt and A. Negri, *Empire* (Harvard University Press, Cambridge MA), 2000).

7   M. Foucault, *The History of Sexuality, Vol. 1* (Penguin, London, 1978): 143.

8   M. Foucault, 'Right of Death, Power over Life', in N. Scheper-Hughes, *Violence in War and Peace* (Wiley-Blackwell, Oxford, 2004): 82.

9   L. McNay, *Foucault, A Critical Introduction* (Polity Press, Cambridge, 1994): 92.

10 M. Hardt and A. Negri, *Empire* (Harvard University Press, Cambridge (MA), 2000): 23.

11 McNay, *Foucault*: 94–95.

12 Foucault adds to this that 'I do not mean to say that the law fades into the background or that the institutions of justice tend to disappear, but rather that the law operates more and more as a norm, and that the judicial institution is increasingly incorporated into a continuum of apparatuses (medical, administrative, and so on) whose functions are for the most part regulatory' (Foucault, *The History of Sexuality, Vol. 1*: 144).

13 Ibid: 144, my emphasis.

14 Ibid: 145.

15 This should be clarified a little. There are a number of Foucaults when it comes to human rights. For a very different reading of the Foucauldian texts on rights, see: B. Golder, 'Foucault's Critical (Yet Ambivalent) Affirmation: Three Figures of Rights' (2011) *Social & Legal Studies*, B. Golder, 'What is an Anti-Humanist Human Right?', 16.5 *Social Identities* (2010): 651–668 and B. Golder, 'Foucault and the Unfinished Human of Rights', 6.3 *Law, Culture and the Humanities* (2010): 354–374.

16 This is despite the fact, as Kelly argues, that by the *College de France* lectures of 1978 and 1979 (now published in English as *Security, Territory, Population* (Palgrave Macmillan, 2007) and *The Birth of Biopolitics* (Palgrave Macmillan, 2010), Foucault had already moved away from the concept of biopower and instead replaced it with 'governmentality' or governmental management (M. Kelly, *The Political Philosophy of Michel Foucault* (Routledge, Abingdon, 2009): 60).

17 H. Arendt, *The Origins of Totalitarianism* (Harvest Books, New York, 1973).

18 E. Balibar, '(De)Constructing the Human as Human Institution: A Reflection on the Coherence of Hannah Arendt's Practical Philosophy', 74.3 *Social Research* (2007): 732.

19 J. Rancière, 'Who is the Subject of the Rights of Man', 103.2/3 *South Atlantic Quarterly* (2004): 302.

20 Ibid: 302.

21 Ibid: 303.

22 J. Rancière, 'Ten Theses on Politics' available at http://abahlali.org/node/3434 (accessed 08/05/08): 6–7.

23 E. Balibar, *We the People of Europe, Reflections on Transnational Citizenship* (University of Princeton Press, Princeton (NJ), 2004): 72.

24 Although there are significant differences with Rancière's distribution of the sensible, I would like to note the similarities between McNay's description of biopower (earlier) and Rancière's description here.

25 Ranciere, 'Who is the Subject of the Rights of Man': 303.

26 N. Nesbitt, *Toussaint L'Ouverture, The Haitian Revolution* (Verso, London, 2008): xlv.

27 Ranciere, 'Who is the Subject of the Rights of Man', 305.

28 Ibid: 304.

29 Ibid: 306.

30 J. Whyte, 'Particular Rights and Absolute Wrongs: Giorgio Agamben on Life and Politics', 20.2 *Law and Critique* (2009): 155.

31 G. Agamben, *Homo Sacer–Sovereign Power and Bare Life* (University of Minnesota Press, Minneapolis, 1998): 6, emphasis in original.

32 P. Festus, quoted in Agamben, *Homo Sacer*: 71.

33 C. Schmitt, *Political Theology: Four Chapters on the Concept of Sovereignty* (University of Chicago Press, Chicago, 2005).

34 M. Ojakangas, 'The Impossible Dialogue on Biopower: Agamben and Foucault', 2 *Foucault Studies* (2005): 7.

35 Whyte, 'Particular Rights and Absolute Wrongs': 158.

36 Ibid: 159, quoting Marx in G. Agamben, *The Time That Remains: A Commentary on the Letter to the Romans* (Stanford University Press, Palo Alto (CA), 2005): 31.

37 Whyte, 'Particular Rights and Absolute Wrongs': 159.

38 S. Sorial, *Heidegger and the Problem of Individuation: Mitsein (Being-with), Ethics and Responsibility* (unpublished PhD thesis, UNSW, Australia (2005)): 89.

39 If such a division were possible (and it is not), it is all for the Agamben of the politics of 'whatever singularity' in *The Coming Community* (University of Minnesota Press, Minneapolis, 1993) and *Means Without End: Notes on Politics* (University of Minnesota Press, Minneapolis, 2000), but against the Agamben of the camps and *homo sacer*. Of course, such a distinction is not possible to draw.

40 Whyte, 'Particular Rights and Absolute Wrongs': 159.

41 It should be noted that singularity is at once the fundamental manner in which each existent manifests its being, and so in this sense, everything that comes to being, comes as singularity. However, it particularly attests to the being of the human or *dasein*, in the Heideggerian sense of the one that is concerned with its own being. My usage will be this latter sense.

42 J.-L. Nancy, *The Sense of the World* (University of Minnesota Press, Minneapolis, 1997): 71.

43 Ibid: 71.

44 Agamben, *The Coming Community*: 1.

45 Nancy, *The Sense of the World*: 72.

46 Agamben says that 'Singularity is . . . freed from the false dilemma that obliges knowledge to choose between the ineffability of the individual and the intelligibility of the universal . . . In this conception, such-and-such being is reclaimed from its having this or that property, which identifies it as belonging to this or that set, to this or that class (the reds, the French, the Muslims) and it is reclaimed not for another class nor for the simple generic absence of any belonging, but for its being-*such*, for belonging itself' (Agamben, *The Coming Community*: 1–2).

47 Nancy, *The Sense of the World*: 72.

48 Agamben, *The Coming Community*: 1.

49 Nancy, *The Sense of the World*: 73.

50 Ibid: 74.

51 Ibid: 74.

52 Ibid: 74.

53 Nancy, *The Inoperative Community*: 3.

54 Ibid: 6–7.

55 J.-L. Nancy, *Being Singular Plural* (Stanford University Press, Palo Alto (CA), 2000): 156.

56 See P. Virno, *A Grammar of the Multitude* (Semiotext(e), Los Angeles, 2004). Nancy says: '[T]he *singular being*, which is not the individual, is finite being. What the the-

matic of individuation lacked . . . was a consideration of singularity, to which it none-theless came quite close. Individuation detaches closed off entities from a formless ground – whereas only communication, contagion, or communion constitute the being of individuals. But singularity does not proceed from such detaching of clear forms or figures . . . Singularity perhaps does not *proceed* from anything. It is not a work resulting from an operation. There is no process of "singularization", and singularity is neither extracted, nor produced, nor derived' (Nancy, *The Inoperative Community*: 27).

57   More on this in the next chapter.

58   Nancy would rely on the Heideggerian experience of death as an event of singulariza-tion, but he couples it with Bataille's view that death is revealed in community: 'Death is indissociable from community, for it is through death that the community reveals itself – and reciprocally' (Nancy, *The Inoperative Community*: 14). Community reveals death and so it exposes finitude. Singularity is finite, it is touched by its birth and death. However, death is mediated by the other, it is not revealed in the purity of one's ownmost projection, as *per* Heidegger.

59   That said, I have used 'singularization' already in the discussion of whatever singular-ity. For clarity's sake, this is a slightly different sense. Singularity is not a set state that one could reach. Instead, it is a constant shifting in which singularity constantly singularizes.

60   Ibid: 27.

61   Ibid: 27.

62   Agamben, *The Coming Community*: 85, emphasis of the entire sentence in original has been removed.

63   Agamben, *The Coming Community*: 85–86.

64   *Ecotechnics* is first deployed in *Corpus*, which Nancy wrote between 1990 and 1992 (J.-L, Nancy, *Corpus* (Fordham University Press, New York, 2008)).

65   M. Foucault, *The History of Sexuality, Vol. 1* (Penguin, London, 1978).

66   J.-L. Nancy, *The Creation of the World or Globalization* (State University of New York Press, New York, 2007): 94.

67   Ibid: 94.

68   Hardt and Negri, *Empire*: 23.

69   Ibid: 24.

70   Nancy, *The Creation of the World*: 95.

71   Ibid: 95.

72   D. Kujundžic, 'Empire, Glocalization, and the Melancholia of the Sovereign', 29 *The Comparatist* (2005): 86.

73   Ibid: 86.

74   Ibid: 28.

75   F. Raffoul and D. Pettigrew, 'Translator's Introduction', in Nancy, *The Creation of the World*: 1.

76   Ibid: 1.

77   Ibid: 2.

78   Ibid: 2.

79   Nancy, *The Creation of the World*: 34.

80   Ibid: 34.

81   S. Žižek, *The Parallax View* (MIT Press, Cambridge (MA), 2006): 318.

82   Although as the translators of *The Creation of the World or Globalization* make clear, it is a play with the literal senses of unworld and the French usage as 'base', 'vile' and 'foul' (Nancy, *The Creation of the World*: 117).

83   J.-L. Nancy, 'Introduction', in P. Connor, E. Cadava and J.-L. Nancy, *Who Comes After the Subject* (Routledge, London, 1991): 1.

84   Raffoul and Pettigrew, 'Translator's Introduction', in Nancy, *The Creation of the World*: 8.

85 Ibid: 10.

86 It is worth mentioning that while Nancy uses 'the word *creation* . . . in a preliminary or provisional way, reserving the hope of being able to transform it. [But] In the end, this word cannot suffice for it is over-determined with and overused by monotheism, although it also indicates in this entire philosophical context the wearing out [*usure*] of monotheism itself . . ., and even if, furthermore, I do not know what word could replace it, unless it is not a matter of replacing it but of allowing it to be erased in the existing of existence' (Nancy, *The Creation of the World*: 67), this cryptic denial of 'creation' is further explained when he suggests that the *ex* of *ex nihilo* is the same as the *ex* of existence. He also suggests that the world-ing of the world is itself world creation. This makes clear that what Nancy is challenging is the sense in which creation has an efficient cause, a creator that produces the entity without remainder.

87 Raffoul and Pettigrew, 'Translator's Introduction', in Nancy, *The Creation of the World*: 10.

88 Read: the pre-given, accepted wisdom, dogma, banalities, even might we say inauthentic chatter, although it is perhaps too far, unless it is clear that we are talking about what passes in the media and elsewhere for what the 'common' 'ordinary' people think, rather than in an anti-populist sense.

89 Ibid: 10.

90 'The world is a fact without cause and without reason, it is a fact without reason or end, and it is our fact" ' (ibid: 11).

91 Ibid: 22.

92 Nancy, *The Creation of the World*: 54.

93 Raffoul and Pettigrew explain that 'the creation of the world . . . is literally the work of justice. As world-forming, the world *is* justice-in-act. This justice is a justice that is appropriate, a justice that is due' ('Translator's Introduction', in Nancy, *The Creation of the World*: 23). However, in each instance, this justice would be singular; unique in each instance, but the same justice somehow everywhere it is done. In this 'Justice would be a world constituted by this inexhaustible creation of meaning. This does not mean, however, that justice or meaning cannot be achieved, but means that each time it is enacted and each time it remains to be created or re-created.'

Chapter 9 On right-ing: constituent power and human rights

1 J.-L. Nancy, 'The Confronted Community', in 6.1 *Postcolonial Studies* (2003): 24. Nancy is referring to the conflagrations of October 2001.

2 W. Brown, *States of Injury: Power and Freedom in Late Modernity* (Princeton University Press, Princeton (NJ), 1995): 98.

3 This would be the soft totalitarianism that Nancy discusses. Equally, this biopolitics is central to human rights, as Douzinas sets out in Chapter 5 of *Human Rights and Empire* (Routledge, London, 2007).

4 For a superbly thorough and terrifying instantiation of the very worst role of human rights and civil society in military–humanitarianism, see Peter Hallward's *Damning the Flood* (Verso, London, 2007) on Haiti's very recent humanitarian history.

5 As the last right of the UDHR's Preamble.

6 The deconstructive significance of this term should not be overlooked. The remains are at once the traditional supplement of the Cartesian subject. That which literally remains behind once the soul has departed. A material, bodily, supplement. The remains of the day are those remnants that lie discarded after an event. They remain as the traces of something else. However, my assertion is that 'it remains'. This is meant in the double sense of the verb, remaining 'passively' but also remaining in an active sense. The corpse or remains of an event are inert in a sense, simply the detritus of another event. However, in an active sense they disturb a normalcy. In this sense, 'it remains' is meant

to sound an active dissonance with the traditional narrative of human rights. It suggests a non-identity, a difference of human rights from itself.

7 R. Vaneigem, *The Revolution in Everyday Life* (Practical Paradise Publications, London, 1975): 6.

8 R.Vaneigem, *A Declaration of the Rights of Human Beings: On Sovereignty of Life as Surpassing the Rights of Man* (Pluto Press, London, 2003).

9 Ibid: 12.

10 Ibid: 17.

11 Ibid: 17.

12 Ibid: 19.

13 Ibid: 31.

14 http://www.notbored.org/human-rights.html#_edn6 (accessed 26/10/09).

15 Ibid.

16 Vaneigem, *A Declaration of the Rights of Human Beings*: 48.

17 Ibid: 89.

18 Ibid: 57.

19 Ibid: 15.

20 Ibid: 67.

21 Vaneigem, *The Revolution of Everyday Life*: 8.

22 Ibid: 9.

23 D. Mitchell, *The Right to the City; Social Justice and the Fight for Public Space* (Guilford Press, New York, 2003): 17.

24 Ibid: 18.

25 Ibid: 18.

26 A. Merrifield, *Henri Lefebvre: A Critical Introduction* (Routledge, New York, 2006): 71.

27 H. Lefebvre, 'The Right to the City', in *Writings on Cities* (Blackwell, Oxford, 1996): 174, also quoted in Mitchell, *The Right to the City*: 18.

28 M. Gottdiener, 'A Marx for Our Time: Henri Lefebvre and the Production of Space', in 11.1 *Sociological Theory* (1993): 133.

29 M. Tushnet, 'An Essay on Rights' 68.2 *Texas Law Review* (1984): 1363.

30 S. Elden, *Understanding Henri Lefebvre; Theory and the Possible* (Continuum, London, 2006): 153.

31 Lefebvre talks of 'the festival' as a crucial event. Elden summarizes: 'The festival of the city amplifies rural traditions of transgression and disorder. [Speaking of the Paris Commune] The organized space of Haussmann's boulevards is challenged by the barriers erected, by the use of the road, café and the festival, which constitute the social space of the poor. It was, for Lefebvre, the first urban revolution, understood, as I suggested, not merely as a revolution in an urban setting, but one that had the potential to challenge that context fundamentally. The people of Paris come into the streets, into all the quarters of the city. They flood (*inonde*) the streets, they drown out existing power. The workers reappropriate the space from which they had been excluded by Bonapartism – and therefore the Commune demonstrates the contradiction of space, and not simply the contradictions of historical time' (ibid: 154). Merrifield assures us, in the vein of Bataille, that the festival 'consumes unproductively, without any other advantage other than pleasure' (A. Merrifield, *Henri Lefebvre*: 69).

32 Elden, *Understanding Henri Lefebvre*: 227. See also S. Elden, 'Introduction', in H. Lefebvre, *State, Space, World: Selected Essays* (University of Minnesota Press, Minneapolis, 2009).

33 Lefebvre, quoted in Elden, *Understanding Lefebvre*: 229.

34 See Lefebvre, *State, Space, World*.

35 Mitchell, *The Right to the City*.

36 Ibid: 26.

37 He says that discourse does not produce, rather it 'helps set the context within which social practices occur and are given meaning. This power lies in the ability of words organized as discourse to *instruct*' (ibid: 26). Instead, he takes a fairly straightforward Marxist line that it is not the Foucauldian disciplinary discourse that prevents people engaging in secondary boycotts, rather it is '*police power*'. It is too late in the day to re-explain the importance and power of discourse. Needless to say, while I acknowledge the direct force of law, and have done throughout, I would also emphasize the disciplinary power of discourses of normalization (see, in particular, Chapter 8). However, it is also worthwhile asking exactly what Mitchell is rejecting in this rejection. Foucault, Derrida and Lyotard are clearly in the firing line. However, if I were to problematize this aspect of his work further, I would question Mitchell's reliance on Lefebvre who moves smoothly between Marx and, crucially, *Heidegger*. I wonder if Mitchell is reading Lefebvre simply as a Marxist?

38 Ibid: 22.

39 Tushnet explains indeterminacy: 'The language of rights is so open and indeterminate that opposing parties can use the same language to express their positions' (ibid: 23, quoting Tushnet, 'An Essay on Rights': 1371).

40 Mitchell, *The Right to the City*: 25.

41 Ibid: 26.

42 J.-L. Nancy, *The Experience of Freedom* (Stanford University Press, Palo Alto (CA), 1993).

43 Mitchell, *The Right to the City*: 19.

44 I must say that there is still much of the radical in Mitchell's work. While, I argue it misses the difference of rights, it clearly enunciates a radical political agenda: 'The abrogation of rights becomes a focus of political action, of social struggle' (ibid: 27).

45 And I mean this in the simple sense, without the philosophical over-determination.

46 See, for instance, Chapter 1 of B. S. Turner, *Vulnerability and Human Rights* (Pennsylvania State University Press, Old Main, 2006). There, Turner suggests that the vulnerability of human beings implies the necessity of the state: 'Human beings are ontologically vulnerable and insecure, and their natural environment, doubtful. In order to protect themselves from uncertainties of the everyday world, they must build social institutions (especially political, familial, and cultural institutions) that come to constitute what we call "society" ' (ibid: 26). With this vulnerability, the necessity of the state is written in human nature. Fineman does something similar in M. Fineman, 'The Vulnerable Subject: Anchoring Equality in the Human Condition', 20.1 *Yale Journal of Law and Feminism* (2008): 1. For further discussion of this use of vulnerability, see I. Wall, 'On Pain and the Sense of Human Rights', 29 *Australian Feminist Law Journal* (2009): 53.

47 B. Mazlish, *The Idea of Humanity in a Global Era* (Palgrave Macmillan, London, 2009).

48 In 'The Last of the Rogue States', Derrida writes a beautifully deconstructive footnote on the relation between majesty and sovereignty. He says: '[L]ike the word sovereignty, its synonym majesty suggests the greatest in size (*majestas* comes from *majus*, for *magius*, major, greatness, height, superiority, the supreme or supremacy, that which, like the *superanus* of the sovereign, comes *above*). Sovereign majesty: a question of size, therefore, as with the democratic majority that assures sovereignty. But it is a question of calculable-incalculable size, for if the majority is numerical, the general will of the sovereign or of the monarch cannot be divided. And the One (of God, of the monarch, or of the sovereign) is not greater, very great (comparatively or superlatively), superiorly great or supremely high. It is absolutely great, and thus above measurable greatness. Higher than height, incommensurable in any case, even if it can sometimes take the form and have the supreme power of the smallest and most invisible. In a modernity of nanotechnosciences, power is also measured in terms of how

well it measures up to the potency of the smallest possible. The sovereign One is a One that can no longer be counted; it is more than one (*plus d'un*) in the sense of being more than a one (*plus qu'un*), beyond the more than one of calculable multiplicity' (J. Derrida, 'The Last of the Rogue States: The "Democracy to Come," Opening in Two Turns', 103.2/3 *South Atlantic Quarterly* (2004): fn3, 339).

49 M. Heidegger, *Logic as the Question Concerning the Essence of Language* (State University of New York Press, New York, 2009): 19.

50 J.-L. Nancy and P. Lacoue-Labarthe, *Retreating the Political* (S. Sparks (ed.)) (Routledge, London, 1997): 158.

51 Hallward, *Damning the Flood*.

52 M. Taylor, 'English Defence League: New Wave of Extremists Plotting Summer of Unrest' (the Guardian, 28/05/2010) http://www.guardian.co.uk/uk/2010/may/28/english-defence-league-protest-bnp (accessed 23/01/2011) or, for further discussion, see J. Puar, 'To be Gay and Racist is no Anomaly' (the Guardian – Comment is Free, 02/06/2010) http://www.guardian.co.uk/commentisfree/2010/jun/02/gay-lesbian-islamophobia (accessed 23/01/2011).

53 C. Douzinas, *The End of Human Rights* (Hart Publishing, Oxford, 2000): 215–216, my emphasis. This connection to writing is important, but I do not have the space here to engage with it properly. Like writing, right-ing is precisely a form of creation that ultimately becomes levelled down to the given, to dogma. He argues that right-ing is the Levinasian irruption of the saying in the said. It is a Benjamanian divine violence that suspends the law-making and law-preserving violence of the state. I would tie it to Nancy's thought of political writing in *The Sense of the World*: 'The writing of the sense of the world, or better the sense of the world as writing, does not reside, first of all, in a worldliness of cultural variegation and "hybridity" as new identity – no more than it can reside in the uniformity of the world "order". It resides in what maintains the world as *existentiale of worldliness:* resistance to the closure of worlds within the world as well as resistance to the closure of worlds-beyond-the-world: the tracing out [*fryage*], in each instant, of this world *here*' (Nancy, *The Sense of the World*: 120). Writing is what maintains the openness of the world. Later he adds: 'Identities must *write* themselves, that is, they must know and practice themselves as non-identifiable (k)nots of sense' (ibid: 122). Here, identity is confounded in writing itself, because this reveals its status as non-identifiable. Writing is the performance of possibility which ruptures the apparent givenness of the world.

54 C, Douzinas, 'The "End" of Human Rights', *The Guardian*, 10/12/2008.

55 Douzinas, *End of Human Rights*, Douzinas, *Human Rights and Empire*.

56 Douzinas, *Human Rights and Empire*: 292.

57 Ibid: 380.

58 Nancy and Lacoue-Labarthe, *Retreating the Political*: 158.

Bibliography

Adorno, T. *The Jargon of Authenticity* (Routledge, Oxford, 2007)

Agamben, G. *The Coming Community* (University of Minnesota Press, Minneapolis, 1993)

Agamben, G. *Homo Sacer – Sovereign Power and Bare Life* (University of Minnesota Press, Minneapolis, 1998)

Agamben, G. *Means without End: Notes on Politics* (University of Minnesota Press, Minneapolis, 2000)

Agamben, G. *The Open; Man and Animal* (Stanford University Press, Palo Alto (CA), 2004)

Agamben, G. *Potentialities* (Stanford University Press, Palo Alto (CA), 1999)

Agamben, G. *Profanations* (Zone Books, New York, 2007)

Agamben, G. *State of Exception* (University of Chicago Press, Chicago, 2006)

Agamben, G. *The Time That Remains: A Commentary on the Letter to the Romans* (Stanford University Press, Palo Alto (CA), 2005)

Anstey, R. *The Atlantic Slave Trade and British Abolition* (Gregg Revivals Macmillian, Basingstoke, 1993)

Arditi, B. *Politics on the Edges of Liberalism; Difference, Populism, Revolution, Agitation* (Edinburgh University Press, Edinburgh, 2008)

Arendt, H. *Between Past and Future: Eight Exercises in Political Thought* (Viking Press, New York, 1968)

Arendt, H. *On Revolution* (Penguin, London, 1973)

Arendt, H. *On Violence* (Penguin, London, 1970)

Arendt, H. *The Origins of Totalitarianism* (Harvest Books, New York, 1973)

Arnould, E. 'The Impossible Sacrifice of Poetry: Bataille and the Nancean Critique of Sacrifice', 26.2 *Diacritics* (1996)

Asad, T. *Formations of the Secular: Christianity, Islam, Modernity* (Stanford University Press, Palo Alto (CA), 2003)

Axelos, K. *Alienation, Praxis, and Techne in the Thought of Karl Marx* (University of Texas Press, Austin, 1976)

Axinn, S. 'Kant, Authority and the French Revolution', 32.3 *Journal of the History of Ideas* (1971)

Badiou, A. *Metapolitics* (Verso, London, 2005)

Balakrishnen, G. (ed.) *Debating Empire* (Verso, London, 2003)

Balibar, E. '(De)Constructing the Human as Human Institution: A Reflection on the Coherence of Hannah Arendt's Practical Philosophy', 74.3 *Social Research* (2007)

Balibar, E. *Masses, Classes, Ideas – Studies on Politics and Philosophy before and after Marx* (Routledge, New York, 1994)

Balibar, E. 'Possessive Individualism Reversed, From Locke to Derrida', 9.3 *Constellations* (2002)

Balibar, E. *We the People of Europe, Reflections on Transnational Citizenship* (University of Princeton Press, Princeton (NJ), 2004)

Bass, A. *Interpretation and Difference* (Stanford University Press, Palo Alto (CA), 2006)

Bataille, G. *The Accursed Share, Volume I* (Zone Books, New York, 1991)

Bataille, G. *The Accursed Share, Volumes II and III* (Zone Books, New York, 1993)

Bataille, G. *Visions of Excess* (Stoekl, A. ed.) (Minnesota University Press, Minneapolis, 1985)

Bates, E. 'History', in Moeckli, D. Shah, S. and Sivakumaran, S. (eds) *International Human Rights Law* (Oxford University Press, Oxford, 2010)

Baxi, U. *The Future of Human Rights* (Oxford University Press, Oxford, 2005)

Beardsworth, R. *Derrida and the Political* (Routledge, London, 2006)

Beck, L. W. 'Kant and the Right of Revolution', *Journal of the History of Ideas* (1971)

Beistegui, M. de, *Heidegger and the Political, Dystopias* (Routledge, London, 1997)

Beistegui, M. de, *The New Heidegger* (Continuum Press, New York, 2005)

Belden Fields, A. *Rethinking Human Rights for the New Millennium* (Palgrave, New York, 2003)

Ben-Dor, O. *Thinking about Law, In Silence with Heidegger* (Hart Publishing, Oxford, 2007)

Benjamin, A. and Osborne, P. *Destruction and Experience* (Clinamen Press, Manchester, 2000)

Benjamin, W. *Reflections* (Schoken Books, New York, 1978)

Berlin, I. 'Georges Sorel', *Times Literary Supplement*, 31/12/1971

Bertram, B. 'New Reflections on the "Revolutionary" Politics of Ernesto Laclau and Chantal Mouffe', 22.3 *Boundary* (1995)

Bhambra, G. K. and Shiliam, R. *Silencing Human Rights: Critical Engagements with a Contested Project* (Palgrave, New York, 2009)

Blanchot, M. *The Unavowable Community* (Station Hill Press, New York, 1988)

Blattner, W. *Heidegger's Being and Time: A Readers Guide* (Continuum, New York, 2006)

Bloch, E. *Natural Law and Human Dignity* (MIT Press, Cambridge (MA), 1987)

Bloch, E. *The Principle of Hope, Volume. I* (MIT Press, Cambridge (MA), 1986)

Bobbio, N. *The Age of Rights* (Polity Press, Cambridge, 1996)

Bottici, C. 'Imagining Human Rights: Utopia or Ideology', 21.2 *Law and Critique* (2010)

Bowring, B. *The Degradation of International Law* (Glasshouse Press, Abingdon, 2008)

Breton, A., Caillois, R., Char, R., Crevel, R., Eluard, L., Monnerot, J.-M. et al., 'Murderous Humanitarianism', (S. Beckett trans.) available at http://racetraitor.org/murderoushumanitarianism.html (accessed 19/08/10)

Brettschneider, C. *Democratic Rights: The Substance of Self-Government* (Princeton University Press, Princeton (NJ), 2007)

Brown, W. *States of Injury: Power and Freedom in Late Modernity* (Princeton University Press, Princeton (NJ), 1995)

Brown, W. *Walled States, Waning Sovereignty* (MIT Press, Cambridge (MA), 2010)

Burton, R. D. E. *Blood in the City – Violence and Revelation in Paris, 1789–1945* (Cornell University Press, Ithaca (NY), 2001)

Butler, J. 'Benjamin's Critique of Violence', in *Political Theologies* (Sullivan, L. and de Vries, H. (eds)) (Fordham University Press, New York, 2006)

Butler, J. *Precarious Life: The Power of Mourning and Violence* (Verso, London 2006)

Canovan, M. *The People* (Polity Press, Cambridge, 2005)

Caputo, J. D. *Demythologizing Heidegger* (Indiana University Press, Bloomington (IN), 1993)

Carens, J. H (ed.) *Democracy and Possessive Individualism – The Intellectual Legacy of C. B. Macpherson* (State University of New York Press, New York, 1993)

Castoriadis, C. *World in Fragments* (Stanford University Press, Palo Alto (CA), 1997)

Cavarero, A. and Bertolino, E. 'Beyond Ontology and Sexual Difference: An Interview with the Italian Feminist Philosopher Adriana Cavarero', 19.1 *Difference* (2008)

Christodoulidis, E. 'Against Substitution, The Constitutional thinking of Dissensus', in Loughlin, M. and Walker, N. (eds) *Paradox of Constitutionalism* (Oxford University Press, Oxford, 2007)

Christodoulidis, E. 'The Aporia of Sovereignty: On the Representation of the People in Constitutional Discourse', 12.1 *King's College Law Journal* (2001)

Christodoulidis, E. and Tierney, S (eds) *Public Law and Politics: The Scope and Limits of Constitutionalism* (Ashgate, Aldershot, 2008)

Clark, D. and Williamson, R. *Self-Determination, International Perspectives* (Macmillan, Basingstoke, 1996)

Clark, O. 'Heidegger and the Mystery of Pain', 10.3 *Man and World* (1977)

Clark, O. 'Pain and Being: An Essay in Heideggerian Ontology', 4.3 *Southwestern Journal of Philosophy* (1973)

Connolly, W. E. *Political Theory and Modernity* (Blackwell, Oxford, 1988)

Connor, P., Cadava, E. and Nancy, J.-L. *Who Comes After the Subject* (Routledge, London, 1991)

Corns, T. Hughes, A. and Loewenstein, D (eds) *The Complete Works of Gerrard Winstanley* (Oxford University Press, Oxford, 2010)

Cover, R. *Justice Accused* (Yale University Press, New Haven (CT), 1975)

Critchley, S. *The Ethics of Deconstruction: Derrida and Levinas* (Edinburgh University Press, Edindurgh, 1992)

Critchley, S. *Ethics, Politics, Subjectivity: Essays on Derrida, Levinas and Contemporary French Thought* (Verso, London, 1999)

Critchley, S. *Infinitely Demanding: Ethics of Commitment, Politics of Resistance* (Verso, London, 2007)

Critchley, S. 'Retracing the Political: Politics and Community in the Works of Lacoue-Labarthe and Jean-Luc Nancy', in Campbell, D. and Dillon, M. (eds) *The Political Subject of Violence* (Manchester University Press, Manchester, 1993)

Critchley, S. 'Violent Thoughts about Slavoj Žižek, 1 *Naked Punch Supplement 1*: 1

Curtin, P. D. 'The Declaration of the Rights of Man in Saint-Domingue, 1788–1791' 30 *Hispanic American Historical Review* (1950)

Daes, E.-I. 'The Right of Indigenous Peoples to Self-Determination in the Contemporary World Order', in Clark, D. and Williamson, R. *Self-Determination, International Perspectives* (Macmillan, Basingstoke, 1996)

Debord, G. *Society of the Spectacle* (Rebel Press, London, n.d.)

Derrida, J. *Acts of Religion* (Routledge, London, 2002)

Derrida, J. *Aporias* (Stanford University Press, Palo Alto (CA), 1993)

Derrida, J. 'Declarations of Independence', 15 *New Political Science* (1986)

Derrida, J. *The Gift of Death* (University of Chicago Press, Chicago, 1996)

Derrida, J. 'The Last of the Rogue States: "The Democracy to Come", Opening in Two Turns', 103.2/3 *South Atlantic Quarterly* (2004)

Derrida, J. *Margins of Philosophy* (Harvester Press, Brighton, 1982)

Derrida, J. *Of Grammatology* (Johns Hopkins University Press, Baltimore (MD), 1978)

Derrida, J. *Of Spirit: Heidegger and the Question* (University of Chicago Press, Chicago, 1991)

Derrida, J. *On Touching – Jean-Luc Nancy* (Stanford University Press, Palo Alto (CA), 2005)

Derrida, J. *Points . . . Interviews, 1974 – 1994* (Stanford University Press, Palo Alto (CA), 1995)

Derrida, J. *The Politics of Friendship* (Verso, London, 2005)

Derrida, J. *Rogues – Two Essays on Reason* (Stanford University Press, Palo Alto (CA), 2005)

Derrida, J. *Spectres of Marx* (Routledge, London, 1994)

Derrida, J. *Writing and Difference* (Routledge, London, 2003)

Douzinas, C. *The End of Human Rights* (Hart Publishing, Oxford, 2000)

Douzinas, C. 'The "End" of Human Rights', *the Guardian*, 10/12/2008

Douzinas, C. *Human Rights and Empire* (Routledge, London, 2007)

Douzinas, C. and Gearey, A. *Critical Jurisprudence; The Political Philosophy of Justice* (Hart Publishing, Oxford, 2005)

Dreyfus H. L. *Being-in-the-World, A Commentary on Heidegger's Being and Time, Division I* (MIT Press, Cambridge (MA), 1991)

Dubois, L. *Avengers of the New World, The Story of the Haitian Revolution* (Belknap Press of Harvard University Press, Cambridge (MA), 2004)

Dubois, L. and Gorrigus, J. D. *Slave Revolution in the Caribbean 1789–1804: A Brief History with Documents* (Bedford/St Martins, New York, 2006)

Eggington, W. 'The Sacred Heart of Dissent', 2.3 *New Centennial Review* (2002)

Elden, S. *Speaking Against Number* (Edinburgh University Press, Edinburgh, 2006)

Elden, S. *Understanding Henri Lefebvre; Theory and the Possible* (Continuum, London, 2006)

Emad, P. 'Heidegger on Pain: Focusing on a Recurring Theme in his Thought', 36.6 *Zeitschrift für Philosophische Forschung* (1982)

Engler, M 'Toward the 'Rights of the Poor': Human Rights and Liberation Theology', 28.3 *Journal of Religious Studies* (2000)

Escalante Gonzalbo, F. *In the Eyes of God–A Study on the Culture of Suffering* (University of Texas Press, Austin, 2006)

Esposito, R. *Communitas: The Origin and Destiny of Community* (Stanford University Press, Palo Alto (CA), 2010)

Evans, T. *The Politics of Human Rights* (Pluto Press, London, 2001)

Evans, T. 'Universal Human Rights: 'As Much Round and Round as Ever Onward',' 7.4 *International Journal of Human Rights* (2003)

Fanon, F. *Black Skin, White Masks* (Pluto Press, London, 1967)

Fanon, F. *The Wretched of the Earth* (Penguin, London, 2001)

Feenberg, A. *Heidegger and Marcuse: The Catastrophe and Redemption of History* (Routledge, New York, 2005)

Ffrench, P. *After Bataille, Sacrifice, Exposure, Community* (LEGENDA. London, 2007)

Fick, C. *The Making of Haiti: The Saint Domingue Revolution from Below* (University of Tennessee Press, Memphis, 1990)

Fitzpatrick, P. *Law as Resistance* (Ashgate, Aldershot, 2008)

Fitzpatrick, P. and Tuitt, P. (eds) *Critical Beings: Law, Nation and the Global Subject* (Ashgate, Aldershot, 2004)

Flahault, F. *Malice* (Verso, London, 2003)

Forsyth, M. *Reason and Revolution, The Political thought of the Abbé Sieyès* (Holmes and Meier Publishers, New York, 1987)

Foucault, M. 'The Art of Telling the Truth', in Foucault, M. *Politics, Philosophy, Culture: Interviews and Other Writings* (Routledge, London, 1988)

Foucault, M. *The Birth of Biopolitics* (Palgrave Macmillan, London, 2010)

Foucault, M. *Discipline and Punish: The Birth of the Prison* (Vintage Books, New York, 1977)

Foucault, M. *The History of Sexuality, Volume 1* (Penguin, London, 1978)

Foucault, M. *Madness and Civilization: A History of Insanity in an Age of Reason* (Routledge, London, 1989)

Foucault, M. *Politics, Philosophy, Culture: Interviews and Other Writings* (Routledge, London, 1988)

Foucault, M. 'Right of Death, Power over Life', in Scheper-Hughes, N. *Violence in War and Peace* (Wiley-Blackwell, Oxford, 2004)

Foucault, M. *Security, Territory, Population* (Palgrave Macmillan, London, 2007)

Foucault, M. *Society Must Be Defended* (Picador, London, 2003)

Frank, J. 'The Abyss of Democracy: Antonio Negri's Democratic Theory', 4.1 *Theory and Event* (2000)

Fraser, N. 'The French Derrideans, Politicizing Deconstruction or Deconstructing the Political?' 33 *New German Critique* (1984)

Fried, G. *Heidegger's Polemos: From Being to Politics* (Yale University Press, New Haven (CT), 2000)

Fynsk, C. 'Foreword', in Nancy, J.-L. *The Inoperative Community* (University of Minnesota Press, Minneapolis, 1991)

Fynsk, C. *Language and Relation, That There is Language* (Stanford University Press, Palo Alto (CA), 1996)

Gearty, C. *Can Human Rights Survive* (Cambridge University Press, Cambridge, 2006)

Gelven, M. *A Commentary on Heidegger's Being and Time* (Harper Torchbooks, New York, 1970)

Gibbons, L. *Edmund Burke and Ireland – Aesthetics, Politics and the Colonial Sublime* (Cambridge University Press, Cambridge, 2009)

Girard, R. *Violence and the Sacred* (Continuum, London, 2005)

Golder, B 'Foucault's Critical (Yet Ambivalent) Affirmation: Three Figures of Rights', *Social & Legal Studies* (forthcoming, 2011)

Golder, B. 'Foucault and the Unfinished Human of Rights' 6.3 *Law, Culture and the Humanities* (2010)

Golder, B. 'What is an Anti-Humanist Human Right?', 16.5 *Social Identities* (2010)

Golder, B. and Fitzpatrick, P. *Foucault's Law* (Routledge, London, 2009)

Goldhammer, T. *The Headless Republic* (Cornell University Press, Ithaca (NY), 2005)

Gooch, G. P. *Germany and the French Revolution* (Longmans, Green and Co., London, 1920)

Gordon, A. S. *Ghostly Matters; Haunting and the Sociological Imagination* (University of Minnesota Press, Minneapolis, 2004)

Gottdiener, M. 'A Marx for Our Time: Henri Lefebvre and the Production of Space', 11.1 *Sociological Theory* (1993)

Gross, D. M. and Kemmann, A. (eds) *Heidegger and Rhetoric* (State University of New York Press, New York, 2005)

Grovogue, S. N. 'No More, No Less: What Slaves Thought About Their Humanity', in Bhambra, G. K. and Shiliam, R. *Silencing Human Rights: Critical Engagements with a Contested Project* (Palgrave, London, 2009)

Guardiola-Rivera, O. *Being Against the World; Rebellion and Constitution* (Birkbeck Law Press, London, 2008)

Guignon, C. B. *The Cambridge Companion to Heidegger* (Cambridge University Press, Cambridge, 1993)

Haas, M. *International Human Rights: A Comprehensive Introduction* (Routledge, Abingdon, 2008)

Habermas, J. *The Philosophical Discourse of Modernity: Twelve Lectures* (Polity Press, Cambridge, 1987)

Hallward, P. *Damning the Flood: Haiti, Aristide, and the Politics of Containment* (Verso, London, 2007)

Hamacher, W. 'Afformative, Strike, Benjamin's "Critique of Violence" ', in Benjamin, A. and Osborne, P. *Destruction and Experience* (Clinamen Press, Manchester, 2000)

Hamacher, W. 'The Right not to Use Rights: Human Rights and the Structure of Judgments', in de Vries, H. and Sullivan, L. E. *Political Theologies; Public Religions in a Post-Secular World* (Fordham University Press, New York, 2006)

Hardt, M. and Negri, A. *Commonwealth* (Harvard University Press, Cambridge (MA), 2009)

Hardt, M. and Negri, A. *Empire* (Harvard University Press, Cambridge (MA), 2000)

Hardt, M. and Negri, A. *The Labor of Dionysus: A Critique of the State-form* (University of Minnesota Press, Minneapolis, 1994)

Hardt, M. and Negri, A. *Multitude, War and Democracy in the Age of Empire* (Penguin, New York, 2004)

Harman, G. *Heidegger Explained: From Phenomenon to Thing* (Open Court Publishing, Chicago (IL), 2007)

Harman, G. *Tool-Being: Heidegger and the Metaphysics of Objects* (Open Court Publishing, Chicago (IL), 2002)

Harris, P. *The Right to Demonstrate* (Rights Press, Hong Kong, 2007)

Harvey, D. 'Contested Cities: Social Process and Spatial Form', in Legatus R. T. and Stout, F. *The City Reader* (Routledge, Abingdon, 2007)

Heidegger, M. *Basic Concepts in Aristotelian Philosophy* (Indiana University Press, Bloomington (IN), 2007)

Heidegger, M. *Basic Writings, From Being and Time to the Task of Thinking* (Harper & Row, London, 1977)

Heidegger, M. *Being and Time* (Robinson E. Macquarrie, trans.) (Blackwell, Oxford, 1962)

Heidegger, M. *The Essence of Human Freedom* (Continuum, New York, 2002)

Heidegger, M. *The Fundamental Concepts of Metaphysics: World, Finitude, Solitude* (Indiana University Press, Bloomington (IN), 1995)

Heidegger, M. *Introduction to Metaphysics* (Yale University Press, New Haven (CT), 2000)

Heidegger, M. *Introduction to Phenomenological Research* (Indiana University Press, Bloomington (IN), 1994)

Heidegger, M. *Logic as the Question Concerning the Essence of Language* (W. T. Gregory and Y. Unna, trans.) (State University of New York Press, New York, 2009)

Heidegger, *On the Way to Language* (Harper & Row, New York, 1971)

Heidegger, M. *Parmenidies* (Indiana University Press, Bloomington (IN), 1998)

Heidegger, M. *Philosophical and Political Writings* (Stassen, M. ed.) (Continuum, New York, 2003)

Heidegger, M. *Supplements: From the Earliest Essays to Being and Time and Beyond* (van Buren, J. ed.) (State University of New York Press, New York, 2002)

Heimonet, J.-M. 'From Bataille to Derrida: *Différance* and Heterology' 12 *Stanford French Review* (1988)

Hewlett, N. *Badiou, Balibar, Rancière – Rethinking Emancipation* (Continuum, New York, 2007)

Hobbes, T. *Leviathan* (Penguin, London 1975)

Hobsbawm, E. *The Age of Capital, 1848–1875* (Vintage Books, New York, 1996)

Hobsbawm, E. *The Age of Empire, 1875–1914* (Vintage Books, New York, 1989)

Hobsbawm, E. *The Age of Revolution: Europe 1789–1848* (Vintage Books, New York, 1996)

Hollier, D. *Against Architecture: The Writings of Georges Bataille* (MIT Press, London, 1989)

Hollier, D (ed.) *The College of Sociology (1937–39)* (University of Minnesota Press, Minneapolis, 1988)

Honig, B. 'Declarations of Independence: Arendt and Derrida on the Problem of Founding A Republic', 85.1 *American Political Science Review* (1991)

Honig, B. *Democracy and the Foreigner* (University of Princeton Press, Princeton (NJ), 2001)

Hunt, L. *Inventing Human Rights – A History* (Norton & Co., New York, 2007)

Hutchens, B. C. *Jean-Luc Nancy and the Future of Philosophy* (McGill-Queens, Montreal, 2005)

Ibhawoh, B. *Imperialism and Human Rights: Colonial Discourses of Rights and Liberties in African History* (State University of New York Press, New York, 2007)

Ingram, D. 'The Retreat of the Political in the Modern Age: Jean-Luc Nancy on Totalitarianism and Community', 18 *Research in Phenomenology* (1988)

Inwood, M. J. *A Heidegger Dictionary* (Blackwell, Oxford, 1999)

Irwin, A. *Saints of the Impossible – Bataille, Weil and the Politics of the Sacred* (University of Minnesota Press, Minneapolis, 2002)

Ishay, M. *The History of Human Rights: From Ancient Times to the Globalization Era* (University of California Press, Berkeley (CA), 2008)

James, I. *The Fragmentary Demand* (Stanford University Press, Palo Alto (CA), 2006)

James, I. 'On Interrupted Myth', 9.4 *Journal for Cultural Research* (2005)

Jenckes, K. 'Thinking the Multiple: Alain Badiou and Jean-Luc Nancy', 9 *Theory @ Buffalo* (2002)

Johnson, Capt. *A General History of the Pyrates* (Dover Edition, New York, 1999)

Joris, P. 'Translator's Preface', in Blanchot, M. *The Unavowable Community* (Station Hill Press, New York, 1988)

Kain, P. *Marx and Modern Political Theory; from Hobbes to Contemporary Feminism* (Rowman & Littlefield, Lanham (MD), 1993)

Kälin, W. and Künzli, J. *The Law of International Human Rights Protection* (Oxford University Press, Oxford, 2009)

Kamuf, P. 'On the Limit', in Miami Theory Collective (eds) *Community at Loose Ends* (University of Minnesota Press, Minneapolis, 1991)

Kelly, M. *The Political Philosophy of Michel Foucault* (Routledge, Abingdon, 2009)

Kennedy, D. *A Critique of Adjudication* (Harvard University Press, Cambridge (MA), 1977)

Kennedy, D. 'The International Human Rights Law Movement, Part of the Problem?' 3 *European Human Rights Law Journal* (2001)

King, M. *A Guide to Heidegger's Being and Time* (State University of New York, New York, 2001)

Klein, N. *The Shock Doctrine; The Rise of Disaster Capitalism* (Penguin, London, 2008)

Klossowski, P. *The College of Sociology (1937–39)* (Hollier, D. ed.) (University of Minnesota Press, Minneapolis, 1988)

Klossowski, P. *Nietzsche and the Vicious Circle* (Continuum, New York, 2005)

Knight, F. W. 'The Haitian Revolution', 105.1 *American Historical Review* (2000)

Kochi, T. *The Other's War: Recognition and the Violence of Ethics* (Birkbeck Law Press, Abingdon, 2009)

Korsgaard, C. 'Taking the Law into our own Hands; Kant on the Right to Revolution', in Reath, A., Herman, B. and Korsgaard, C. (eds) *Reclaiming the History of Ethics, Essays for John Rawls* (Cambridge University Press, Cambridge, 1997)

Koskenniemi, M. 'The Effects of Rights on Political Culture', in Alston, P. *The European Union and Human Rights* (Oxford University Press, Oxford, 1999)

Kouvelakis, S. *Philosophy and Revolution: From Kant to Marx* (Verso, London, 2003)

Krasner, S. D. *Sovereignty: Organised Hypocrisy* (Princeton University Press, Princeton (NJ), 1999)

Kujundžic, D. 'Empire, Glocalization, and the Melancholia of the Sovereign', 29 *The Comparatist* (2005)

Laclau, E. *Emancipation(s)* (Verso, London, 1996)

Laclau, E. *On Populist Reason* (Verso, London, 2005)

Laclau, E. *Politics and Ideology in Marxist Theory* (Verso, London, 1977)

Laclau, E. and Mouffe, C. *Hegemony and Socialist Strategy* (Verso, London, 2001)

Lacoue-Labarthe, P. *Heidegger and the Politics of Poetry* (University of Illinois Press, Chicago, 2007)

Lacoue-Labarthe, P. *Poetry as Experience* (Stanford University Press, Palo Alto (CA), 1999)

Laing, G. 'The Origin of the Cult of the Lares', 16.2 *Classical Philology* (1921)

Lauren Gordon, P. *The Evolution of International Human Rights – Visions Seen* (University of Pennsylvania Press, Pittsburgh, 2003)

Lefebvre, H. *State, Space, World: Selected Essays* (University of Minnesota Press, Minneapolis, 2009)

Lefebvre, H. *Writings on Cities* (Blackwell, Oxford, 1996)

Lefort, C. *Democracy and Political Theory* (Polity Press, Cambridge, 1988)

Lefort, C. *The Political Forms of Modern Society: Bureaucracy, Democracy, Totalitarianism* (Polity Press, Cambridge, 1986)

Lenin, V. I. *State and Revolution* (Martin Laurence Ltd, London, 1933)

Lescallier, D. *Reflections sur le sort des noirs dans nos colonies* (Paris, 1789)

Levett, N. C. *Finitude, Singularity, Community: An Introduction to the Thought of Jean-Luc Nancy* (unpublished PhD thesis, University of Sussex, 2002)

Levinas, E. *Alterity and Transcendence* (Athlone, Linton (IN), 1999)

Levinas, E. *God, Death and Time* (Stanford University Press, Palo Alto (CA), 2000)

Levinas, E. *Otherwise than Being, or, Beyond Essence* (Martinus Nijhoff, The Hague, 1981)

Levinas, E. *Totality and Infinity, an Essay on Exteriority* (Martinus Nijhoff, The Hague, 1969)

Levy, D. and Sznaider, N. *Human Rights and Memory* (Pennsylvania State University Press, Old Main, 2010)

Lindahl, H. 'A-legality: Postnationalism and the Question of Legal Boundaries', 73.1 *Modern Law Review* (2010)

Lindahl, H. 'Collective Self-Legislation as an *Actus Impurus*: A Response to Heidegger's Critique of European Nihilism', 3 *Continental Philosophy Review* (2008)

Lindahl, H. 'Constituent Power and Reflexive Identity: Towards an Ontology of Collective Selfhood', in Loughlin, M. and Walker, N. (eds) *Paradox of Constitutionalism* (Oxford University Press, Oxford, 2007)

Lindahl, H. 'Dialectic and Revolution: Confronting Kelsen and Gadamer on Legal Interpretation', 24.3 *Cardozo Law Review* (2003)

Lindahl, H. 'The Opening: Alegality and Political Agonism', in Schaap, A. *Law and Political Agonism* (Aldershot, Ashgate, 2009)

Linebaugh, P. *The London Hanged: Crime and Civil Society in the Eighteenth Century* (Verso, London, 1991)

Linebaugh, P. *The Magna Carta Manifesto, Liberties and Commons for All* (University of California Press, Berkeley (CA), 2008)

Linebaugh, P. and Rediker, M. *The Many Headed Hydra: The Hidden History of the Revolutionary Atlantic* (Verso, London, 2002)

Lingis, A. *Foreign Bodies* (Routledge, London, 1994)

Locke, J. *Locke: Political Essays* (Cambridge University Press, Cambridge, 1997)

Locke, J. *Second Treatise on Government* (Cambridge University Press, Cambridge, 1963)

Lotringer, S. and Marazzi, C. (eds) *Autonomia: Post-Political Politics* (Semiotext(e), Los Angeles, 2007)

Loughlin, M. *The Idea of Public Law* (Oxford University Press, Oxford, 2004)

Loughlin, M. and Walker, N. (eds) *Paradox of Constitutionalism* (Oxford University Press, Oxford, 2007)

Luszczynska, A. 'The Opposite of the Concentration Camp, Nancy's View on Community', 5.3 *New Centennial Review* (2005)

Luxemburg, R. *The Mass Strike: The Political Party and the Trade Unions* (Merlin Press, London, 1928)

Macpherson, C. B. *The Political Theory of Possessive Individualism: Hobbes to Locke* (Oxford University Press, Oxford, 1962)

Mahoney, J. *The Challenge of Human Rights: Origin, Development and Significance* (Blackwell, Oxford, 2007)

Manning, E. *Politics of Touch: Sense, Movement, Sovereignty* (University of Minnesota Press, Minneapolis, 2007)

Marchart, O. 'In the Name of the People; Populist Reason and the Subject of the Political', 35.3 *Diacritics* (2005)

Marchart, O. *Post-foundational Political Thought: Political Difference in Nancy, Lefort, Badiou and Laclau* (Edinburgh University Press, Edinburgh, 2007)

Marcuse, H. *A Study on Authority* (Verso, London 2008)

Martinon, J.-P. *On Futurity – Malabou, Nancy and Derrida* (Palgrave, London, 2007)

Martis, J. *Philippe Lacoue-Labarthe: Representation and the Loss of the Subject* (Fordham University Press, New York, 2005)

Marx, W. *Heidegger and the Tradition* (Northwestern University Press, Evanston (IL), 1989)

Marx, K. and Engels F. *The Communist Manifesto* (Lawrence & Wishart, London, 1990)

Matlock, J. 'Ghostly Politics', 30.3 *Diacritics* (2000)

Mazlish, B. *The Idea of Humanity in a Global Era* (Palgrave Macmillan, London, 2009)

Mbembe, A. 'Necropolitics', 15.1 *Public Culture* (2003)

McNay, L. *Foucault, A Critical Introduction* (Polity Press, Cambridge, 1994)

Merrifield, A. *Henri Lefebvre: A Critical Introduction* (Routledge, New York, 2006)

Miami Theory Collective (eds) *Community at Loose Ends* (University of Minnesota Press, Minneapolis, 1991)

Miami Theory Collective (eds) *Rethinking Technologies* (University of Minnesota Press, Minneapolis, 1993)

Milchman, A. and Rosenberg, A. (eds) *Foucault and Heidegger: Critical Encounters* (University of Minnesota Press, Minneapolis, 2003)

Minkkinen, P. *Sovereignty, Knowledge, Law* (Glasshouse Press, Abingdon, 2009)

Mitchell, D. *The Right to the City: Social Justice and the Fight for Public Space* (Guilford Press, New York, 2003)

Moeckli, D., Shah, S. and Sivakumaran, S. (eds) *International Human Rights Law* (Oxford University Press, Oxford, 2010)

Morris, D. B. *The Culture of Pain* (University of California Press, Palo Alto (CA), 1993)

Motha, S. and Zartaloudis, T. 'Law, Ethics and the Utopian End of Human Rights', 12.2 *Social & Legal Studies* (2003)

Mouffe, C. *The Democratic Paradox* (Verso, London, 2009)

Mouffe, C. *The Return of the Political* (Verso, London, 2005)

Moyn, S. http://www.youtube.com/watch?v=oqtFJZB27M8 (accessed 04/01/11)

Moyn, S. *The Last Utopia: Human Rights in History* (Harvard University Press, Cambridge (MA), 2010)

Mulhall, S. *Heidegger and Being and Time* (Routledge, London, 2005)

Mutua, M. *Human Rights: A Political and Cultural Critique* (University of Pennsylvania Press, Pittsburgh, 2002)

Mutua, M. 'Savages, Victims and Saviours: The Metaphor of Human Rights', 42 *Harvard International Law Journal* (2002)

Nancy, J.-L. *Being Singular Plural* (Stanford University Press, Palo Alto (CA), 2000)

Nancy, J.-L. *The Birth to Presence* (Stanford University Press, Palo Alto (CA), 1993)

Nancy, J.-L. *The Creation of the World or Globalization* (State University of New York Press, New York, 2007)

Nancy, J.-L. 'Church, State, Resistance' (paper presented at the Critical Legal Conference, 2005)

Nancy, J.-L. (Strong, T. B. trans.) 'The Compearance: From the Existence of Communism to the Community of Existence', 20.3 *Political Theory* (1992)

Nancy, J.-L. 'The Confronted Community', 6.1 *Postcolonial Studies* (2003)

Nancy, J.-L. *Corpus* (Fordham University Press, New York, 2008)

Nancy, J.-L. *Dis-enclosure – The Deconstruction of Christianity* (Fordham University Press, New York, 2008)

Nancy, J.-L. 'Is Everything Political (A Brief Remark)', New Centennial Review (2002)

Nancy, J.-L. *The Evidence of Film: Abbas Kiarostami* (Yves Gevaert, Brussels, 2001)

Nancy, J.-L. *The Experience of Freedom* (Stanford University Press, Palo Alto (CA), 1993)

Nancy, J.-L. *A Finite Thinking* (Stanford University Press, Palo Alto (CA), 2003)

Nancy, J.-L. *The Gravity of Thought* (Humanity Books, New York, 1997)

Nancy, J.-L. *The Ground of the Image* (Fordham University Press, New York, 2005)

Nancy, J.-L. *Hegel: The Restlessness of the Negative* (University of Minnesota Press, Minneapolis, 2002)

Nancy, J.-L. *The Inoperative Community* (University of Minnesota Press, Minneapolis, 1991)

Nancy, J.-L. 'The Insufficiency of "Values" and the Necessity of "Sense" ', 9.4 *Journal of Cultural Research* (2005)

Nancy, J.-L. 'Introduction', in Connor, P. Cadava, E. and Nancy, J.-L. *Who Comes After the Subject* (Routledge, London, 1991)

Nancy, J.-L. 'Love and Community, Roundtable Discussion at the EGS' http://www.egs.edu/faculty/nancy/nancy-roundtable-discussion2001.html (accessed 02/01/2009)

Nancy, J.-L. *Multiple Arts – The Muses II* (Stanford University Press, Palo Alto (CA), 2006)

Nancy, J.-L. *The Muses* (Stanford University Press, Palo Alto (CA), 1994)

Nancy, J.-L. *Noli Me Tangere – On the Raising of the Body* (Fordham University Press, New York, 2008)

Nancy, J.-L. 'Of Being-in-Common', in Miami Theory Collective (eds) *Community at Loose Ends* (University of Minnesota Press, Minneapolis, 1991)

Nancy, J.-L. 'On Finitude and Sovereignty', (transcription by Gilbert Leung of Seminar during the *Adieu Derrida* Series at Birkbeck College) available at http://www.critical-legalthinking.com/?p=128

Nancy, J.-L. 'Of the One, Of Hierarchy', 57 *Cultural Critique* (2004)

Nancy, J.-L. *Philosophical Chronicles* (Fordham University Press, New York, 2008)

Nancy, J.-L. 'Two Secrets of the Fetish', 31.2 *Diacritics* (2001)

Nancy, J.-L. *The Sense of the World* (University of Minnesota Press, Minneapolis, 1997)

Nancy, J.-L. *The Speculative Remark (One of Hegel's Bon Mots)* (Stanford University Press, Palo Alto (CA), 2001)

Nancy, J.-L. 'The West Battles against Itself', 57 *Cultural Critique* (2004)

Nancy, J.-L. and Hall, M. M. 'The War of Monotheism: On the Inability of Civilization to Expand: The West Battles against Itself', 57 *Cultural Critique* (2004)

Nancy, J.-L. and Lacoue-Labarthe, P. *Re-treating the Political* (Sparks, S. ed.) (Routledge, London, 1997)

Nancy, J.-L. and Stockwell, C. 'Of the One, of Hierarchy', 57 *Cultural Critique* (2004)

Negri, A. *Books for Burning: Between Civil War and Democracy in 1970s' Italy* (Verso, London, 2005)

Negri, A. *Insurgencies* (University of Minnesota Press, Minneapolis, 1999)

Negri, A. *Time for Revolution* (Continuum, New York, 2005)

Nesbitt, N. *Toussaint L'Ouverture, The Haitian Revolution* (Verso, London, 2008)

Nietzsche, F. *Beyond Good and Evil* (Penguin, London, 1975)

Nietzsche, F. *The Birth to Tragedy, and the Genealogy of Morals* (Doubleday & Anchor Books, New York, 1956)

Nietzsche, F. *Thus Spoke Zarathustra, A Book for None and All* (Penguin, New York, 1966)

Nietzsche, F. *The Will to Power* (Vintage Books, New York, 1968)

Norris, A. 'Giorgio Agamben and the Politics of the Living Dead', 30.4 *Diacritics* (20

Noys, B. *Georges Bataille, A Critical Introduction* (Pluto Press, London, 2000)

Ojakangas, M. 'The Impossible Dialogue on Biopower: Agamben and Foucault', 2 *Foucault Studies* (2005)

Orend, B. *Human Rights: Concept and Context* (Broadview Press, Peterborough (ON), 2002)

Orford, A. *Reading Humanitarian Intervention: Human Rights and the Use of Force in International Law* (Cambridge University Press, Cambridge, 2003)

Ortega y Gasset, J. *The Revolt of the Masses* (W.W. Norton, New York, 1994)

Osiatynski, W. *Human Rights and their Limits* (Cambridge University Press, Cambridge, 2009)

Pagden, A. 'Human Rights, Natural Rights and Europe's Imperial Legacy', 31.2 *Political Theory* (2003)

Palumbo, M. *Human Rights: Meaning and History* (Robert E. Krieger Publishing, Miami, 1982)

Parekh, S. 'Resisting 'Dull and Torpid' Assent: Returning to the Debate over the Foundations of Human Rights', 29 *Human Rights Quarterly* (2007)

Paust, J. J. 'The Human Right to Participate in Armed Revolution and Related Forms of Social Violence: Testing the Limits of Permissibility', 32 *Emory Law Journal* (1983)

Pearlman, C. 'The Safeguarding and Foundation of Human Rights', 1.1 *Law and Philosophy* (1982)

Perry, M. J. *Human Rights: Religion, Law, Courts* (Cambridge University Press, Cambridge, 2007)

Plate, S. B. *Walter Benjamin, Religion and Aesthetics* (Routledge, London, 2005)

Polt, R. *Heidegger, An Introduction* (UCL Press, London 1999)

Pryor, B. S. 'Law in Abandon: Jean-Luc Nancy and the Critical Study of Law', 15.3 *Law and Critique* (2004)

Raffoul, F. *Heidegger and the Subject* (Humanity Books, New York, 1999)

Raffoul, F. and Pettigrew, D. 'Translator's Introduction', in *The Creation of the World or Globalization* (State University of New York Press, New York, 2007)

Rancière, J. *Dis-agreement – Politics and Philosophy* (University of Minnesota Press, Minneapolis, 1999)

Rand, R. *Futures of Jacques Derrida* (Stanford University Press, Palo Alto (CA), 2001)

Rancière J. *The Ignorant Schoolmaster* (Stanford University Press, Palo Alto (CA), 1991)

Rancière, J. *The Nights of Labor – The Workers Dream in 19th Century France* (Temple University Press, Philadelphia, 1989)

Rancière, J. *On the Shores of Politics* (Verso, London, 2007)

Rancière, J. *The Philosopher and His Poor* (Duke University Press, Durham (NC), 2004)

Rancière, J. *The Politics of Aesthetics* (Continuum, London, 2004)

Rancière, J. 'Ten Theses on Politics' available at http://abahlali.org/node/3434 (accessed 08/05/08)

Rancière, J. 'Who is the Subject of the Rights of Man' 103.2/3 *South Atlantic Quarterly* (2004)

Rediker, M. 'Thomas Clarkson and History from Below', 8 *Naked Punch* (2006)

Rees, A. M. 'Pitt and the Achievement of Abolition, 39.3 *Journal of Negro History* (1954)

Richardson, W. J. *Heidegger: Through Phenomenology to Thought* (Martinus Nijhoff, The Hague, 1974)

Richman, M. 'Reviewed: Georges Bataille in "La Critique Sociale" ', 14.3/4 *South Central Review*

Robinson, C. J. 'Capitalism, Slavery and Bourgeois Historiography', 23 *History Workshop* (1987)

Rockhill, G. 'Translator's Introduction', in Rancière, J. *The Politics of Aesthetics – The Distribution of the Sensible* (Continuum, New York, 2004)

Rodríguez-Salgado, M. J. 'How Oppression Thrives where Truth is not Allowed a Voice: The Spanish Polemic about American Indians', in Bhambra, G. K. and Shiliam, R. *Silencing Human Rights: Critical Engagements with a Contested Project* (Palgrave, London, 2009)

Rousseau, J.-J. *Emile or Education* (J. M. Dent & Sons, London, 1925)

Rousseau, J.-J. *The Social Contract and the Discourses* (Everyman's Library, London, 1993)

Saccamano, N. 'Rhetoric, Consensus, and the Law in Rousseau's *Contrat Social*', 107 *MLN* (1992)

Said, E. W. *Orientalism* (Penguin, London, 1987)

Salama, M. R. 'The Interruption of Myth: A Nancean Reading of Blanchot and Al-Bayati', 33 *Journal of Arabic Literature* (2002)

Sayers, S. 'Review of "The Politics of Aesthetics", *Culture Machine*' http://scm-rime.tees. ac.uk/Reviews/rev54.htm (accessed 08/05/08)

Scarry, E. *The Body in Pain, The Making and Unmaking of the World* (Oxford University Press, Oxford, 1985)

Schalow, F. *The Incarnality of Being: The Earth, Animals and the Body in Heidegger's Thought* (State University of New York Press, New York, 2006)

Schmitt, C. *Constitutional Theory* (Duke University Press, Durham (NC), 2008)

Schmitt, C. *Political Theology – Four Chapters on the Concept of Sovereignty* (University of Chicago Press, Chicago, 2005)

Schurmann, R. *Heidegger, On Being and Acting: From Principles to Anarchy* (Indiana University Press, Bloomington (IN), 1990)

Shaw, M. *International Law*, 6th edn (Cambridge University Press, Cambridge, 2008)

Sherwood, M. 'Britain, the Slave Trade and Slavery, 1808–1843', 46 *Race Class* (2004)

Shestov, L. *All Things are Possible – The Apotheosis of Groundlessness* (BiblioBazaar, reprint of Robert M. McBride & Co., New York, 1920)

Shuler, J. *Calling Out for Liberty, The Stono Slave Rebellion and the Universal Struggle for Human Rights* (University Press of Mississippi, Missouri, 2009)

Sieyès, E. J. *Political Writings* (Sonenscher, M. ed.) (Hackett Publishing Co., Indianapolis (IN), 2003)

Skinner, Q. *The Foundations of Modern Political Thought, Volume 2* (Cambridge University Press, Cambridge, 1978)

Slaughter, J. R. *Human Rights, Inc. – The World Novel, Narrative Form, and International Law* (Fordham University Press, New York, 2007)

Smith, A. *An Inquiry into the Nature and causes of the Wealth of Nations* available at http://oll.libertyfund.org (accessed on 12/12/09)

Smith, A. D. 'Nations and History', in Guibernau, M. and Hutchinson, J. (eds) *Understanding Nationalism* (Polity Press, London, 2001)

Smith, A. *The Theory of Moral Sentiments* (Liberty Fund, Indianapolis (IN), 1984)

Smith, M. B. 'Translator's Foreword', in Nancy, J.-L. *Dis-enclosure – The Deconstruction of Christianity* (Fordham University Press, New York, 2008)

Somerville, J. 'A Key Problem of Current Political Philosophy: The Issue of Force and Violence', 19.2 *Philosophy of Science* (1952)

Sorel, G. *From Georges Sorel – Essays in Socialism and Philosophy* (Stanley, J. L. ed.) (Oxford University Press, Oxford, 1976)

Sorel, G. *Reflections on Violence* (George Allen & Unwin, London, 1916)

Sorial, S. *Heidegger and the Problem of Individuation: Mitsein (Being-with), Ethics and Responsibility* (unpublished PhD thesis, UNSW, Australia, 2005)

Sparks, S., Sheppard, D. and Thomas, C. *The Sense of Philosophy, On Jean-Luc Nancy* (Routledge, London, 1997)

Sprinker, M. (ed.) *Ghostly Demarcations, A Symposium on Jacques Derrida's Spectres of Marx* (Verso, London, 1999)

Suglia, J. 'The Communication of the Impossible', 31.2 *Diacritics* (2001)

Sullivan, L. and de Vires, H. (eds) *Political Theologies* (Fordham University Press, New York, 2006)

Thornton, J. K. ' "I am the Subject of the King of Congo": African Political Ideology and the Haitian Revolution', 4.2 *The Journal of World History* (1993)

Todd, M. *Reconsidering Difference – Nancy, Derrida, Levinas and Deleuze* (Penn State University Press, Old Main (PA), 1997)

Tomuschat, C. *Human Rights: Between Idealism and Realism* (Oxford University Press, Oxford, 2003)

Trouillot, M-R. *Silencing the Past: Power and the Production of History* (Beacon Press, Boston (MA), 1995)

Turner, B. *Vulnerability and Human Rights* (Pennsylvania State University Press, Old Main (PA), 2006)

Turner, V. 'Sacrifice as Quintessential Process: Prophylaxis or Abandonment?' 16.3 *History of Religions* (1977)

Tushnet, M. 'An Essay on Rights' 68.2 *Texas Law Review* (1984)

Tuttle, H. N. *The Crowd as Untruth – The Existential Critique of Mass Society in the Thought of Kierkegaard, Nietzsche, Heidegger and Ortega y Gasset* (Peter Lang, New York, 1996)

Universal Declaration of Human Rights available at http://www.un.org/Overview/rights.html

Ure, M. 'The Irony of Pity: Nietzsche contra Schopenhauer and Rousseau', 32 *Journal of Nietzsche Studies* (2006)

Urpeth, J. R. *The Language of Pain: Heidegger, Difference and Distance* (PhD thesis, University of Essex, 1989)

Vail, L. M. *Heidegger and Ontological Difference* (Pennsylvania University Press, London, 1972)

Vaneigem, R. *A Declaration of the Rights of Human Beings: On Sovereignty of Life as Surpassing the Rights of Man* (Pluto Press, London, 2003)

Vaneigem, R. *The Revolution in Everyday Life* (Practical Paradise Publications, London, 1975)

Villa, D. R. *Arendt and Heidegger, The Fate of the Political* (Princeton University Press, Princeton (NJ), 1996)

Virno, P. *A Grammar of the Multitude* (Semiotext(e), Los Angeles, 2004)

Voltaire, *Candide* (Bedford/St Martins, Boston (MA), 1999)

Vries, H. de and Sullivan, L. E. *Political Theologies; Public Religions in a Post-Secular World* (Fordham University Press, New York, 2006)

Wall, I. 'On Pain and the Sense of Human Rights', 29 *Australian Feminist Law Journal* (2008)

Watkin, C. 'A Different Alterity: Jean-Luc Nancy's 'Singular Plural',' 30.2 *Paragraph* (2007)

Weil, S. *Gravity and Grace* (Routledge, London, 2002)

Weil, S. *Notebooks I & II* (Routledge & Kegan Paul, London, 1956)

Weingrad, M. 'The College of Sociology and the Institute of Social Research', 84 *New German Critique* (2001)

Whyte, J. 'Particular Rights and Absolute Wrongs: Giorgio Agamben on Life and Politics', 20.2 *Law and Critique* (2009)

Williams, E. *Capitalism and Slavery* (University of North Carolina Press, Chapel Hill, 1944)

Williams-Myers, A. J. 'Slavery, Rebellion and Revolution in the Americas: A Historiographical Scenario on the Theses of Genovese and Others', 26.4 *Journal of Black Studies* (1996)

Willson, M. *Technically Together – Rethinking Community within Techno-society* (Peter Lang, New York, 2006)

Wolin, R. 'From the 'Death of Man' to Human Rights: The Paradigm Change in French Intellectual Life', in Bevir, M., Hargis, J. and Rushing, S. *Histories of Postmodernism* (Routledge, Abingdon, 2007)

Wolin, R. *Heidegger's Children* (Princeton University Press, Oxford, 2001)

Wrathall, M. A. and Malpas, J (eds) *Heidegger, Authenticity and Modernity, Essays in Honour of H. L. Dreyfus, Volume 1* (MIT Press, Cambridge (MA), 2000)

Young, A. F. *Liberty Tree: Ordinary People and the American Revolution* (New York University Press, New York, 2006)

Young, J. *Heidegger, Philosophy, Nazism* (University of Cambridge Press, Cambridge, 1997)

Zartaloudis, T. *Giorgio Agamben: Power, Law and the Uses of Criticism* (Routledge, Abingdon, 2010)

Žižek, S. *The Fragile Absolute* (Verso, London, 2000)

Žižek, S 'The Lesson of Rancière' in Rancière, J., *The Politics of Aesthetics* (Continuum, London, 2004)

Žižek, S. *The Metastases of Enjoyment* (Verso, London, 2005)

Žižek, S. *The Parallax View* (MIT Press, Cambridge (MA), 2006)

Žižek, S (ed.) *Revolution at the Gates: Selected Writings of Lenin from 1917* (Verso, London, 2002)

Žižek, S. *The Sublime Object of Ideology* (Verso, London, 1999)

Žižek, S. *Violence* (Profile Books, London, 2008)

Index